'If David Morgan agrees to be CEO, and puts some of his own money in, I'm in.'
Warren Buffett, chairman of Berkshire Hathaway

'David was the principal engine of the 1985 tax reform.

'The cabinet decided to embark on the biggest fiscal consolidation in the history of the OECD. From 1983 until 1989, he was the officer most charged with the burden of these responsibilities. Somebody had not just to coordinate it, but to guide it, and David did.

'He had a prodigious capacity for work. Conscientious, perfectionist.

'He would have made an effective secretary to the Treasury, just as he made an effective CEO of Westpac.'
Paul Keating, former treasurer and prime minister of Australia

'I believe that everyone should be treated equal in the company, including the janitor, the receptionist and the people who clean the kitchen. David thinks about things the same way. He's a very engaging guy.'
Jamie Dimon, chairman and CEO of J.P. Morgan

'David's leadership is truly transformative. It's infectious.'
Ken Henry, chairman of National Australia Bank and former secretary to the Treasury

'David systematically strengthened the risk framework of the bank. That manifested itself quite powerfully in the years from 2008 to 2010, when we were clearly better, absolutely and relatively, than both other major banks within Australia and other banks globally.'
Gail Kelly, former CEO of Westpac

'David was regarded as one of the strongest banking CEOs of the last couple of generations in Australia. There was a level of professional management that he brought to it – and discipline – which was more akin to the global markets than the domestic market.

'David is very focused on the nature of leadership, the values of the leader. The natural intellect and social curiosity around matters of leadership make him something of an expert. It makes him valuable to other CEOs.

'He was really successful and on top of the pile. Not just as a bank CEO – he was legit. I don't know that I've come across any CEOs who are quite that methodical, disciplined, diligent, prepared.'
James Gorman, chairman and CEO of Morgan Stanley

'The most remarkable thing about David was his incredible desire to improve and learn, and an ability to take feedback and actually change. Not many people can do that. It was pretty amazing.

'During his nine years as CEO of Westpac, it really became a highly regarded institution – which it wasn't when I left.'
Bob Joss, former CEO of Westpac and professor and dean emeritus, finance, of the Stanford Business School

'I thought he had the most successful outcome in his tenure of the banks.'
John McFarlane, chairman of Barclays and former CEO of ANZ

'I think David is the most successful of the people who left the public sector and went into the private sector.'
Ian Macfarlane, former governor of the Reserve Bank of Australia

'David was never one of these self-made people who ended up despising his origins. He actually has some sense of them.'
Don Watson, author

'From a strategy point of view, David was probably the first to really grasp the potential of wealth management in banking.

'He has an enviable track record of hiring extremely high-quality people.

'One key legacy of David is the sustainability focus. At the time it was pretty out there. Westpac ended up being recognised as the world's most sustainable bank, and that really set a benchmark for others to pursue.'
Brian Hartzer, CEO of Westpac

'He was very successful as a chief executive. David had to give Westpac a new future. I thought he managed all that superbly.'
John Uhrig, former chairman of Westpac

'He was the stand-out banker of his generation. David correctly saw a lot of the big shifts of the era, notably banks moving away from personal finance and into wealth management. Critically, he was also really clinical on banks having to be safe, resilient and able to withstand shocks. Although he left before the global financial crisis hit in 2008, the bank was in such a strong position because of him.'
Andrew Cornell, ANZ executive and former chief financial writer and associate editor at *The Australian Financial Review*

'When Westpac entered the global financial crisis it was in a much stronger position than its peers by virtue of what David had done.'
Brian Johnson, bank equity analyst

'David has the highest work rate of anyone I have ever known, to this day.'
Phil Chronican, non-executive director of NAB and former senior executive of Westpac and ANZ

To Dear John and Richard,

David Morgan

An Extraordinary Life

OLIVER BROWN

Best

David

Hardie Grant

BOOKS

Published in 2019 by Hardie Grant Books,
an imprint of Hardie Grant Publishing

Hardie Grant Books (Melbourne)
Building 1, 658 Church Street
Richmond, Victoria 3121

Hardie Grant Books (London)
5th & 6th Floors
52–54 Southwark Street
London SE1 1UN

hardiegrantbooks.com

 A catalogue record for this
book is available from the
National Library of Australia

David Morgan: An Extraordinary Life
ISBN 978 1 74379 350 3

10 9 8 7 6 5 4 3 2 1

Cover design by Nada Backovic
Cover photo: David Morgan at Westpac offices, Kent Street, Sydney,
    30 June 2006, Jessica Hromas, *The Australian Financial Review*
Typeset by Kirby Jones
Printed by McPherson's Printing Group, Maryborough, Victoria

 The paper this book is printed on is certified against the
Forest Stewardship Council® Standards. FSC® promotes
environmentally responsible, socially beneficial and
economically viable management of the world's forests.

CONTENTS

INTRODUCTION

By any gauge, the life of David Morgan is an intoxicating Australian story. The boy brought up in a broken home, in the shadow of his father's financial ruin and racked by anxiety about whether the butcher could be paid on time, morphed into the man who would steer Westpac from the edge of oblivion to its position as a global top-20 bank. It was, in every sense, a road less travelled. As a child actor, he savoured a life beyond his peers' most exotic imaginings, singing alongside Olivia Newton-John and completing his high-school studies aboard a schooner in the South Pacific. As a young economist at the International Monetary Fund, he was parachuted into some of the world's most benighted spots, accused of being a CIA agent by the kleptocratic ruler of Sierra Leone and forced to beat his retreat under the watch of armed guards. As a senior Treasury bureaucrat, and one of Paul Keating's inner sanctum, he held sufficient influence to wipe $1.5 billion off the projected federal Budget deficit with barely more than the stroke of a pen.

All of this he could claim before even crossing the threshold of Westpac. It was little wonder that the bank's more reactionary executives, accustomed to lavish expense accounts and a jobs-for-life culture, scorned him at first as an academic socialist, an interloper who threatened to disrupt the status quo. A budding thespian he might have been, but as a banker, Morgan was anything but a product of central casting. A profile in *The Mail on Sunday* in 2010, conducted soon after his relocation from Sydney to London with private equity firm J.C. Flowers, depicted him as a 'big-hitter who defies stereotypes'. Brian Johnson, the Australian banking analyst who has credited Morgan with steeling Westpac against the ravages of the global financial crisis, was even more succinct when I met him. 'David,' he smiled, 'is a bloody interesting guy.'

Initially, Morgan was torn about the notion of a book. Eighteen years at Westpac, including nine as CEO, had convinced him that the lessons of leadership were far too complex and multi-faceted to be condensed under such boilerplate eighties slogans as 'true grit' or 'only sharks can swim'. Equally, his daughter, Jessica, knew enough about his passion for economics to caution against the dangers of producing a dry academic textbook. But over dinner one evening, at the family farm in the Southern Highlands, we agreed that the greatest value lay in documenting his extraordinary path in full.

For a start, there was the unusual dimension of public service versus private sector, and his record of success on both sides of the fence. There was also the richest historical backcloth. During graduate study at the London School of Economics, Morgan was not so much learning his craft as living it, as the global oil and energy crisis of the early seventies tipped the UK into painful austerity. In Washington DC, his office at the IMF was just three blocks removed from the White House, affording him a front-row seat for every twist of Watergate. Even in Treasury, he bore witness to a fundamental shift, as the calcified hierarchies of seventies Canberra gave way to a far more audacious spirit, with the Labor government of Bob Hawke and Paul Keating seeking to liberalise Australia's economy in ways that would once have been unthinkable.

The schedules of a leading financier and a full-time journalist seldom neatly intersect, but for this project Morgan sat for around 100 hours of interviews. While our sessions would explore his Westpac feats and his pivotal contribution to tax reform in the closest detail, they touched, too, upon the deeply personal: the sense of abandonment by his mother, the shattering loss of his kindred spirit Chris Higgins, the joys of fatherhood, and the ordeal that his wife, Ros Kelly, Labor's first female minister in the House of Representatives, experienced with breast cancer. For the inquisitor, these were priceless insights behind the defences that many CEOs construct around themselves. For the subject, they served, dare one say it, as a form of therapy.

Naturally, a balanced picture requires a multitude of outside perspectives. It became clear at an early stage that this would not be a problem, with Don Watson, Morgan's flatmate at La Trobe University – not to mention a master of biography, as author of the award-winning *Recollections of a Bleeding Heart*, on his years as Keating's speechwriter – agreeing to speak on the condition he could tell me 'absolutely everything'. For two hours at a wine bar in Fitzroy, Watson was true to his word, offering a stream of indiscretions about Morgan's student girlfriends, as well as a compelling portrayal of how his friend's trappings of success masked some acute vulnerabilities.

While Morgan acknowledged that his constant striving had been motivated by a fear of failure, Watson traced this directly to the paternal struggles that had framed his childhood. 'The defeat of the father,' he said, 'is in David forever.'

The depth of any biography owes much to the diversity of source material, and my work has been hugely helped by the number of people willing to speak so candidly. After research trips stretching from Melbourne to New York, Sydney to San Francisco, this book comprises interviews with a former prime minister, two Wall Street titans, two former Reserve Bank governors, four secretaries to the Treasury, Morgan's predecessor and successor as Westpac CEO, not to mention dozens of no-holds-barred conversations with his chairmen, colleagues, chiefs of staff and, in some cases, his critics. Keating, a long-time confidant of Morgan's and now the godfather to his son, rather liked the fact that this book would not be autobiographical. As one who has inspired six biographies, but always steered clear of the self-penned memoir, he once said: 'If you're any good, someone else will write about you.'

In the final analysis, Morgan's body of work stacks up as rather better than 'good': he played a pivotal role in reshaping the country's economic fabric at Treasury, turned Westpac into a byword for resilience and sustainability, and continues to command such respect that he acts as an informal mentor to several of the world's premier CEOs. In uncertain times, his experience carries profound weight, whether in highlighting the dangers of neglecting the Australian Public Service, in Morgan's view an invaluable national asset, or in explaining why the recent Royal Commission can be a 'circuit-breaker' for banks desperate to rehabilitate their image.

Even at 71, Morgan has an irrepressible energy. He attempted the retired life of leisure once before, upon his departure from Westpac, and quickly grew exasperated with it, feeling that he still had far more to give. For this reason, he has spent the past decade in a dynamic, cross-cultural role with J.C. Flowers, holding board positions simultaneously in six different countries. Some contemporaries have long urged him to step back and relish the chance to appreciate his achievements. But perhaps Morgan's perpetual restlessness points to a more universal truth. 'The only real failure in life is not to try,' he told me, towards the end of this process. 'I certainly tried.' It has been both my pleasure and privilege to chronicle those efforts.

CHAPTER 1

Stage Fright

It came as a curdling horror to David Morgan to return from school one afternoon and find a 'For Sale' sign plastered across the family home. For as long as David could recall, he had lived in the elegant two-storey house in a neat slice of Glen Iris suburbia – just a few streets removed from where Sir Robert Menzies had retired after his second, sixteen-year stretch as Australia's prime minister. The Morgan family had a live-in maid, not to mention a sparkling new Chevrolet every couple of years. David and his elder sister, Cherry, could tinkle the ivories on a choice of two pianos, a grand and an upright. Their evenings would be framed by the convivial hubbub of black-tie parties.

In that world of quintessential Melbourne gentility, there had been no warning, not an inkling that his parents were in financial peril. But ten-year-old David understood, as he stood frozen in front of that grimly definitive sign, that the certainties in his life were dissolving before his eyes.

Ray Morgan had been declared bankrupt in 1957. The paternal millinery business, Raymor Hats, which at its zenith employed close to 100 people, had become a victim of shifting fashions. Ray's section of Flinders Lane was once a street paved with gold for Melburnian milliners, but shops were left flailing to adapt to the shift in emphasis from hats to hair. The late fifties saw the rise of the bouffant, upon which the Melbourne Cup's highly coiffed habitués perched small, decorative fascinators. Even the staunchly conservative Catholic women saw a relaxation of the papal edict that they had to wear hats for Mass. A gentle soul, not given to rage or self-pity, Ray would often voice thanks that at least the Queen, her headwear imprinted on Australian consciousness from the state visit in 1954, would never be so fickle as to go out without a hat.

Where her husband was concerned, Verna Morgan drew no distinction between the failure of the business and the failure of the man. David's exacting and rather judgmental mother would disparage Ray viciously, often within earshot of the children. She would exacerbate these wounds by keeping newspaper cuttings about more successful businessmen and sticking them in a scrapbook. Ray, born in 1903, would let slip his vintage on visits to the local car showroom by talking indulgently about Rolls-Royces manufactured in the twenties; for Verna, at least a decade younger (although she upheld the Wildean wisdom that one should never trust a woman who told her age), this became another stick with which to beat him. She would seldom pass up an opportunity to remind Ray of how old he was. Behind the curtains of an ostensibly happy household, there was, Morgan reflects, an 'utter humiliation of a very decent individual'.[1]

The privations that Ray's bankruptcy wrought are etched upon his son's memory. Whenever David spotted the piano teacher, who had not been paid, he would cross the road. If he happened to pass the butcher's shop, knowing that the man was chasing payment for the latest meat delivery, he would walk on the other side of the street. Bills about which he had once been blasé assumed a horrible urgency. Out of the embarrassment, however, emerged a quiet, implacable resolution. As a child, he glimpsed the distress that was consuming and crushing his docile father, and decided it was a pain too acute to risk enduring himself. He would, he promised himself, do everything within his power not to fail in his own life, either emotionally or economically.

Their straitened circumstances put paid to maid service and forced the family into a rented weatherboard house in about the only part of East Malvern that was not refined. What magnified the desolation for David and Cherry was that their mother did not want to go with them.

While divorce was rare enough in Australia in 1957, the notion of a mother forsaking her brood bordered on unconscionable. The country was just beginning to adjust, too, to a change from the old divorce rule, where the only path out of a doomed union was for one spouse to demonstrate that the other was guilty of cruelty, desertion or adultery. Although this proviso had been softened in 1956, Ray enlisted a private investigator to confirm his suspicions about his wife's infidelities.

One evening, after weeks of stake-outs, the detective knocked on his door. 'Is it all right if I talk in front of the boy?' he asked, pointing to David. Reassured that it was, he announced, solemnly: 'I'm sorry to have to tell you this, but she spent the night with Keith Horsley.' Horsley, nicknamed Horse, was a local gin salesman with whom Verna had been involved for some time. It had, it transpired, been far from her only dalliance.

For all that a young boy might struggle to grasp the dynamics of a disintegrating marriage, the fact that he did not defend his father's honour more vigorously in these situations has troubled Morgan ever since.

'I wasn't terribly supportive, and yet I would come to the realisation that he was a far more admirable person than my mother, with a more laudable set of values,' Morgan says. 'He never blamed her for any of her terrible conduct. He never looked at another woman, never blamed her for any of her affairs. He was just somebody everybody liked, a thoroughly good egg who wasn't dealt the cards I think he deserved.'[2]

The loss of self-esteem that these revelations inflicted upon Morgan was severe. The twin agonies of his mother's exit and Ray's sense of defeat lodged themselves deep in his psyche. As he puts it: 'One has sufficient insecurities at that stage of life without the most powerful parent piling them on by rejecting you.'[3]

For his teenage sister, it was crippling. Already Cherry had, in Morgan's estimation, a debilitating lack of confidence in her own talents. She could rarely abide company beyond her close circle of friends. The stigma attached to the strife at home was such that she had difficulty forming most other relationships. A mother of one of the boys she courted was even heard to say: 'Don't go out with that girl, her parents are divorced.' Cherry detested her experiences at Korowa Anglican Girls'

School with such ferocity that she decided, within days of her parents' divorce and in the week of her fifteenth birthday, to walk out. 'I don't know how you have stuck it for this long,' said the headmistress, whom Cherry abhorred.

Verna did little to elaborate her reasons for leaving, besides telling the children: 'There's no use me trying to keep you. Your father will only fight me in court.'

'She simply wasn't into slumming it,' Cherry reflects. 'So, she lost interest pretty quickly. She was terribly selfish. It was "me first", all the time.'[4]

It is a curiosity of Morgan's relationship with his mother that for all he has come to deplore her maligning of Ray, he retained more than a few special dispensations as the younger child. 'He was the golden boy, and I was the damn nuisance,' Cherry says. 'I was often whacked with her wooden spoon.'[5]

Thrust prematurely into a role as the de facto matriarch, Cherry felt, not unreasonably, that the greater burden of her parents' marriage fell upon her. In their ramshackle lodgings, with no washing machine and no vacuum cleaner, every household task was hard work, especially when she returned home one evening to find that her little brother and his friends had thrown ice-cream all across the living room. Confronted by such behaviour – about which David later wrote a letter of apology – Cherry elicited scant sympathy from Verna. 'She would say to me, over the telephone, "Cherry, he's just a little boy." And I would reply, indignantly, "Yes, Mum, and I'm just a little girl."'[6]

The chronic lack of money meant it was not long before David gave up his school place at the fee-paying Malvern Grammar. This was a mark of scalding shame. In the cossetted, cliquey, distinctly non-meritocratic postwar Melbourne that David knew – where the values of a long-term Liberal government held sway – society and business were rigidly stratified along the lines of where one was educated. It is something of an Australian aphorism that in Sydney, people's initial instinct is to inquire how much your house is worth, whereas in Melbourne, they first want to know where you went to school. David was convinced that the lack of an elite education would put him at a serious competitive disadvantage.

In keeping with Ray's noble streak of defiance, he insisted on trying to keep David at a prestigious school. 'My dear dad would say, "If you really want to go, I'll find a way to send you there,"' Morgan recalls. 'He didn't have a hope in hell, the poor chap, but it was very sweet of him to offer.'[7]

To be knocked so abruptly off the comfortable path prescribed by the old school tie felt both wrenching and disorientating. Only when, in 1960, David won one of the few free places at the selective Melbourne High, the first public secondary school in Victoria and not shy of claiming to be the best, did his anxieties start to be assuaged.

'Brains, not money, should be the passport to the higher realms of knowledge,' argued Frank Tate, the state's inaugural director of education, upon founding Melbourne High in 1905. It was an ethos that the school encapsulated, and one that David upheld as if the words were inscribed on tablets of stone. Any environment that happened not to be hidebound by cronyism was, he decided, one where he could thrive. So it would prove.

As if to validate the notion that, in order to flourish, a pupil depended not so much on the overall standard of teaching as on a single pedagogue with the power to inspire, David became the protégé of one Neville Drohan, a fellow whose fearsome directness could be a source of amusement. One can discern Drohan's polarising character from his obituary in *The Age*, which describes him as 'always provocative, often outrageous'.[8] He cultivated what he called a 'savage' persona and died in 2016 a virtual recluse, having severed contact with most of his admiring former students. One year, he sought to galvanise his economics class by telling them, with a nod to Melbourne's burgeoning Hellenic population: 'It's about time one of you Greeks got the Exhibition.'[9] It was not an insignificant demand, with Exhibitions awarded only to Victoria's top students in their given subjects.

Drohan was imbued with a profound love of economics. He had become fascinated while on an exchange program in the US with how eccentric American entrepreneurs made their millions and would pepper his lessons with stories about 'Flav-R-Straws', a wildly popular innovation that made drinks more palatable for children by lining the straw with a strip of chocolate. Drohan collaborated with his friend John Day to write *The Australian Economic Framework*, first published in 1964 and soon established as the country's essential text for secondary-school students.

David was captivated by Drohan's methods, and in David, Drohan identified a promising protégé. 'I'm grooming you for the Exhibition,' he announced one day, to the surprise of a young man who had arrived with no ideas about economic theory but who was now front of the queue to win the highest academic prize in the state. It was a stunning example of the effect that one teacher could exert, and sowed the seed of an ambition that would never leave him.

'Drohan was an entertainer as well as a serious educator,' Morgan says. 'You need people like that, with a passion for their subject, who can persuade you to take it far more seriously than you otherwise would.'[10]

What reinforced their connection was a love of drama. David, who experienced a delayed adolescence that had left his voice stranded in the higher octaves, grasped a part under Drohan's directorship of the school play in a version of Eugene Labiche's *The Italian Straw Hat* – as a girl. An equally riotous turn as Puck, 'that shrewd and knavish sprite' in *A Midsummer Night's Dream*, was soon added to his repertoire.

It would become a theme of Morgan's formative years, this impression that puberty was something that happened to other people. Between the ages of twelve and sixteen, he barely grew; his insecurities sharpened by his sense of being the only boy who stood four-foot-ten and whose vocal range remained firmly at the falsetto end of the scale. His mother was so perplexed that she sent him for medical tests, a process that was hardly likely to alleviate his self-doubt. But he did discover that his status as what he calls the 'class runt' conferred certain advantages from a thespian perspective. As well as being the sole boy of sixteen who could plausibly tread the boards in a female guise, he also became the first port of call for directors auditioning for the role of an eleven-year-old. It was to be a useful mark of distinction, as he found when an opportunity arose in 1959 to join the cast of a children's television series.

* * *

Morgan's transition to the heady world of TV sprang from his mother's opportunism. Since abandoning Ray, Verna had taken up work as manager of a photographic studio, fielding offers of modelling that she steered shrewdly towards her children. Before he was truly aware of it, Morgan found himself the face of just about every line of boys' clothing north of the Yarra, from fleecy windcheaters to the finest knitwear the Myer Emporium could offer. Cherry, likewise, was in demand as a 'house model', even if it was a bind for a girl of fifteen to spend up to ten hours a day tottering around in high heels. From fashion, at least for Morgan, there flowed a natural route to the glamour of the small screen.

Television was a nascent medium that was teeming with possibilities. Only in 1956 had Bruce Gyngell, original anchor of TCN-9 in Sydney, greeted Australia with the words: 'Good evening, and welcome to television.'

For Roger Mirams, a former war cameraman, the television revolution was intoxicating. Mirams was born in New Zealand but took Australian citizenship after filming the 1956 Olympics in Melbourne. Regarded as rather a Peter Pan character for his habit of turning up for parties in pirate costume, Mirams channelled his passion into the production of *The Terrific Adventures of the Terrible Ten*.

Mirams was planning to shoot this new children's series in the Macedon Ranges, close to the old gold rush town of Woodend – 'Hollywoodend' to the locals – and it was here, as he fleshed out his ensemble cast, that he encountered a young Morgan poised on the cusp of child stardom.

The Terrible Ten, as it was better known, was a charmingly whimsical show based on a group of ten children being left to create their own town, with its own rules. The precocious residents of 'Ten Town' would act out the jobs of police officers or firefighters in their little simulated utopia and encounter all manner of scrapes, from rescuing runaway children to driving a jazzed-up jalopy around Calder Park Raceway.[11] In one scenario, they even tried to launch a space rocket.

The premise was unashamedly folksy and homespun, and filming techniques were not exactly sophisticated, either, with a skeleton crew limited to Mirams, a sound recordist and an assistant cameraman, all relying on the time-honoured clapperboard method. It was not uncommon for scripts to be scribbled on the back of an envelope. But the stories themselves, always touching affirmations of childlike enterprise and exuberance, proved phenomenally marketable.

It was the first Australian series to be sold internationally. Over the run of fifty-one episodes, Mirams managed to hawk his concept to eighty-one foreign markets, stretching from Germany to Nigeria, from Sweden to Hong Kong. The swelling revenues from these sales did not filter down to the actors themselves though.

'We were on about two pounds a day to start with,' says Gary Gray, then the lead narrator. 'We never made much money out of it, but I suppose somebody must have.'[12] The compensating factor was that they were scattered with the first grains of global stardust. They were celebrities, in a modest sense, even if they never quite perceived the experience as such. Within the Australian entertainment world, the notion of celebrity was still evolving, with the corollary that child actors were grateful just to be given a chance of what seemed an impossibly seductive existence. But Gray remembers receiving fan mail from County Durham, after the UK rights were bought by Granada Television, while Morgan spent one day on set as host to a five-year-old, Graeme Davis, who had travelled with his family from England to satisfy his curiosity about the ways and workings of Ten Town.

A close friendship had been forged between Morgan and Gray from their days taking riding lessons together at Ferntree Gully, a bucolic retreat beyond Melbourne's eastern extremities. 'He would travel there from East Malvern, I from Mornington,' Gray recalls. 'It was *Boys' Own Annual* stuff. There was a farm on site, where you could stay over the weekend. In our minds, it represented an adventure, of the kind that foreshadowed what we went on to do.'[13]

The difference, perhaps, was that Gray was the more earnest about envisaging acting as his calling. An only child, Gray had determinedly nurtured his talents, first by completing an elocution course and then by attending 'art of television' classes that his widowed mother subsidised at a guinea a time. In Morgan, by contrast, he detected signs of uncertainty that this could ever be a viable vocation. 'David was eager, not to mention generous in the creative sense,' Gray says. 'He might have had the idea, but I'm not sure he genuinely had the conviction that acting was what he would pursue.'[14]

Nevertheless, by the end of 1963, at the age of sixteen, Morgan had left full-time study at Melbourne High because of his many acting commitments, centred on the lead role of Tom Thumbleton in Mirams' latest brainchild, *The Magic*

Boomerang. The show transplanted the exploits depicted in *The Terrible Ten* to a fresh realm of fantasy, investing Tom with the power to use his enchanted boomerang – an Aboriginal relic discovered in his parents' attic – to thwart the attempts of an unscrupulous solicitor to take over the family sheep farm. The boomerang, so the script decreed, was capable of stopping any living creature from moving while in flight, and was possessed of a magic limited to doing good. 'It was pretty raw stuff,' Morgan reflects. 'I blush at the recollection.'[15]

A sense of embarrassment continues to colour his attitude to his acting career. He looks back at himself as a 'third-rate actor', even if the popularity of *The Magic Boomerang* was widespread. The thirty-nine episodes resonated with children from Canada to Southern Rhodesia (present-day Zimbabwe). They were directed mostly by Joe McCormick, who had already enjoyed prominence as a long-time Australian radio actor. Morgan was inundated with letters from English schoolgirls critiquing his horse-riding technique (some of whose addresses he tried to look up, on subsequent visits to the UK, to no avail).

Morgan's fame also brought him into contact with a blonde singer by the name of Olivia Newton-John. They were booked to appear together in McCormick's 1966 feature film *Funny Things Happen Down Under*, relating the tale of resourceful children who raise money by dyeing their sheep's wool in bright colours and then selling it as a naturally occurring phenomenon. It was long before Newton-John shot to stratospheric renown through her lead role in *Grease*, – indeed she was identified more then as 'Lovely Livvy' from Channel Seven's *The Happy Show*.

Newton-John exuded an effortless stage presence that left Morgan feeling somewhat eclipsed. He was billed initially as the co-star but was disabused of any delusions of grandeur when it came to rehearsing his eight-stanza duet with the leading lady. 'We did the first take and the director said, "David, drop off your first stanza, and we'll just start with Olivia." So, we tried again, and he said, "We'll do another take, and this time we'll just run Olivia's last two stanzas together."'[16] Suffice to say, once the film was released, he had been reduced to humming in the background.

A belief was crystallising in Morgan that, for the sake of his future happiness, he should follow what he was competent at, as opposed to what he loved. Impressionable young minds tend not to be conditioned to such sober, pragmatic thinking, but it was noticeable how his growing list of TV credits did little to dilute his dedication to his studies. Even after a gruelling day's filming, he could be found wide-awake with a fountain pen in one hand and a spiral notebook in the other.

'What I remember vividly about David is that he had the most enormous capacity for hard work,' Gray says. 'Even if we had gone out to some local dance, I could go to his room for a chat at any time during the night. He would always be sitting up in bed, chewing his tongue, studying furiously.'[17]

Partly, this was a case of anxiety, borne of being withdrawn from private school. But it was also a question of necessity. Instinctively, Morgan understood that his acting days were numbered. For a start, his voice had finally broken, even if he attempted at first to pass it off as a cold. Thus was he deprived of the versatility that had enabled him to play characters far younger than his actual age. Plus, his sidelining by Newton-John fed the sobering suspicion that, among the hordes of actors harbouring great visions of Hollywood, he was in the front rank of the also-rans. After years spent observing every nuance of TV production, a desire simmered inside him to make the grade as a director.

When a chance arose to become assistant director on the *Adventures of the Seaspray*, a co-production between Mirams' Pacific Films company and Screen Gems in the US, he grasped it with alacrity. It helped that there was the promise of a reunion with Gray, despite his old friend having beaten him to the central role of Mike Wells, the son of a widowed journalist aboard a charter schooner – the eponymous *Seaspray* – as it plied the South Pacific. It was appealing, too, to have a project that he could treat essentially as a sabbatical, having finished his studies for his Matriculation Certificate by correspondence. But most enticing of all was the idea of spending an indeterminate length of time sailing between paradise islands, untethered from anything resembling normality.

It proved to be one of those rare phases of life that was as exhilarating to live as it was to imagine. For eighteen months, Morgan's version of an office was the 112-foot *Seaspray*, known in real life as the *Fifeath Ban* (Gaelic for 'White Raven'), a majestic topsail schooner still used today for tourist excursions from its dock in Fiji. As for living quarters, it was scant hardship to be put up on the *Romunda*, a Fairmile cruiser that had been built during World War Two as a submarine chaser. Refitted, heated, and serviced by waiters who could cater to the cast's every whim, it was just the scene a young man might draw if he were planning his perfect escape from the shackles of everyday living.

When Morgan was not spending a working day looking out across pristine turquoise waters, he was left to his own devices. 'We were very independent,' Gray says. 'We didn't need much looking after, so we grew up pretty quickly.'[18]

Wherever the *Seaspray* docked, from the outer atolls of Fiji to the jungles of New Guinea, life for Morgan and Gray was touched by a spirit of exploration and bravado. The two young men savoured the times when the *Seaspray* cast and crew would wind up a day's filming at four in the afternoon by drinking a crate of gin on the cool, wide verandahs of Suva's colonial-era Grand Pacific Hotel. Together they revelled in night-time bacchanals on the streets of Suva, wooing twin sisters at the Golden Dragon, an upstairs bar across the road from the Grand Pacific. 'Gary was successful, I wasn't,' Morgan acknowledges. 'But that didn't stop him from waking me at 4 am on the boat to tell me that he had lost his virginity.'[19]

When they docked to film in Kioa, a verdant Melanesian paradise, they were assimilated so deeply into island life that their hosts even staged a valedictory dance, a *tralala*, in their honour. Kioa was an unusual case, a place that Fiji had bequeathed to Ellice Islanders who had been forced from their own communities by the scarcity of land. Until 1947, the only signs of habitation were a small wooden house, built by the island's former European owner, and a few wild pig tracks. 'The whole purpose of going there was to find out about people who embraced the subsistence life,' Gray says.[20] He discovered, with Morgan, that it was a happy coexistence. When the day came for them to set sail once more, the local people lavished them with gifts and saw them slip away into the sunset with a soft, haunting refrain of 'Isa Lei', the traditional Fijian song of farewell:

Isa, Isa you are my only treasure,
Must you leave me, so lonely and forsaken?
As the roses will miss the sun at dawning,
Every moment my heart for you is yearning.[21]

Even with a half-century's distance, the images have not lost their lustrous sheen of perfection. 'It was out of this world,' Morgan reflects. 'As teenage boys, you're saying, "Pinch me, is this reality?"'[22]

During one ten-week shoot in New Zealand, the crew was flown on to the Tasman Glacier beneath Mount Cook, only for a vast blizzard to engulf them and cut off all routes for an airborne rescue. Eddie Davis, the veteran American director celebrated for his work on *The Cisco Kid* and *Highway Patrol*, was one of sixteen people left stranded by the storm. To escape, he, Morgan, Gray and the rest of their bedraggled party roped themselves together for the perilous descent from the mountain, dodging deep crevasses as they went. The collective response, once they were down, was to head for the bar and drink all day, even if the New Zealand beer, notoriously under-strength in 1966, did not furnish the levels of inebriation desired.

While other young men his age found solid employment as bank tellers or trainee actuaries, Morgan's occupation was the very definition of chasing rainbows. Professionally, did he want the short-term rush of show business or the long-term crutch of a safe, signposted career path? The choice, at the age of nineteen, was ambivalent; to a degree, he craved both.

As Gray, who to this day addresses Morgan by the Fijian variant of Tevita, puts it: 'Our parents never had to say, "You must keep doing this." We just thought, Why would we ever want to give it up? No one else is having the life we're having.'[23] They felt utterly, invigoratingly adrift in the world, earning a more than respectable wage while enjoying a taste of exotica unthinkable to their contemporaries. Morgan wrestled with the question of why he should abandon a lifestyle of such thrilling daring and indulgence, but he knew that the decadence could not last.

Together with his awareness of his shortcomings as an actor, and the pressures of elevating himself from a crowded field, was the fact that Morgan had come to detest the insecurity of it all. He had worked alongside enough head-in-the-clouds vagabonds, whose delusions of the silver screen persisted in spite of having no TV bookings for three months. Some of his companions, including Paul Caro, were still living out of a caravan in Melbourne. Fred Parslow confided to Morgan that there were perhaps only five people in the land who could support themselves on acting earnings alone. Having watched his father's business go to the wall, Morgan struggled to sustain his appetite for the rootlessness or the risk. 'There are some people who can live with economic insecurity,' he explains. 'But I knew, from my background, that it was like a dagger in my heart.'[24]

Morgan allowed himself one last hit of razzle-dazzle on a pilot of *Birds of Paradise College*, an affectionate rendering of life at a girls' finishing school in the Australian bush envisaged as the female equivalent of Timbertop, the rural outpost of Geelong Grammar that Prince Charles attended as a teenager. Morgan would play the headmaster's son, while Liza Goddard, the English actress best remembered as Clarissa 'Clancy' Merrick in *Skippy the Bush Kangaroo*, would be among the schoolgirls versed in proper deportment and in such essential etiquette as how to butter a scone when hosting a luncheon. Sadly, the concept did not take off and the coveted order of thirteen episodes never materialised.

It was time to let this particular dream slide. The part of Morgan that viewed acting as wild and electrifying was becoming overwhelmed by the part that saw it as a precarious way to make a living. He could be consoled by no less an authority on the subject than Marlon Brando, who once memorably dubbed acting a bum's life. 'It is the expression of a neurotic impulse,' Brando said. 'The principal benefit acting has afforded me is the ability to pay for my psychoanalysis.'[25] The conclusion that Morgan drew was just as stark: that the talent he saw manifested in his acting rivals was necessary but not always sufficient for success. He could not countenance a future clouded by so much uncertainty and struggle. Besides, he had a university place to consider.

Morgan had never forgotten a promise he once made to Drohan, his old economics master and one who had not stinted in praise for Morgan's academic prowess, that he would complete his secondary education, come what may. His parents saw it differently. Ray, having lived through the Great Depression, believed above all else in the necessity of finding a trade, while Verna was inherently sceptical of students, keeping articles in her scrapbooks about graduates who could never hold down a steady job. She also enjoyed the reflected glory of seeing her son's name at the top of a TV credits reel.

However, in Morgan's mind there could, in the contest between show business and study, be only one winner. This, of itself, brought a certain catharsis.

While his grades had suffered slightly from the distance learning mandated by his strange and wonderful japes at sea, they still earned him entry to La Trobe, a newly founded university campus at Bundoora, north of Melbourne, in what were once sheep paddocks. There was also an offer from Monash, created in 1961 as a rival to Melbourne University, but the thought of joining the foundation class at La Trobe, with a blank canvas and an unfettered freedom of ideas, held much the greater appeal – and he had no time to prevaricate. When he telephoned the admissions officer at La Trobe, he was informed that unless he took up his place within twenty-four hours, it would be withdrawn. What seemed a decision of immense import was made, ultimately, with startling clarity.

So it was that he found himself, on the morning of 14 March 1967, his twentieth birthday, driving out to La Trobe in his mother's Triumph Herald, with an uncharted road ahead and his acting aspirations receding irrevocably in his rear-view mirror.

CHAPTER 2

Escaped Hamsters

Deep in winter, when the paddocks turned to quagmires and a bitter wind howled between the outhouses, La Trobe felt like the frontier. It had been envisaged by Melbourne's captains of industry as a quasi-Oxbridge, where students would wear gowns to dinner and earn Blues for sporting accomplishment, but this was a place unencumbered by the weight of institutional privilege. On a campus located between a drive-in theatre and the Mont Park Mental Hospital, rough-hewn boys from the Victorian bush, most of them the first from their families to go to university, matriculated alongside private schoolgirls steeped in the finer points of enunciation and social grace. They were a motley band, this founding class of 450 students, a mix of sharpies and suburbanites, where conservative minds mingled with the kind of free, existentialist spirits that the late sixties produced. This was 1967, the year of psychedelia and the Summer of Love, framed by the rise of hippiedom and the dawning sexual revolution. It was a world in tumult, and La Trobe was its logical mirror: an unkempt slice of

Bundoora where, in a reversal of the national average, there were twice as many Catholics as Protestants, and where even academic faculties adopted a devil-may-care view to make of it what they would. All shades of politics were tolerated, from fervent Maoism to the inaugural Society for Restoration of the Plantagenets on the English Throne. What La Trobe lacked in surface aesthetics, it compensated for through the vibrancy and optimism of the atmosphere it fostered.

'We were like escaped hamsters,' reflects Don Watson, who went on to become an author and political speechwriter. He belied his conformist upbringing near Korumburra by reinventing himself as pseudo-bohemian. 'Many were pretty rough characters – some were still members of gangs. There was a fair degree of violence on campus in the first year, a lot of fornication, and several suicides. You had to watch what you were doing.'[1]

The gap between the straitlaced governors and their *bon vivant* subjects could scarcely have been more glaring. Starchy drinks parties designed to stir the subtle arts of conversation degenerated into competitions to see who could quaff sherry straight from the bottle fastest. One black-tie ball unravelled to the extent that Ralph Locke, a lecturer in the sociology department, ended up standing on the dinner table, frantically fending off the fists of Garry Weaven and Ian Court, future trade union luminaries both. Watson, claiming to be guilty of nothing more than trying to protect the women caught up in the melee, had a chair broken over his head for his trouble and spent the night in Preston Hospital.

Even at La Trobe's formal opening, a report in *The Australian* wryly noted that the 'caps, gowns and coloured satin didn't quite fit the bush setting'.[2] If the environment seemed feral, it was also extraordinarily intimate: a few swathes of reclaimed countryside in which the students' political, philosophical, social and sexual lives overlapped. Those reading politics would make close acquaintance of others specialising in botany. Anybody with the slightest connection to the campus, from staff at the Plaka Coffee Lounge to the proprietor at the Heidelberg Road garage, was known by name. Even the hastily created drinking clubs could be strikingly niche: one, called the Beaker Society, was devoted to the consumption of a particularly rough form of cider from the Kinglake Ranges. As for attempts to keep the sexes apart at night with guards and heavy locks on the college doors, these were gleefully resisted, as more intrepid souls just arranged their assignations by day. This being the defining age of youth and liberation, everything took place through a thick haze of sexual tension.

Watson, in an essay aptly entitled 'Unsettled, Panicky, Astray', described how, in his subsequent meetings with La Trobe's lecturers from that time, it was the young women, many with a fondness for Lark cigarettes or a brandy, lime and soda, whom they tended to recall. He wrote: 'The fragrance of tutorials wafted back and up their leathery noses. The mini-skirt. The attempts to talk about Cervantes and Voltaire. They reached for whisky. They spoke in tones inaudible to their wives and children. One became quite catatonic for an hour or more, while another's teeth began to chatter uncontrollably and he left the room complaining lamely of a fever.'[3]

Morgan approached La Trobe's swirl of passions and urges not with trepidation but a disarming sense of certainty.

It helped that he was twenty, less callow than some of his peers and better versed in the mysteries of life from his acting explorations. He could also fall back on that most unfamiliar advantage of money. Despite lacking a scholarship in his first year, he had accrued healthy savings from his television days and had no need to augment his funds by waiting on tables or working behind a bar. As such, he fast acquired an image as the slick, urbane alpha male, having replaced the Triumph Herald with a racing-green MGB while his friends made do with dilapidated Singers. He derided Watson's faded Vauxhall as a pensioner's vehicle.

'He had a charisma aided by acquisition,' says Bill Kelty, who had enrolled in the same economics course, and who subsequently became secretary of the Australian Council of Trade Unions (ACTU). 'He drove the best car, attracted all the girls. He was just one of those stars.'[4]

Morgan's and Kelty's visions of what they wanted from their La Trobe experiences were starkly different. Where Kelty was blinkered in his industriousness, perceiving a degree as his ticket to join the trade unions, Morgan coveted a far more immersive experience, pouring himself into just about every leadership position available. Within a few months he had risen to be president of the sports union, head of the economics society, not to mention captain, opening batsman, wicketkeeper and chief purchasing officer for the cricket team. In Australian Rules football, which he had not even played between the ages of eleven and nineteen, his anointment as captain and full-forward was immediate. 'When David Morgan walked in at La Trobe, 99 per cent of his peers would have said: "One day he is going to be prime minister, or at least a person of great significance,"' Kelty says. 'He had natural leadership and he was confident in his own abilities. Confidence is not enough, though. You have to be smart as well.'[5]

Watson, observing from close quarters as Morgan's friend and third-year flatmate, viewed this rather differently. To him Morgan was a curiosity, anthropologically speaking, a product of an unusual childhood and one for whom the outward lashings of bravado concealed deep-seated vulnerabilities. 'David was a piece of raw material, essentially, something that had been hacked off,' he explains. 'If you were looking for an equivalent in literature, you would go perhaps to Balzac, to one of those characters that constantly buzzes around. There was something unformed about him, which could be galling at times, but also very intriguing.'[6]

This restless energy would manifest itself in a hostility towards anybody Morgan thought had had it easy, and a contempt for any semblance of a 'born to rule' culture. For students who owed their places in tertiary education purely to their parents' money, he reserved particular disdain. 'The first words he ever said to me at La Trobe were, "Are you here on a scholarship or a fathership?"' Watson says. 'The second words were, "Why don't you get a haircut and take that ridiculous scarf off?"'[7]

Instinctively, Morgan railed against anything that could be construed as pretentious, from scarf habits to film tastes. La Trobe would often host cinema evenings, where Philippe Mora, a student who moonlighted as an accomplished director, projected black-and-white movies on to the Glenn College walls while Max Merritt and the Meteors played their medleys of rock and roll. But where Watson gladly embraced the more esoteric productions, Morgan was agnostic. At one stage, Watson, a literature student whose college room was furnished with little save for a turntable, an ashtray and a Judy Henske record, sought to convince his friend of the merits of Ingmar Bergman's *Through a Glass Darkly*, with little success.

'I had been in the film business, and I still found it utterly impenetrable,' Morgan says. 'My preferences were more mainstream, I suppose.'[8] He would never belong, he realised, among the avant-garde wing of the student body, opposed as he was to the idea of hangovers or those who inclined towards sloth.

Watson, who by his own admission spent his first year in a state of delirious disorientation, thought Morgan's self-discipline remarkable. It remains his theory that most males of student age are hormonally unable to do what they should on the academic front, but in Morgan he saw someone exceptionally capable of keeping work and play in proper proportion. 'He would have his Ovaltine in the morning and then work ferociously. He was driven, never finding much time to sit around and talk. He would take students to task for wearing sunglasses in the library. "Bit glary in here, pal?" he would ask. I was halfway between finding him fascinating and regarding him as like a father to me. He would drink, for example, but he wouldn't have the patience for dealing with hangovers. Somehow, he got his hormones functioning in conjunction with his study, but I'm not sure how. Most of us can't do that.'[9]

The pedigree of his teachers helped. As one of twelve in the economics honours class, Morgan gravitated naturally towards the instruction of Donald Whitehead, an effervescent professor in his late thirties who had already been widely published in the fields of macro-economics and economic history. Far from being an ivory-tower academic, Whitehead was deeply enmeshed in the public policy debates of the day. A Liberal supporter, he advised the Employers' Federation on national wage cases and lobbied hard to have an income system linked to productivity introduced in Australia.

'The guy was phenomenal,' Morgan says. 'His lectures were like economic poetry. Sometimes, when he was fleshing out the business of trade, he would use the example of England, where the idea that old landed wealth was the only legitimate form of money faded out to the point where trade and commerce became respectable. Suddenly, he would throw a piece of chalk over our heads and ask, "Why? Why did that happen? What was the motivation? Did I just get bored or was I trying to get your attention?"'[10] This technique, of challenging students' assumptions and steering them – gently or otherwise – to alternative standpoints, was the essence of the La Trobe way. This was a university governed by academics rather than administrators. It was a reflection of the intellectual electricity on campus that lecturers did not feel burdened, unlike at Melbourne University, by a 120-year history that they had to honour obediently.

'Whitehead was the best teacher I ever had,' Kelty says. 'He would make me develop issues, formulate arguments. You would be marked accordingly: firstly, for getting a basic proposition right, and secondly, for showing initiative, for looking at an issue from a different perspective. You were being examined for creativity of thought.'[11] For Kelty, just as for Morgan – who acknowledges that he was consciously trying at La Trobe to escape the shadow of his mother's casual prejudices – this openness to other forms of thinking was the very symbol of education's power.

Across Australia, the fabric of conservatism was fraying. When Harold Holt disappeared, presumed drowned, in the waters off Portsea in December 1967, he seemed to take the ballast of the Liberal Party with him. While Labor was furnished with the visionary Gough Whitlam, the Liberals were poised to throw in their lot with the despised William McMahon. An internal leadership crisis, allied to a growing revolt against the Australian government's policy of conscription for the Vietnam War, stirred an enthusiasm among the young men and women of La Trobe for upsetting the old political order.

'Their complacency was surpassed only by their supineness, their arrogance, their Anglophilia,' Watson argues. 'We wanted to blow marijuana up their noses and make them laugh, helplessly.'[12]

There was no better lightning rod for rebellion than Vietnam. Holt, an arch-disciple of Lyndon Johnson's presidency in the United States, had expanded Australian involvement in the war under the slogan 'All the way with LBJ!' Galvanised by the mutinous climate of 1968, the students took conflict as their cue to embarrass the ruling elite. It is a stretch to imagine that an event such as the Tet Offensive, waged within a month of Holt's death, could have had so visceral an effect upon a tiny campus far away, but the backlash was instant. Photographs of Viet Cong soldiers in the heart of Saigon spoke of an American military campaign that was ill-conceived, deceitful and hurtling towards failure.

Demonstrations were mobilised along Waterdale Road, while the university newspaper *Rabelais* – named, with no little affectation, after the French Renaissance writer – produced thunderous editorials to match. Interventions by the police, led by Inspector Keith Plattfuss, were horribly heavy handed. The arrogance of Plattfuss, whose name felicitously translated as 'Flat Foot' in German and who infamously said that the protestors 'got some baton today and they'll get a lot more in the future', gave extra impetus to the uprising. In one incident, members of the university council were blockaded inside their own committee meeting. Even Neville White, a physical sciences student who had served in Vietnam, joined marches intended to highlight not so much military folly as the abhorrence of conscription at a time when Australia was not engaged in a global conflict.

It was a doctrine, perfectly literally, of life or death. With the country unwilling to commit the resources required to train up a volunteer army, it alighted instead upon the dreaded 'Birthday Ballot'. Marbles would be drawn out of a barrel, in a bi-annual lottery-style ritual that came to be nationally televised, and if your date of birth was inscribed on one, you could consider it a call-up. This was the fate that befell Kelty, at least until he registered as a conscientious objector, ultimately winning his case at Heidelberg Court. Kelty had a predetermined view of life from which he could not possibly be swayed, despite all the letters he received at La Trobe, ordering him to fight. 'I was driven for causes,' he says. 'I was there to get a good result, get a job with the unions, and to get out of the war. I was using university for those instruments alone.'

Morgan, as it turned out, was never thrust into the same predicament. To his immense relief, his date of 14 March was not declared. He headed straight to the telegram office, intending to send his parents a message about his 'bloody good news', only for the lady on duty to inform him soberly that she would not agree to such language in print. There could be no exaggerating how great a mercy it was. In June 1968, when twenty-five Australians were killed near Saigon in the Battle of Coral-Balmoral, Morgan and Watson, who had also avoided the draft, were on their way to Brisbane to play intervarsity football.

* * *

Of course, football was never a mere frivolity to a Melburnian. As Bruce Dawe had recognised in his 1967 poem, 'Life Cycle', Australian Rules was the city's cult, its creed, its invention, its abiding obsession: 'When children are born in Victoria / They are wrapped in club colours, laid in beribboned cots, / Having already begun a lifetime's barracking.'[13] It was the dream of every Melbourne boy to read his name on the back page of *The Age* on a Friday morning.

On the face of it, the sport was not one to which Morgan seemed innately suited. He did not resemble the archetypal athlete, being neither the tallest nor the quickest, but he compensated through brilliant reflexes and an intuitive understanding of how balls bounced. 'It was unorthodox, the way he was made up,' Watson says. 'He was all bones and hips, but he was insanely strong.'[14] He was heavy enough to hold his position in a pack and equipped with a prodigious leap that enabled him to take a high mark at will. While dexterous with his hands, he made by far his most eye-catching contributions with the boot.

In the halls of La Trobe, there has never been a goal-kicker to bear comparison with 'Mushrooms Morgan' – a nickname honouring his outstanding displays on an oval overgrown with fungi – before or since. In 1969, his third full season for the University Blacks, he kicked 175 goals. Little wonder, then, that Jim Main of the *Melbourne Herald*, struck by the feats of this unusually slight full-forward, acclaimed him as a 'goal goliath'.

The La Trobe team's rivals were rough; unsuspecting young undergraduates faced off against men. The very place names – Whittlesea, St Andrews, Lalor – are recalled by Tony Sheehan, La Trobe's stalwart of a ruck rover and later treasurer in the Victorian government, with a shudder. Sheehan had come from a rural background himself, in Bendigo, but nothing could quite steel him for the primal intensity with which students were loathed out in the Victorian hinterland. 'We were kids, they were bloody thugs,' he says. 'These were small towns, mostly struggling communities. With the backdrop of Vietnam, we would also be associated with anti-conscription sentiment. We were everything they weren't.'[15] Many of the darker transgressions went unreported. 'I happened to challenge one umpire,' Sheehan reflects. 'He said, "You don't think I'm coming back out here for the tribunal on Tuesday night, do you?" He wasn't about to risk life and limb.'[16]

Morgan, in his isolated position up the field, bore the brunt of the punishment. Since his was an era when a match had only one umpire, full-forwards could be beaten up without anyone noticing. In one game against Lalor, he received such a fearful going-over that he was knocked unconscious and had his nose broken, prompting Keith Horsley, by now Morgan's stepfather after marriage to Verna, to run out into the fray in outrage.

Watson, who observed many such scenes, reflects: 'It was like Princeton versus the Okies. Even the women on the boundary wanted to kill him. He might be sixty yards from goal, and they would still be howling abuse at him, saliva running down their faces.'[17]

It was Morgan's natural instinct, even so, to screen out the worst of the invective. A close friend of Blair Campbell, the earliest progenitor of the 'banana kick' in Australian Rules, he had the resilience to stand mere inches from his tormentors on the touchline and still send the ball screaming between the posts on a reverse cycle. The brutality was a curiously fortifying experience for him. In the grand final against Mernda in 1969, there was a price on his head, a bounty on offer to any enterprising belligerent who could take him out. It was testament, perhaps, to the bull-headedness he had built up by this point that he not only foiled his opponents' worst intentions but also kicked ten goals that helped seal the Blacks' first league title. 'It was rough, but it was something you inured yourself to,' he says. 'With one goal, the pain would miraculously seep away.'[18]

But the memories of confronting such vitriol remain seared upon his subconscious. In a speech to mark La Trobe's fortieth anniversary in 2007, Morgan told the audience: 'As long as I live, I will never forget the female supporters of Mernda, the shrillness of their screams, the distilled hatred on the faces, or the certainty of their views – including, and despite all evidence to the contrary, their opinion about my sexual preferences.'[19]

Sheehan, who still holds La Trobe's appearance record with 321 games, names Morgan without hesitation among the club's team of the half-century. It is his contention, too, that their full-forward's irrepressible qualities had a dimension far beyond the playing oval. 'He took terrible punishment, but he still got up. That tends to be overlooked in the reflections on him. I have no doubt that it was useful to David, this understanding that he could cope in such situations. If you played against some of those guys, you had nothing else to fear in life.'[20]

There is a consensus among Morgan's contemporaries in these years that he was guided by an earnestness of purpose, that he was at La Trobe to work and not – or at least not exclusively – to play. He removed himself from revolutionary politics, from the pamphleteering and the polemics in *Rabelais* or *Red Moat*, the resident Marxist broadsheet, in favour of an unwavering focus on his scholastic ambitions. University, he understood, was his chance to repudiate the stifling conservatism he had grown up with in East Malvern. For Morgan, the longer he was exposed to the independence of thought championed at La Trobe, the more any vestigial preconceptions from his youth fell away.

His father, for instance, had been friendly with Norman Banks, Melbourne's reactionary pioneer of talkback radio, who used to speak passionately in defence of monarchy and even of apartheid in South Africa. 'Banks was a horrible, sleazy figure, who belonged somewhere in the American Midwest,' Watson says. 'He was full of unction, even if he would have called himself civilised all the same.'[21]

His Protestant mother was also very bigoted towards Catholics and Jews. 'This was despite the contradiction that her two best friends were Catholics. We would ask, "But what about Marge and Joan?" "Yes, but they're different," she replied. I had gone to Sunday school and Bible classes until I started acting. I was never a great believer but never a sufficient disbeliever, either. Education was life changing. You could formulate your own view on politics and religion, rather than carrying your parents' prejudices.'[22] From the moment that he learned to think for himself Morgan was, essentially, an atheist.

Marks of academic distinction mattered profoundly to him. This arose, in part, from his pathological dread of failure, but also from the rare calibre of his peers in La Trobe's small economics cohort. Run a rule across these students and the unifying theme is that they went on, almost without exception, to forge careers of considerable eminence. Take Sheehan, who, shelving his football dreams, became treasurer of Victoria under the premiership of Joan Kirner. Weaven, negating his insistence that he had only enrolled at university 'for the beer and the girls', steered a path to the assistant secretaryship of the ACTU, establishing himself as a central figure in the country's superannuation revolution.[23] Pasquale Sgro was so smitten by what he was studying that he made it his vocation, rising to be head of economics at Deakin University in Geelong, while Ghazzali Sheikh Abdul Khalid's skills as a diplomat elevated him to the role of Malaysian ambassador to the United States. As for Sue Dao – who Weaven describes as a 'one-in-a-million student, off the charts' – she decided at first to take up nursing in her native Vietnam, tending to soldiers maimed in the unremitting bloodshed.[24]

The contest for top intellectual honours was waged, largely, between Morgan and Kelty, even if the two brought distinct qualities to their chosen discipline. Both were enamoured of the intrinsic elegance of their tuition from the likes of Whitehead and Roy Webb, but few could rival Kelty for sheer remorselessness of work ethic.

For all Kelty's name would later become indivisible, in his capacity as head of the ACTU, from the economic transformation of Australia, he showed scant interest in any of the Marxist agitation convulsing the La Trobe campus. 'Bill was a strange fellow,' Watson reflects. 'People knew him by reputation, but seldom saw him. He would attend Whitehead's lectures and go straight back to his mother's place in Brunswick, scribbling down notes.' It is an account that Kelty himself does little to deflect. 'I was an unbelievable scholastic warrior,' he says. 'For every essay I was told to write, I would write twenty. I would do the work of four students. Nobody ever worked as hard as me at economics in any place, I reckon, in the whole world.'[25]

And yet it is to Morgan that Kelty ascribes the more agile intuition. 'Whatever skill I had was honed out of bloody steel,' he explains. 'David, by contrast, had a very clear mind, one that could understand processes. There was a sense of brilliance about him, in how he could take a complex proposition and distil it to something simple very rapidly.

I would have to take it home, analyse it, write out all my workings. I would take two days to come to a result that he would reach within a few minutes. There's a great advantage in life from being quick.'[26]

Not that Morgan would always wear his erudition lightly. It is Weaven's carefully worded judgment that Morgan made a lack of modesty an endearing characteristic, while Sheehan admits to having found his ebullience overwhelming at times. There was also a certain fixation with keeping up appearances, or at least an idea, in the eyes of his close friend Elizabeth Welsh, that being perceived as one of life's achievers was half the battle.[27]

One particular episode proved illustrative. Morgan had just collected his third-year results – formidably strong, it turned out – when he jumped into his MGB with his girlfriend at the time, Judy McPherson, and headed off to a Panton Hill reception honouring his record goal-kicking exploits for the season. Despite the summer rain he drove, as was his wont, at a fair clip, only to veer out of control on treacherous roads and wedge his vehicle under the tray of a parked truck. Judy hit her head on the windscreen in the impact, but such was the importance of the function to him, he insisted on taking her along to an evening through which she had to suffer with a broken nose. 'That was David,' Watson says, indulgently. 'Says it all, really.'[28]

There is a tendency in life for the memories of one's alma mater to become steeped in sepia. In Morgan's case, though, there is no false romanticising required. He regarded his escapades in Bundoora as affectionately then as he does today, even with the benefit of a half-century's reflection. He would live in the moment with such intensity that he has no need to look back upon those years wistfully, wondering why he had not appreciated it more. 'I understood at the time,' he explains. 'All the while, I had a feeling that this might be as good as it would ever get.'

Even so, his edifying rite of passage at La Trobe did not breed in him an appetite for becoming a career academic. Instead, inspired by Whitehead, who would encourage him to draw connections between lectures and articles in *The Australian Financial Review*, he was enthusiastic about applying his learnings to some practical use.

A chance conversation with Richard Wright, a classmate who later reinvented himself in law, becoming a magistrate in Bendigo, brought clarity to his thinking. In 1969, the pair were strolling across the university moat, from Glenn College to the library, when Wright let slip that he was applying for a cadetship at the Treasury. It was one of those innocuous disclosures that turned out to be life changing.

Morgan, competitive to his core, followed where Wright had led, advancing within weeks to a final interview in Canberra. Across the desk at Treasury was Bill Cole, later Sir William and a secretary of finance, no less, whom Morgan urged to gloss over the acting section of his CV, lest he deem it frivolous. 'Oh, fear not,' Cole shot back. 'That will be very relevant in the Cabinet Room.'[29]

* * *

The august corridors of Treasury were an invigorating habitat. For the first time, Morgan sensed, even on the lowly cadet duties that he assumed in 1970, how it felt to have one's hands on the levers of power. 'Rightly or wrongly, I had this image as a cloistered academic, sitting in a room, scribbling away on an article,' he says. 'But I found that I relished the camaraderie of a team.'[30]

The thought that he could make this his métier was by no means far-fetched. Aspirational students of the time, buoyed by continuous improvement in postwar quality of life, did not think twice about whether they would have a job after graduation. Rather, the question was one of which institution should be given the gift of employing them. It became an attitude that Morgan upheld in almost everything he did. One morning, on the drive to Canberra, he stopped off at a pharmacy to buy some shaving equipment. 'Instead of going for the lather, I said, "No, I'll have the pressure pack." You could see the cashier reel back in surprise. But I thought, Of course I'll go for the more expensive option. Living standards doubled every thirty years, right? That was the mindset we had.'[31]

Essentially, he took a decision that he would succeed in whatever he discovered an aptitude for – and it was clear, under Whitehead's tutelage, that he had an uncommon skill for grasping the subtleties of how economies functioned. But success, in his estimation, equated to something far grander than job satisfaction or financial security, even if Treasury had agreed to pay his way through his fourth year at La Trobe. It mattered to him that he should be, in his chosen sphere, a person of significance. Welsh sat with him one afternoon while he worked out his best route of advancement. He told her, quite baldly, that he wanted to be the finest economist in Australia.

And here again there was a choice to be made. To be the finest economist in Australia, he would need to set his fledgling football career to one side.

Given his propensity for setting records wherever there was an oval bladder to be kicked, Morgan had advanced beyond the quaint informality of football at La Trobe, where it had been his obligation as foundation captain to scour Glenn College at 1.15 pm on Saturdays and drag would-be players out of their obscenely worse-for-wear state. In 1970, his fourth and last year as an undergraduate, Morgan switched his football allegiance to Melbourne University – ranked at the highest 'A' grade by the Victorian Amateur Football Association, while La Trobe would be forced to start at the lowest 'F' – while also earning selection for the All-Australian Universities team. It was here that his coach, Peter O'Donohue, a former customs officer and a captain of Hawthorn in the early fifties, espied a talent that could potentially propel him all the way to the Victorian Football League (VFL).

Frank Dunin, chairman of selectors at Australian National University (ANU) in Canberra, whose team Morgan joined as a fresh-faced Treasury official in 1971, was inclined to agree. His latest recruit was conspicuously accomplished, amassing 108 goals in a season, en route to signing a one-year professional contract at Eastlake. The Eastlake name carried kudos, the club having nurtured the virtuoso Alex Jesaulenko, who had taken the 'mark of the century' playing for Carlton in the VFL grand final of 1970. It fell to Morgan to break an ACT record that had stood since 1948, kicking an eye-watering 134 goals in the 1972 campaign. Nobody had accumulated more in one year in the entire annals of football in the Australian Capital Territory.

The allure of pursuing a future in the VFL, where men such as Jesaulenko would be feted as minor deities, was becoming irresistible. It was doubly powerful on the training fields at Richmond, where Morgan earned a trial by virtue of Dunin's recommendation. Two Premiership triumphs in the previous five years had bestowed a cachet upon the Tigers, where Royce Hart and Kevin Bartlett occupied the type of pedestal befitting gladiators at the Colosseum. They were searching, though, for a recognised forward, and Morgan seemed ready-made to meet their prescription. As such, he was pitched straight into a deceptively billed 'practice game' against Carlton, their implacable rivals. It was a fiery baptism that he survived sufficiently well to earn a spot in the Richmond team for his first league match, against Collingwood at the Melbourne Cricket Ground.

The stumbling block was that his club transfer had become tangled in red tape, as Eastlake held out for more money than Richmond were willing to pay. One Eastlake official, speaking anonymously, said: 'I don't think he will make the grade on the half-forward flank, because he is too slow. Richmond say they will not play him at full-forward, because he is not tall enough. We can't really afford to let him go – he is our most valuable player.'[32]

Ultimately, the impasse left Morgan's grand designs upon sporting greatness dead in the water. He had been prepared to fly each week to Melbourne if Richmond could prove that they wanted him, but the lingering uncertainty threatened a slide back into the insecurity he abhorred. And Morgan understood that while he could have made a tolerable living on the fringes of the VFL, he was never likely to win the Brownlow Medal. 'It would be hard to exaggerate what an agonising decision it was,' he reflects. 'Football is Melbourne's religion.'[33] But this decision would help determine, in ways he could barely have envisaged at twenty-five years old, how the rest of his life played out.

* * *

'A lot of intelligent people in the world disappear,' Kelty argues. 'They have incredibly high IQs, but they vanish, because of their own self-interest. All the intellect in the world leads them nowhere. But David was one who applied his intellect for a purpose.'[34]

A conviction had hardened within Morgan, to the point where he felt able to shelve football altogether, that his degree was an asset worth bringing to its fruition. La Trobe could not lay any claim to academic pre-eminence in Australia. It could not even purport to be in the top two in Melbourne. But there was an incalculable value in what a smaller university, still forging its way in the world, could give to students who might have struggled for recognition at a sprawling, impersonal campus elsewhere.

The story of Jack Welch, who rose from unprepossessing origins as the son of a rail conductor to become one of the iconic business leaders of his generation at General Electric, is instructive here. Welch was dismayed at first to discover that his two preferred seats of learning, Columbia and Dartmouth College, had rejected him, but upon walking into the University of Massachusetts' modest Amherst division in the autumn of 1953, everything changed. 'In 1957, I was one of the university's top best students graduating, with a degree in chemical engineering,' Welch wrote in his memoir, *Straight from the Gut*. 'If I had gone to MIT [Massachusetts Institute of Technology], I might have been in the middle of the pile.'[35]

The lesson that Morgan gleaned from his flourishing at La Trobe was strikingly similar. 'Had I just rolled on to Melbourne University, the more conventional destination, I could have been buried among 30,000 others,' he says.[36] Instead, he graduated top of his class, even if he suspects that Kelty could have run him close had he not left before the honours year to join the Storemen and Packers' Union. He thrived, like Welch, on teaching that placed a premium on creative thought processes, rather than on finite, rigidly defined answers. Similarly, just as Welch had been the 'pet project' of one particular professor at UMass, Ernie Lindsey, Morgan relished the presence of a father figure in Whitehead. 'He loved our little group of students,' Morgan says, and the bond was mutual. Morgan later visited Whitehead in hospital as he lay dying from stomach cancer.

The confidence that Morgan derived from his first-class degree at La Trobe would never leave him. Elites, he knew from bitter observation of the tyranny of Melbourne's private schools, had a tendency to recreate themselves. It remains a feature, for example, of the UK's 'elite' – technically defined as the top six per cent – that admission to this highest social caste invariably depends on possession of a degree from Oxford, Cambridge or a mere five other of the country's grandest universities. But Morgan was persuaded beyond the faintest doubt by his La Trobe years that there could be a different way, outside an educational straitjacket in which societies simply replaced one form of aristocracy with another.

One of Whitehead's parting wishes was that Morgan should consider postgraduate study, a possibility that struck him with renewed force as his football prospects dwindled. As such, one mid-September afternoon, straight after the Eastlake premiership win, he sidled towards the gate at Canberra Airport, his bags packed and his hand clutching a boarding pass marked for London.

CHAPTER 3

Journey Without Maps

For anybody who has ever entertained visions of becoming a Rhodes Scholar, there is a certain etiquette to follow. Candidates for this most coveted postgraduate bursary, among whose Australian recipients can be counted one governor-general, two Nobel Prize winners and three prime ministers, are traditionally judged not only on scholarly prowess and moral rectitude, but also on the poise with which they hold a knife and fork. When Michael McFaul, the United States' former ambassador to Russia, pitched up for his final interview in the mid-eighties, he was asked how he could reconcile his keenness to study at Oxford with the fact that Cecil Rhodes, the award's benefactor, had been a British imperialist and white supremacist. What, his inquisitor asked mischievously, would he do with this 'blood money'? 'I will use it to bring down the regime,' McFaul replied.[1]

Spool back a decade, and a remarkably similar scene played out within the neoclassical splendour of Government House in Melbourne.

At the table for lunch, in late 1971, as prospective 'Rhodies' were examined on such essentials as how well they handled their drink, sat Sir Rohan Delacombe, governor of Victoria and a gentleman of impeccable military bearing. Beside him was Morgan, who, in a less than subtle reading of his environment, began holding forth about the wrong-headedness of the war in Vietnam and why he believed marijuana use was no more pernicious than that of alcohol. 'Sir Rohan was this typical Colonel Blimp figure,' he says. 'If you put him in a film, he was the guy the Brits would always send over to be governor of a state.'[2] Politically, this cut-glass grandee, a Harrow-educated major-general who once commanded the British occupation forces in Berlin, found little fellow feeling with a left-wing student emboldened by a couple of glasses of wine. This became painfully clear when he inquired of Morgan how Rhodes might be regarded in seventies Australia. 'As a racist,' Morgan shot back, to uncomfortable silence.[3] The meal over, the other judges sheepishly suggested that he ought to apologise to his affronted host.

It was scant surprise when Morgan, among the final four in Victoria in line for the scholarship, found that the letter of congratulation never came.

Morgan recognised that he had been guilty of 'phenomenal naïveté'.[4] And yet his route to the broadening pleasures of graduate study abroad was far from closed. A second tilt at Rhodes prestige was out of the question, since he was about to pass the cut-off age of twenty-five, but a successful quest for a Commonwealth Scholarship afforded him the freedom to attend any UK university he chose.

For a restless young economist, the London School of Economics (LSE) was the finest place in Europe to refine one's craft. By 1972, the institution had among its doyens Harry Gordon Johnson, erstwhile member of Milton Friedman's Chicago School and one who all but rewrote the manual on international trade, and Alan Prest, known to every economics undergraduate in Britain by virtue of his definitive textbook on public finance. Even today, it is ranked close to Oxford or Cambridge in its field.[5]

For Morgan, fresh off the flight from Australia, the exhilaration of a first taste of northern-hemisphere life was tempered by a sense of panic that he had not prepared diligently enough. He had arrived a month late in London for his masters course, having stayed to honour his final commitments at Eastlake by playing in the ACT grand final against Ainslie, and discovered his classmates deep in intensive, mandatory modules on mathematics and statistics. 'I was beside myself,' he reflects. 'I thought, I've made a horrible mistake here, I'll never catch up, I'll fail my exams. The only solution was to work my toenail off.'[6]

The LSE in 1972 formed a fascinating nexus of time and place. Muhammad Ali had recently visited, to deliver a barnstorming speech about boxing and Black Power. Protests against the directorship of Walter Adams, unpopular to many due to his background teaching in Rhodesia under white nationalist ruler Ian Smith, bubbled up frequently. All around, too, a gathering global oil and energy crisis was conspiring to create the most volatile economic landscape for industrialised countries since the Great Depression. Anybody signed up to study economics in the heart of London was not so much reading the subject as living it. 'It was a wild ride,' Morgan says. 'The economics profession was being turned on its head by "stagflation", an ugly combination of stagnation and inflation. High prices and high unemployment were not supposed to coexist. This wasn't in the rulebook.'[7]

The first oil price shock, in 1973, had raised generalised inflation while increasing unemployment, a phenomenon that could not be explained by any conventional macro-economic models. The consequences in Britain were grievous. Inflation hit double digits, the national debt ballooned, and prime minister Edward Heath was bulldozed by striking coal miners into enforcing the Three-Day Week, limiting consumers to only three consecutive days of electricity use in seven. 'We shall have a harder Christmas than we have known since the war,' an ashen-faced Heath declared, even if Londoners bore the privations with the spirit of the Blitz, lighting their offices with candles and fitting their homes with camping stoves to fend off the chill.[8] Morgan's love for acerbic British humour was sparked by the merciless depictions in satirical magazine *Private Eye* of Heath, who had once negotiated for the country at a Common Market food prices conference, as 'the Grocer'.[9]

The working patterns that Morgan set for himself at LSE mirrored the austerity of the times. Terrified of falling behind, he committed to a lifestyle of scrupulous self-denial. His room at London House, the residence for graduate men from the Commonwealth, was directly opposite the women's quarters on Mecklenburgh Square in Bloomsbury, but he inhabited a bubble far removed from the loose antics permissible at La Trobe. 'Whenever I caught sight of his course notes, I was always struck by the level of detail,' says Bronwyn Curtis, who had plied the same path to LSE from Bundoora. 'I went to enjoy London, while David was utterly focused.'[10]

Centralised campus life was notable by its absence. For all LSE's merits as a seat of learning, it was physically unprepossessing, lacking the dreaming spires of Oxford or the bucolic Backs of Cambridge, and instead merging imperceptibly with the metropolis around. Jeffrey Golden, an American student who later returned as a visiting fellow, recalls his dismay at discovering that an institution of such international renown was contained within three buildings and an alleyway.[11] Morgan, so myopically absorbed in his work that extramural activities extended little further than a few evenings at the film society, claims that he 'would have felt cheated if this had been my undergraduate experience'.[12] As it was, he treated his ascetic masters year almost as a necessary sacrifice, mindful that success far from home could be his ticket to greater glories.

* * *

Not that he knew it immediately, a career of international dimension was already taking shape. Through LSE connections, an opening had arisen to spend a summer at the International Monetary Fund (IMF) in Washington, a body so close to the epicentre of global power that its headquarters lay just three blocks along from the White House. The offer was non-committal – presented, according to Morgan, as a 'chance for us to look at the IMF, and for them to have a look at us' – but it was one that he seized with alacrity.[13] Even a nerve-shredding first night in New York, his first on American soil, could not dissuade him.

Having landed late at night, he checked into a dive of a hotel on Times Square, where the door of his room had, ominously, been quadruple-locked. In the early seventies, this slice of Manhattan was a benighted place, rife with pimps and prostitutes, the drug-filled New York streets calling to mind less a jaunty Frank Sinatra melody than a scene from *Taxi Driver*. Morgan was shocked when a short walk from his hotel brought an encounter with NYPD officers armed to the teeth with Magnum revolvers. 'At that point I went straight back to my fleapit hovel, put each of the four locks on, and watched some television,' he says. 'Only to be greeted by a news report about violent crime.'[14]

If he were discombobulated by New York, he found the ambience of Washington soothingly Canberra-esque. Both cities occupied federal districts not far from the coasts of their respective continents, both were planned from scratch on farmland sites dictated by compromise, and both owed their very identities to the business of government.

The one flaw in the bureaucratic machine was Watergate, as Sam Ervin's Senate hearings on Capitol Hill became not just a fixation of the Washington establishment but a national television event. All three major networks carried the broadcast simultaneously, as the extent of President Nixon's malfeasance was unmasked. In one session, John Dean, a former White House counsel, acknowledged that Watergate was a 'cancer on the presidency', while in another, Alexander

Butterfield, among Nixon's closest advisors, revealed the existence of Oval Office tapes that would soon show the president to be scheming, profane, and complicit in the most infamous political cover-up of the twentieth century.[15] Morgan, still finding his level among Washington's small army of summer interns, drank it all in. 'It was unfathomably exciting to think that the biggest story in the world was happening in the same city,' he reflects. 'Bob Woodward and Carl Bernstein had a new revelation in the *Washington Post* every morning, and it would be leading the MacNeil/ Lehrer Report every evening. You just could not believe what you were seeing. This was the president of the United States, supposed to be the most sophisticated politician in the world.'[16]

When Morgan first set foot in Washington, thoughts of his master's result preoccupied him. Had he passed? Had those hundreds of hours spent burning the midnight oil in his LSE room translated into success in the final examinations? After all, his credibility in the eyes of the IMF brains trust depended on it. It was with a quickening pulse, then, that on his first day in his Georgetown apartment, he took a call from Professor Prest. His worry eased little when Prest – characterised by Morgan as a 'classic phlegmatic soul, a good egg but dry as dust' – adopted a monotone that gave nothing away. 'You've done tolerably well,' he began.

'Any more?' Morgan asked, uneasily.

'You've passed.' A pause. 'Actually, you managed a high distinction in your special subject.' Another pause. 'You managed a high distinction in all the other subjects, too. Oh, and you won the Ely Devons Medal for top student.' Finally,

Prest added, in what sounded almost like an afterthought: 'It was also by a margin managed by only one other person in the history of the course.'[17]

Morgan, struggling to comprehend what he had just heard, felt like letting out a scream of triumph. Indeed, it is testament to how much this conversation meant to him that he can still recount it verbatim. It was one matter to finish top of the class at La Trobe, but quite another to do so at LSE, against a far more diverse spectrum of agile economic minds. 'It convinced me,' he says, 'that I was capable of doing serious things in my life.'[18]

At a stroke, Washington's broad avenues and monumental grandeur appeared to symbolise the priceless professional kudos he had just unlocked. But as a neophyte in the ways and workings of the District of Columbia, he could still benefit from a guiding hand. It was a theme of his early life that wherever he went, Morgan leant naturally towards father figures, older male influences who could furnish the type of wisdom that his unstable upbringing had done little to provide.

At Melbourne High it was Drohan who fulfilled this quasi-paternal role, at La Trobe it was Whitehead, and in the hothouse environment of the IMF's Fiscal Affairs Department it was a resolutely unpretentious fellow Australian by the name of Bill Beveridge. The embodiment of his country's best characteristics of dry humour, unaffected charm and a skill for telling it straight, Beveridge identified abilities in Morgan, in particular an unusual level of macro-economic astuteness, worth nurturing. It helped, too, that the latest recruit had an expressiveness of character that could stop the IMF's sober worthies in their tracks. Peter Boxall, who had joined the organisation's cadre of young Australians straight from ANU, recalls: 'If some of the Americans walked into a room and all of a sudden got hit by David, they were inclined to take a step back. He was outgoing, flamboyant, the kind of person people noticed. It wasn't long before Beveridge took him under his wing.'[19]

For Morgan, this friendship had a significance beyond any professional tête-à-têtes over tax theory. In a sign that his increasingly luminous résumé had not fully papered over the hang-ups of his youth, he says: 'I undoubtedly enjoyed becoming something of a fourth son to Bill. He would invite me home to meet his children, where we would share meals and I could taste the happy family life I had not enjoyed before.'[20]

At first, Morgan felt so invigorated by the internationalism of the IMF that he told Beveridge he had no wish to return to London to pursue the doctorate that his stellar masters performance seemed to mandate. Beveridge, believing otherwise, told him: 'Go and get your sheepskin.'[21] Over a cold beer, and a couple more besides, the two started fleshing out the subject that would come to constitute Morgan's PhD thesis – namely, the effect of inflation on progressive personal tax systems and what might be done about it. By 1973, this had morphed into an area of urgent public interest. High-inflation countries of Latin America, not to mention a few Swiss cantons, had already started to head down the route of automatically indexing tax scales for inflation. Recognising that the gap in the academic literature was his to fill, Morgan returned to LSE.

* * *

Composing a PhD treatise could, he found, be an isolating experience. Each Friday evening, he would force himself to forsake the temptations of London altogether, taking the train from Waterloo to the leafy expanse of Windsor Great Park for a weekend's uninterrupted writing. There, the principal of Cumberland Lodge, a grace-and-favour retreat opposite the Queen Mother's then residence, had given Morgan licence to stay for as long as necessary, or at least until the time came to rush back for his Monday morning lecture. Ensconced in his luxurious eyrie, where nothing but the soft rustle of leaves disturbed his thoughts, he worked with Stakhanovite intensity.

It helped his motivation that by 1975, not one but two august institutions, in the shape of the IMF and the Australian government, had a vested interest in his progress. 'Without that, I might never have finished,' he acknowledges. 'It wasn't because I didn't have the capability, but because the thesis was an endurance test. It could be very, very lonely. It doesn't take long, in the field of economics, for you to have knowledge of a topic well ahead of your supervisor's.'[22]

Equally, there was the pressing prospect of a dash back to the homeland. It was a condition of Morgan's scholarship that he was allowed one return boat trip to Australia, first-class, which he put towards his involvement in the Mathews Inquiry, appointed in late 1974 by Gough Whitlam's Labor government to explore the impact of rising prices on the tax system. Peter Wilenski, an early friend of his at Treasury, had since become Whitlam's principal private secretary. Once he became aware of the closeness of Morgan's PhD topic to the task at hand, he arranged for him to meet Professor Russell Mathews, who offered him the job on the spot. He was well qualified, having endured so many days of solitude in suburban London poring over every last nuance of this subject. Credited by his peers for an 'outstanding contribution', he helped draft a report of impressive boldness, calling for income tax scales to be indexed to the rate of inflation, thus holding the real taxation burden in check at a moment when prices were spiralling across the developed world.[23] Phillip Lynch, then deputy leader of the opposition, heralded it as a 'historic document'.[24] The Mathews formula would, predicted Lynch, impose clear statutory controls on government spending, deterring it from using inflation as a hidden tax to finance its own extravagance.

Alas, 'events, dear boy, events', to borrow a phrase often ascribed to Harold Macmillan, blew these best-laid plans dramatically off course. By November 1975, Whitlam had been dismissed amid a budgetary impasse, Labor had revolted, and governor-general John Kerr had essentially fired everyone in Parliament with a proclamation that ended with the words 'God save the Queen'. Set against this constitutional carnage, wholesale tax reform was relegated down the order of political priorities. While watered-down indexation provisions were built into the 1976 Budget, they were abandoned within a year.

Still, Morgan refused to lose faith in his arguments. Squirrelling himself away in another semi-rural sanctuary in Culham, Oxfordshire, he polished off his doctoral opus with exceptional speed. Indeed, when he went to submit, LSE staff said that he was much too early, that he would need to be enrolled for a minimum of six terms when he had only been present for four.

Two whole terms of relative leisure stretched before him until the decisive *viva voce* examination, where he would have to mount a robust oral defence of his ideas. One rare avenue of escapism offered itself at the Alliance Française, the French cultural institute in South Kensington. Morgan had joined full of noble intention, eager to enhance his grasp of all things Gallic, but the make-up of his language class – three males, twenty-two females – ensured a different outcome. 'I took up with this young woman who was trapped in a doomed marriage,' he says. 'I later found out that she was an alcoholic. As a consequence, my French today is as bad as the moment I set foot in the place.'[25]

The viva itself, held in November 1975, was not short on entertainment. Prest had arranged for John Fleming, an economics don from Oxford, to interrogate Morgan about the most arcane minutiae of tax policy. Morgan, in turn, sought to assuage his nerves by chain-smoking, lighting up one cigarette as soon as the butt of another lay smouldering in the ashtray. 'I was trying to seem perfectly at ease,' he explains. 'I ended up looking like a complete idiot.'[26]

Fleming, also an economic advisor to the Bank of England who had written extensively on Morgan's sphere of interest, was an intimidating intellect. But he made one crucial mistake in his questioning, assuming that the interplay of inflation and the personal tax scales would be progressive, with the greatest impact concentrated in higher-income brackets. Instead, Morgan demonstrated through his own work that the reverse was true, that the burden fell most heavily upon those who were worst off. On every point, Prest backed up his pupil, but the effect of Morgan's conclusions would be felt far beyond the confines of the examination room.

They were, quite simply, attuned to their time, dovetailing seamlessly with contemporary public policy in Britain. Between 1973 and 1976, personal income tax in the country had more than doubled, with the strain of that shift borne disproportionately by the largest, poorest families. Uniquely in the developed world, Britain stubbornly continued its practice of separating decisions on expenditure from its choices on tax raising, even when this contributed to a bloated public sector. The ruling Conservative government had, Morgan showed, been exonerated by the huge increases in tax revenue made possible by inflation, since it did not have to ask the electorate explicitly to impose higher tax rates. It was a classic case of taxation by misrepresentation. Morgan's proposed solution was for Britain to increase its personal and dependent allowances at the time of the Budget and automatically in line with inflation. He had seen how this could work in Australia, having essentially authored the Mathews Report. He saw no reason why it could not be effective for the British, too, save for the fact that fiscal policy at Westminster tended to move about as fast as an Alpine glacier.[27]

Mercifully, his enthusiasm was shared by his intended audience. In 1977, the Institute of Economic Affairs published a truncated version of his doctoral findings, the release date auspiciously timed between pamphlets by Friedman and Friedrich Hayek, each Nobel laureates. The reception matched the elevated platform, as the UK's pre-eminent broadsheets lavished praise on its logic. While

The Times called it 'conclusive', a leader in *The Daily Telegraph* echoed Morgan's emphasis on the 'incentive that the absence of indexation gives to the politician to indulge in inflation'.[28] Even denizens of the House of Commons were listening, especially to his eye-watering calculation that Denis Healey, the chancellor of the Exchequer, would need to hand out £5.75 billion in tax cuts – rather than the meagre £2.25 billion he had managed so far that year – to restore the real income tax burden to where it had been before he took office in 1974.

To John Pardoe, then deputy leader of the Liberal Party, the message was unambiguous: only a systematic form of indexing, where all real tax increases were legislated separately, could make the government truly accountable to the people. 'No one who has read Dr Morgan,' he said, 'can fail to be convinced by the argument.'[29] This much was evident in Britain's decision that year to pass a Finance Bill that codified exactly what Morgan had called for, in providing for the automatic adjustment of tax schedules to the rate of inflation.

It was a fragile victory, reforming only a limited part of the sprawling British taxation structure, but for Morgan it was a powerful affirmation of an idea, hatched in his first weeks as a cadet in Canberra's Parliamentary Triangle, that his best course in life was not as a detached academic but as one whose expertise could help enrich the economic fabric of a nation.

***

Under the auspices of the IMF, where Morgan rose from intern to full-time staff member in early 1976, he was empowered to enact that philosophy on a rich and complex canvas. An unusual privilege of working for the Fund, and a potent factor in persuading Morgan to work in Washington, was the trust invested in him to advise even heads of state on how they should manage their countries' finances. For Margaret Kelly, an Australian who followed her studies at the University of New England with IMF missions to over forty countries, this implicit assumption that she would be fast-tracked into multilateral talks at the highest level was central to the institution's allure. 'Even though you were quite junior, you were given major responsibility,' she says. 'You would go straight into meetings with ministers of finance – and you would have the floor. To a young economist, it was a hugely exciting place to be.'[30]

Morgan's initial postings in 1976 had a somewhat *Out of Africa* feel, framed by the lost relics of colonialism and the depredations of sub-Saharan despots. First in his sights was Liberia, a grindingly impoverished state founded for returned slaves but a place that, paradoxically, gave him some hope. Independent for almost 130 years, it derived democratic plausibility from the presidency of William R. Tolbert Jr, a leader elected on a progressive platform and sworn in wearing a short-sleeved safari suit. It also used the US dollar as its sole currency, thereby preventing any unscrupulous politicians from trying to turn on the printing press. Two sources of revenue were critical to its economic survival, one being iron ore – Liberia, by happy quirk of geology, had become the continent's pre-eminent exporter – and the other the so-called 'flags of convenience' that international ships would fly to save on fees and regulations. By 1976, the maritime registry in Monrovia, Liberia's capital, was the most prolific of its kind in the world. 'Africa had been heartbreaking for the IMF, but this experience made me feel optimistic,' says Morgan, who had been brought in to help the government mitigate the effects of a dip in the cyclical iron ore trade. 'I thought, Finally, here is a model that could work.'[31]

Tragically, within four years, Tolbert would be assassinated in a coup d'état, his Cabinet members executed after trials at kangaroo courts, and his people plunged into the most savage civil war.

It took far less time for Morgan's own idealism to be shattered. His very next flight, into neighbouring Sierra Leone, transported him into a realm where all accepted codes of probity and transparency were suspended. Siaka Stevens, the tinpot tyrant whose reign was likened by his opponents to a 'plague of locusts', had no interest in the conventional apparatus of state.[32] The son of a policeman, swept to power in rigged elections in 1971, he made personal gain from public office his signature ideology. Fond of quoting the aphorism that 'the cow grazes wherever it is tethered', he presided over institutionalised corruption, where the state was both customer and provider for Stevens and his moneyed henchmen in the All People's Congress.[33] In particular, he had been quick to spot the lucrative potential of diamond mining, encouraging illicit operations that could help feather his nest. One day, Morgan walked into Sierra Leone's finance ministry to see scores of plastic shoeboxes stuffed with money.

He felt, in more reflective moments, as if he were inhabiting a scene from a novel by Evelyn Waugh or Graham Greene, not least when Morgan, assailed by the thick equatorial humidity, kicked back on his hotel balcony with a pink gin and a copy of Greene's *The Heart of the Matter*. His peregrinations mirrored those of Greene himself, whose wandering through the lawless Liberian interior had been vividly captured in his thirties travelogue, *Journey Without Maps*. The setting was headily, thrillingly foreign, as the heat, the smell and the dust all combined to sharpen his sense that he was 'just a kid, far from home'.[34]

Sierra Leone desperately needed an IMF agreement to shore up this escalating financial chaos, but the snag, not unexpectedly, was that they had yet to convince officials in Washington that the Budget was in proper order. It fell to Morgan, as the IMF's fiscal specialist, to unearth the truth of what was going on. 'To begin with, Stevens was cooperative,' he recalls. 'He gathered all his ministers and the central bank governor together and explained how they wanted the Fund's help. He instructed them, "You are going to open the books up to Dr Morgan." You could see them thinking, Do you really mean this, Siaka?'[35]

What Morgan uncovered was a vast money trail funnelling straight into Stevens' Swiss bank account. It transpired that the autocrat had, quite apart from siphoning off tax revenues for his own ends, been taking payments from diamond smugglers to ensure they would not be prosecuted. Stevens, in connivance with his Afro-Lebanese business associate Jamil Sahid Mohamed, was conspiring to rape the diamond fields and to pocket backhanders galore.

The thorny question was how best to tell him that his cover had been blown. Morgan knew, in light of Stevens' reputation for ordering his thugs to beat up dissidents in the dead of night, that it would not be a smooth conversation. As such, upon requesting a private meeting with Stevens at the dictator's palatial Freetown residence, he decided it was prudent to pack his bags in advance. Barely suppressing his anxiety, Morgan announced to Stevens: 'I regret to say this, Prime Minister, but some of these problems seem to find their way right back to your desk. There is incontrovertible evidence.'[36]

Stevens was ashen-faced, his earlier civility dissolving in an instant. 'I know who you are, Morgan,' he said, gravely. 'I've done my research on you. You're a CIA agent. There is a plane out of here at 2 pm, the only plane all day. I suggest that you are on it.'[37]

Morgan, not needing a second invitation, took his leave with some haste, sweeping out of the building via a long spiral staircase, watched by cruel-looking guards bearing rifles. There could be no starker reminder, as a young bureaucrat thrown headlong into the rotten venality of West African politics, of the stresses he was shouldering.

That Morgan tolerated such pressure, even thrived on it, guaranteed him recognition at the Fund, where Beveridge afforded him the maximum promotion allowable through the ranks. By 1978, he was, according to a letter he wrote to his friend Chris Higgins, a key ally at Treasury, 'starting to earn something of a reputation', as his IMF superiors discussed appointing him as a senior economist, a role typically out of reach for a thirty-one-year-old.[38]

His peers did not always regard his thrust for higher office favourably. 'David had a good eye for where the action was, if I can put it like that,' Boxall says. 'He positioned himself for the more substantive assignments.'[39] Burke Dillon, the division chief for Southern Africa, went further, labelling Morgan the 'most ambitious guy at the IMF'.[40] She did not mean it entirely as a compliment. 'Burke went on one Asian mission with him, and he manoeuvred himself cleverly,' says Christine Bindert, a Belgian-born, multilingual IMF officer with whom Morgan worked closely. 'He would go around a table and switch the place settings to be sure he was next to the most important people. That way, he could see, be seen, and whisper in their ears.'[41] Bindert's own first foreign posting was to Zaire, as the sole Western woman at the court of the bloodthirsty Mobutu Sese Seko. 'At least I didn't have to change the names on the little cards when we were having dinner, because he always placed me, as the only woman, next to him,' Bindert recalls. 'I would tell him what I thought, which was not always friendly. People would say: "You must be out of your mind." Mobutu had a reputation that whenever he didn't like people, he would throw them over the boat to the alligators.'[42]

Judging by the school of thought that most weaknesses are overdone strengths, there is little doubt that Morgan's penchant for managing upwards delivered him the recognition he craved. No sooner had he recovered from his awkward brush with Stevens than he had inherited a brief of equal stress in Egypt. For just as president Jimmy Carter was seeking to broker his peace deal between Egypt and Israel, in negotiations that would culminate in the Camp David

Accords, Morgan had been dispatched to Cairo as the IMF's advance party to resolve a budgetary dispute that threatened the legitimacy of ruler Anwar el-Sadat.

The policy of *infitah*, Sadat's idea of opening the door to private investment in Egypt after the Yom Kippur War, had been a conspicuous calamity, extending the gulf between rich and poor while swelling the national debt to record levels. Egypt's only realistic solution was to cut state subsidies of essential foodstuffs such as rice, flour and cooking oil, sparking a 50 per cent price hike that led directly to the notorious 'bread riots' of 1977, in which seventy-nine people were killed and over 500 injured.

Sadat, having repealed the austerity measures himself, persuaded the IMF to intervene with an A$675 million loan, issued in July 1978 with strict conditions attached. Interest rates had to be increased, the exchange rate system reformed and the fiscal deficit drastically cut. It was Morgan's task to pay the Egyptians a visit, some four months later, and confirm that their obligations were being met.

'There was a lot of pressure on a kid,' he says. 'I was very junior for something so senior. I was just hoping that they had a packet waiting for me at the Nile Hilton. I got in at about midnight, took my envelope, and headed down to the brasserie for a hamburger. I opened the papers and saw that they had done the square root of nothing about the Budget. Ten minutes later, I started having chest pains and thought, My God, I'm having a heart attack.'[43] Returning to his bedroom, he called a doctor, who carried out an electrocardiogram on the spot. 'Sir,' the medic told a panicked Morgan, 'you have acute indigestion.'[44]

Morgan was drawn to turmoil in these years like a moth to a lantern. A trip to Pakistan had coincided with a period of intense strife in Islamabad, where Zulfikar Ali Bhutto, the prime minister, had been overthrown by the military in 1977 and sentenced to death in a travesty of a trial. His successor, army chief of staff General Muhammad Zia-ul-Haq, was in Morgan's estimation 'economically illiterate, as thick as two short planks'.[45]

For travelling diplomats, Pakistan's status as a dry country – one that compelled Morgan to stock up on two litres of Johnnie Walker Black Label at the airport duty-free – was the least of their concerns. The twin evils of Zia's takeover and the ever-present threat of nuclear war with India had created considerable reluctance in global capital markets to provide funds, making it imperative for Morgan and his colleagues to settle nerves and give Pakistan the IMF's seal of approval. This was easier said than done, when he found that the once-powerful secretary of finance had, amid Zia's purges of Bhutto loyalists, simply disappeared. Matters worsened when, in disentangling the fiscal mess, he came across a major tranche of government spending under the letters 'PAEC', instantly recognisable as code for the Pakistan Atomic Energy Commission.

His hosts, however, had a creative excuse ready. 'The senior Budget official was aghast at my discovery,' he says. 'He tried to bullshit me that these initials were an acronym for overspending on politics, agriculture, economic development and councils.'[46]

There were all the hallmarks in Pakistan of a failed state, with a thin bureaucratic talent base and vast swathes of territory beyond government control. This could, when allied to the crookedness Morgan had observed on his African sorties, have bred in him a pessimism about the future for the developing world. What offset it, though, was a merciful diversion to the liberating, fast-changing economic landscape of South Korea.

In Seoul, he worked alongside a political class united by the view that opportunity could be prised from adversity. President Park Chung-hee, the authoritarian leader, had taken a paucity of natural resources and the carnage left by the Korean War as his cue to fashion an economic strategy based firmly on exports. It also placed a high character value on education, which Morgan had long since identified as a vital determinant for any economy to move beyond emerging-market status.

The one problem was that the South Koreans' hunger for foreign expertise was so insatiable, they could occasionally be too eager for their own good. 'You had to be careful, talking to them over a drink at night, criticising anything to do with corporation tax, for instance,' he explains. 'Otherwise, the very next day, they would have a taskforce to abolish it.'[47]

He had glimpsed living proof of a concept that would later be articulated by two MIT professors, Daron Acemoglu and James A. Robinson, in their best-selling 2012 book, *Why Nations Fail*. It was not geography, topography or cultural inheritance that dictated why some nations were rich and some were poor, they said, but institutional and political factors.[48] Morgan had embraced this conclusion wholeheartedly, on the evidence of his dealings in South Korea, confiding to Higgins that they had reinforced a 'resounding belief in the value of applied economics, given the political will to allow its prescriptions to operate'.[49]

Life at the Fund gave rise, by 1979, to a degree of professional satisfaction that made Morgan think twice about returning to Australia. Besides the intellectual fulfilment, some of the accoutrements could be extraordinary: on his last mission to Egypt, and his last for the IMF, he flew on the Concorde from Washington to Paris, eating caviar and sipping Dom Perignon in the company of Richard Goode, who had led the famous delegation to London in 1976, in the depths of the sterling crisis and at the pinnacle of the IMF's power. Demonstrably, Morgan possessed the requisite gifts to make a deep imprint, too. 'David had an ability to convince people that what he was advising, or putting as conditions, added up,' Bindert says. 'Finance ministers might have been disposed to think, Who is this guy David Morgan, telling me what to do? What does he know about my country? But he was never pedantic and he never aggravated them. He had a lot of common sense.'[50]

Ultimately, though, even Morgan's steep upward career trajectory could not keep him in the post indefinitely. When not flying across the world, he could almost see the White House Rose Garden from his office window, and yet he craved to be less an advisor and more a key actor with his hands on the levers of power. While he had the privilege, working for a cornerstone of global bureaucracy, of not having to pay tax, he was also not entitled to vote. 'I would happily have traded taxes for voting,' he argues. 'Washington is a one-company town. And if you're not part of the company, you feel a bit of an outsider.'[51]

In this context, the lure of Canberra, where Treasury made no secret of wanting him back, became irresistible. The Treasury was small, comprising around 500 people at the time, and wielded immense power on diverse, real-world fronts, from monetary policy to setting the exchange rate. For all the globe-girdling glamour of IMF work, for all the scrapes and jousts with shadowy third-world oppressors, his overwhelming sense was that he wanted to come home, to the one place where he could be truly at the centre of the game.

CHAPTER 4

The Stone Age

It is enshrined within the Treasury's own mission statement that its abiding ambition should be to 'improve the wellbeing of the Australian people'. The principle seems self-evident, indisputable, and yet under the aegis of John Owen Stone its validity was a moot point. By the time of Morgan's return to Canberra, early in 1980, Stone had made the department his personal fiefdom, harnessing his power as the Commonwealth's tenth secretary to the Treasury to ensconce himself as the sole conduit to the government of the day.

'Talk about hierarchical, the place was an inverted funnel,' reflects Ken Henry, who joined under Stone's stewardship and later became the second longest-serving secretary of the postwar era. 'Nothing went out of the building without his approval.'[1] Stone was the most unyielding of mandarins, who would never tolerate being second-guessed about the righteousness of his cause. Jack Garrett, a long-standing associate, once said: 'He had no doubts, unlike we ordinary mortals.'[2] Even Dick Rye, one of his most loyal lieutenants and a figure with whom he was ideologically aligned, acknowledged: 'Once he made up his mind, he would never be swayed.'[3]

The paradox was that Stone was indisputably brilliant, his nimbleness of mind mirrored in the fact that he had earned not just one first-class degree but two – the 'brightest public servant I ever dealt with',[4] according to Malcolm Fraser's treasurer, John Howard. But the years in which he had the greatest power to furnish Australia with his economic wisdom would scarcely be regarded as a beacon of success.

Stone's words, in 1979, upon replacing Sir Frederick Wheeler as secretary – 'I'm going to have fun'[5] – found few echoes beyond the walls of his august office. There is a saying beloved of Warren Buffett, iconic Sage of Omaha, that 'Only when the tide goes out do you learn who has been swimming naked,'[6] and nowhere bore out such wisdom better than Australia in the period from the early seventies to early eighties. For decades, the country had bobbed along happily on a system of crony capitalism, high tariffs and made-to-measure protection, where the default solution to industrial inefficiency was simply to provide more government assistance. Increasingly, the complacency of such a position was painfully exposed. A fall in Australia's terms of trade, coupled with the repercussions of a second global oil shock, had left the economy in a dismal, sclerotic state. Inflation and unemployment raged ever closer to double-digit marks.

The response of Fraser's government was distinguished only by its poverty of imagination, which did virtually nothing to bolster Australia's global competitiveness. While Fraser prided himself on an administration much tighter and more disciplined than his predecessor, Whitlam's, his impulse all too often was to do less, not more.

'It was a great do-nothing era,' Morgan argues. 'The fifties, sixties, seventies: they were wasted years. We had ridden up on a global golden age, but we were stuck with these huge tariff barriers that prevented us finding our place in the world.'[7] In 1980, the outlook was bleak enough for Lee Kuan Yew, founding father of Singapore and a man who regarded Fraser as a feeble hand on the tiller, to warn that Australia risked becoming the 'poor white trash of Asia'.[8]

The remark stung, but Treasury had to shoulder its share of the blame. While Stone was a figure of substantial intellectual heft, he could also be the most mulish autocrat. It was Stone who, long before he acquired the secretaryship, propagated the view that inflation lay at the root of many economic ills and who spearheaded a 'fight inflation first' strategy, against the misgivings of Fraser himself. Plus, it was Stone who would stir antagonism with politicians by his sheer bull-headedness.

Ian Macfarlane, en route to a ten-year tenure as governor of the Reserve Bank, worked in this period at the Organisation for Economic Co-operation and Development (OECD) in Paris, where he observed this habit of Stone's first-hand. 'He was strong-willed,' Macfarlane says. 'He used to represent Australia at the OECD, and he paid no attention whatsoever to what the government's views were. He just spoke entirely from his own opinion and was always nearly losing his job because of it. In that case, he wasn't a classic mandarin. If anything, he was a wildcard.'[9]

Economic thought was in the grip of what Don Dunstan, Labor premier of South Australia, dubbed in less than complimentary fashion the 'new Stone Age'. Stone, for all the power of his portfolio, applied an inflexible neo-liberal perspective to the nation's problems, upholding a Treasury line that was tethered less to hard economic facts than to his reactionary conceptions of how society should be organised.[10] The upshot was a political and bureaucratic class conditioned to assume that the country had control of its destiny even when the rest of the world was so palpably in flux. Stone had, in Morgan's assessment, become an 'arch right-winger posing as a quintessential public servant'.

The implication of such a right-wing political bent was that he would impart his views to politicians with a sense of certainty they scarcely deserved, and that a Fraser regime that could have grasped the nettle of reform instead became a byword for timidity and inertia. 'When he was secretary, it was very much a culture of an ivory tower,' Henry argues. 'Treasury was absolutely convinced it was delivering the appropriate advice and thought it wasn't their fault if government took no notice of it. Stone was just so dogmatic – bigoted, really. He was smart, but intolerant, and without sufficient command of his subject matter.'[11]

For all that Stone was an impediment to progress, he had constituted Treasury in such a way that it was impossible for his subordinate officers to succeed without his patronage. Michael Keating, later a secretary of finance, was working at the time in the Department of Prime Minister and Cabinet (PM&C) and saw the lengths to which Stone would go to ensure quiescence in the ranks. 'He surrounded himself with acolytes,' he says. 'They were chosen that way.'[12]

As an example, he cites Stone's decision to elevate John Monaghan to head of the macro-economic policy division at the expense of Chris Higgins, who by 1980 was regarded among Treasury's most agile intellects – rated by Lawrence Klein, his graduate professor at the University of Pennsylvania and winner of the Nobel Prize for economics in 1980, as one of the finest students he had ever taught.[13] 'The problem was that Chris was just a bit too independent. So, Stone put in somebody who was never likely to have an opinion of his own. Chris was shattered. But I wasn't a bit surprised.'[14]

Even before their paths intersected at Treasury, Morgan and Higgins had cultivated a close personal connection. Both were restless for change, both had pursued their studies to doctoral level abroad, and both had emerged from formative years framed by few trappings of privilege: Morgan from the shadow of his father's dire financial state and Higgins, the son of a sawmill worker, from a poor childhood in Murwillumbah, country New South Wales, who did not own a pair of school shoes until sixth grade. Still, their personalities could clash, with the cerebral and understated Higgins sometimes upbraiding his friend for a failure of modesty. During one dinner party at his house, he said to Morgan: 'Why don't you get some humility?' The reproach struck like such a thunderbolt that Morgan can still remember where he was sitting at the table, although the lesson was not altogether heeded. Later, in 1979, he sent a note – on Concorde letterhead, no less – asking for Higgins' help in securing a Treasury position as assistant secretary. Higgins described the missive as 'pathetically ostentatious'.[15] A chastened Morgan replied: 'I feel acutely embarrassed. Your modesty has always provided a mixture of feelings in me, and

I had made a (no doubt feckless) attempt to curb my immodesty. I'm sorry.'[16]

Throughout his Washington period, Morgan was scrupulous about making sure he kept Stone on side. The two had enjoyed an early introduction, when the young Treasury official, fresh out of La Trobe, acquired a copy of his department's critique of the Vernon Committee Report, an extensive exploration of Australia's economic direction after Menzies almost lost the election in 1961. Boldly, Morgan described the document, of which Stone was a principal author and intensely proud, as an unadulterated hatchet job, at best incompetent and at worst dishonest. Stone, sensing that there was nothing quite like the bravado of youth, left him an order to be in his office at 5 pm. Morgan arrived expecting to be witheringly rebuked as an upstart and encountered quite the contrary. Indeed, Stone agreed with much of Morgan's analysis, but argued that Vernon's inquiry had been nothing other than a Machiavellian ploy by Sir John Crawford, permanent secretary of the Department of Trade, to wrest power over economic policy advising from the Treasury. 'Anyway,' he added, apparently impressed by the force of Morgan's views, 'let's have a beer.'[17]

Through this one unlikely exchange, they formed a bond, where each derived a satisfaction from the energetic back-and-forth of their political debates. Over dinner one night in London's Soho, after a second summer at the IMF that had left him blazing with idealism, Morgan referred to Australia as a 'small, rich, smug, industrial country' that ought to be doing far more for the Third World.

'David, they've got to do it for themselves,' Stone said. 'You're never going to do it from within the IMF or the

World Bank. It's a lovely aspiration, but they've got to pull themselves up by their bootstraps.'[18]

As Morgan embarked upon his trans-Pacific adventure at the IMF, Stone persisted in trying to steer him back towards his Treasury calling. 'International bureaucrats,' he sniffed, whenever Morgan's Washington's colleagues were mentioned – with some irony, given that Stone had himself been Australia's representative at the IMF during the late sixties. The pair of them would meet periodically for lunches and dinners inside the Beltway, like master and apprentice. Contemporary correspondence illustrates how, in spite of their disputes, Morgan held his mentor in the highest esteem. 'It was delightful to cross swords with him again,' he confided to Higgins, after one especially bibulous brunch. 'He is a fantastically stimulating bloke, for whom I have enormous affection.'[19]

What complicated the relationship was Stone's ultimatum, delivered in January 1979, that Morgan wake up to himself and commit formally to a future at Treasury within twelve months at the most. The demand struck Morgan as unreasonable: for a start, he was not at all convinced that he would find life in Canberra fulfilling, after the thrills of London and Washington DC, and that was before he considered the growing temptation of staying in the northern hemisphere, specialising – as his IMF adventures encouraged – in fiscal policy. But Stone, characteristically, was adamant, demanding a written commitment of Morgan's intent for fear that he would otherwise vanish into the Washington ether.

By now, Morgan had enough diplomatic *savoir faire* to see that it was not worth his while creating ructions. Instead, he drove a hard bargain with Stone, claiming that Treasury was out of the question unless he could be guaranteed one of the top twenty-six positions. It was a forthright condition, given that the department employed around 500 people, but he felt it was a fair one. From his perspective, he would be turning his back on an enviable arrangement, where the IMF had promoted him rapidly to senior economist and were prepared to pay a salary broadly equivalent to those at New York investment banks to keep him. Ultimately, Stone's confirmation as secretary later that year swung the pendulum, as Morgan secured a coveted assistant secretary's post. Coming with a large office just a short walk from the treasurer's, through the National Rose Gardens and past the Lobby Restaurant, it would give him the proximity to power he craved.

He had also timed his homecoming propitiously. Treasury, by his own admission, would have been a stultifying environment in the seventies. 'It didn't serve anybody well then, including itself,' Morgan says. 'It had been split in two by Fraser in 1976 – into Treasury and the Department of Finance – because it had been so sure of its advice, so dismissive and arrogant, so unconcerned about working with government to achieve beneficial reform. It was more preoccupied with the purity of its own views, such that it was "our way or the highway". We would go down to the Press Clubs most Friday nights and Treasury officials would be bad-mouthing governments of both persuasions.'[20]

Come 1980, the moment was, in theory, ripe for a figure of Morgan's brashness and thespian flair to crash through this bureaucratic pomposity. The nation was sleepwalking towards recession, and at last he had a platform from which to make his ideas heard. He would quickly catch the attention of Bernie Fraser, a Treasury stalwart who through a laconic demeanour and a streak of devilishly dry humour was in many ways his diametric opposite. 'Some public servants are pretty self-effacing – David wasn't in the least,' Fraser recalls. 'Someone told me how he had given a talk to some younger officers in Treasury, which began with the words: "This is not an exercise in economic masturbation". As an actor, he never lost that style of wanting to make a big splash when he was trying to woo people. I adjusted to it, but it could be grating for some.'[21]

* * *

It is an anomaly of Morgan's life that just when he had found a role within the apparatus of state, he let his professional priorities slide. Indeed, his climb to the upper echelons of the public service coincided with the one true fallow period of his career. Five years earlier, he had made his first acquaintance of a striking, passionate young Labor activist called Ros Kelly. Kelly had realised that politics was her calling the instant she rushed out of the National Library to join in an Aboriginal land rights rally. They again met in passing in the US, but it was not until Morgan settled in Canberra that Michael Delaney, a mutual friend and former private secretary to Whitlam, put them back in touch. 'An old mate of mine from Washington is back in town for the holidays,' he said, sticking his head around Kelly's door. 'Would you like to join us for lunch?'[22]

The rendezvous was memorable enough for Kelly to remember exactly what she was wearing – a fuchsia shift dress – and for Morgan to pursue her with a determination that verged on obsessive.

The one rather hulking roadblock was that the thirty-two-year-old Ros was already married. In 1970, she had wed journalist Paul Kelly, then just starting at *The Australian* on his path to becoming the pre-eminent political commentator in the country. It was, as she puts it, 'never a great love affair – I wanted to be married more than Paul did and if I had been wiser, perhaps this fact would have given me pause'.[23] Her husband's father was killed in a car accident in 1971 and at this point, she reflects, she noticed a darkening of his behaviour that put their union under intolerable strain, where only her strict Catholic scruples prevented her leaving.

All the ingredients of a complex love triangle were there: a wife agonising about how to extricate herself from a doomed marriage, a suitor making ever more concerted overtures, and a spouse 'reacting appallingly', in Kelly's words, to being informed that he had a rival. For Morgan, the stress of this situation was profound, dominating his thoughts from dawn until dusk. The emotional torture is writ large in his dispatches to Higgins, who by now had left Australia for the OECD. 'I'm hopelessly besotted,' he wrote. 'My Treasury job has not been the most important thing in my life for the past three months. By and large I have never permitted anything, especially a woman, to intrude on my career.'[24] He courted Kelly with an assiduousness that underlined his conviction that in life, he could have any one thing he desired, so long as he wanted it badly enough.

The symmetries between them were striking: both came from broken homes, Morgan having faced his mother's desertion and Kelly having learned, to her horror, that her father was abandoning the family for a woman he had met in Cyprus while part of a United Nations peacekeeping force. Equally, they complemented one another in terms of vaulting ambition, with Morgan setting out his stall at Treasury as Kelly, who had been a Labor member of the ACT House of Assembly since 1974, launched a campaign for Federal Parliament in the 1980 election.

Slightly more awkward, alas, was the prospect of Morgan breaking news of this romantic entanglement to his mother. Knowing Verna's religious and political predilections only too well, he steeled himself to announce: 'Well, Mum, she's a Catholic and a socialist. Oh, and she's married to someone else.'[25]

Kelly was elected as Labor member for Canberra on 18 October 1980, confounding the prediction of her opponent Frank Brennan, a dyed-in-the-wool Catholic right-winger, that 'she'll never win – women won't vote for a woman'.[26] Detractors had tried all manner of dirty tricks to discredit her, with incumbent Liberal MP John Haslem seizing upon her friendship with the Labor leader to ask voters if they wanted Canberra in the eighties 'to be run by a blue-eyed blonde who jumps out of the box on to Bob Hawke's knee'. A toxic chauvinism seeped deep into the political canvas, although it could not taint Kelly's feat, thanks to ceaseless door-knocking across the division, of triggering a seven per cent swing in her party's favour.

Behind the scenes, the web of personal intrigue was at breaking point. On the one hand, she had sought to present a solid 'Mrs Kelly' façade in public, even including an image of Paul in her campaign pamphlets, while on the other, relations with Morgan had deepened to the stage that he would act as an unofficial support driver. In the heat of that year's electioneering, he would quip that he saw more of the capital's shopping centres than most househusbands did in a lifetime. Chauffeur duties apart, his casting as the other man was far from a recipe for contentment. 'Paul tried desperately to keep her, and Ros was susceptible to that,' he says. 'She left home, went back, and I was terribly hurt. I told her, "Don't contact me ever again." She sent me a gift, a beautiful leather bag, and I sent it back. But she reached out once more, and I weakened.'[27] By February 1981, his patience all but exhausted, he penned a note to Higgins. 'My God,' he wrote. 'How romantic love f---- us around.'[28]

It was hardly doing wonders for his sense of job security, either. On one occasion at the Canberra Hotel, where he and Stone would regularly repair for Friday night drinks, he told Stone of his implacable resolve to wed. 'If you marry that woman,' Stone said, grimly, 'you will never be secretary to the Treasury.'[29] Alarmed by this typically hardline verdict, and wary of the perceived conflict of interest in an assistant secretary – one in charge, no less, of fiscal and monetary policy, easily the most important branch – dating a high-profile Labor MP, he deemed it sensible to inform treasurer John Howard that relations with Ros had crossed a line. 'Thank you, David, that's your business,' replied Howard, who would later admit to Morgan, privately, that such a situation would never be tolerated in the tougher, more forensically scrutinised world of twenty-first century Australian politics.[30]

One consolation, as he strained to refocus his addled mind on Treasury business, was that the upheavals of 1980 signalled the beginning of the end for Fraser's lily-livered government. The Liberal–National Coalition had lost twelve seats, including seven in Victoria alone, as optimism grew that a vast backlog of unimplemented economic reform might finally see the light of day. While Stone had an absolutist idea of running a department – believing that for all the earnest deliberations among his staff, the secretary's filtered advice to the treasurer should be the definitive view – his style of rule was increasingly open to challenge. Fresher voices were demanding to be heard, as Morgan joined forces with Ted Evans, a quiet but fiercely intelligent figure who shared a similar appetite for change.

Evans had risen via an unconventional route, working as a telecoms technician by day and studying for his economics degree at night, but as a Treasury lifer since 1969 he understood Stone's foibles better than most. They were fellow carousers at the Canberra Hotel, where, on one infamous occasion, Stone bristled at being told to leave at 10 pm. Evans recalls, 'We were carrying on a bit, but John said, "I'll leave when I finish this drink." They said, "You'll leave now." So, Stone picked his drink up and tipped it all over the carpet.'[31]

A divide was emerging between the Treasury's stubborn old guard and a different breed of bureaucrat – the so-called 'ginger group', epitomised by Morgan and Evans – agitating for swift and sweeping change. 'It's not a simple, one-dimensional story of ambition,' Henry argues. 'It wasn't all about David. He was ambitious for policy, too.'[32]

For all that Stone had drawn Morgan's admiration and loyalty at first, he was gradually unmasked as a hindrance to reform by his sheer intransigence, inflexibilty and exaggerated right-wing ideology. Stone found reinforcement through the backing of his deputy, Des Moore, another right-wing ideologue who had inherited wealth from a highly successful retailing family in Victoria. It was Whitlam who would later say, acidly: 'Stone and Moore regard themselves as celebrities. They're curiosities.'[33]

Morgan and his cohort were growing weary of the 'John and Des' show, not that they displayed it overtly. 'They got fed up with Stone,' acknowledges Macfarlane, who followed the changing dynamic from his vantage point at the Reserve Bank. 'He had been their hero, but then it all went too far. It was so uncompromising that he wasn't actually achieving things.' With no recourse to Stone, Morgan became involved in a long and bruising confrontation with Fraser in the Cabinet Room about the state of the crucial 1982–83 Budget, designed to control Australia's economic downturn.

Patrick Weller, chronicler of Fraser's years at the helm, records how Morgan refused, with Evans at his side, to take a backward step in arguing that government outlays had to be drastically reduced: 'Two senior officers of the Treasury, led by David Morgan – but not including the secretary, who chose not to attend – strongly argued to Cabinet that their strategy was dangerous. They stood firm in the face of tough questioning by Fraser, who "used every trick, side-flanking, chopping off at the knees", says one observer. That performance helped to turn the debate around.'[34]

Stone's response to his protégé's intervention, which had been dauntless by the standards of a thirty-five-year-old Treasury officer, was proud, even proprietorial. Morgan remembers that an annotation on the note for file of the encounter said that if Stone was to fall under a bus tomorrow he knew that Treasury would be in good hands.

If Stone sounded relaxed about having had his thunder stolen, the impression did not last. There comes a point in the careers of even the most cussed characters when the waning of one's influence becomes a fact of life, and by 1983 the apogee of Stone, once omnipotent on Treasury's turf, was passing. It scarcely helped his cause that Fraser, who had appointed him, was a husk of a leader by the end. Fraser would blame the tanking economy on any number of factors outside his control, from the fall-out since the oil shock to the 1981 drought that had ruined the wheat crop in eastern Australia, but the cold reality was that he lacked the inspiration or even the energy to turn the tide. 'I allowed myself to get tired,' Fraser conceded in his memoir. 'Only by looking back do you realise that you were weary, and that perhaps it was affecting your judgment.'[35] The jaded air of a government in its death throes would soon envelop Stone, whose powerbase was also crumbling. His modus operandi of obstructing urgent economic reforms and corroding an effective working relationship between the Treasury and the government was a strategy that had run its course, ultimately allowing the whip hand in Treasury to be passed from Stone to Morgan, Evans and the rest of the self-styled 'Young Turks'.

This reaches to the heart of a notion that personalities are the key drivers of reform in its broadest sense. For all that Australia had the classic burning platform, with parlous economic conditions necessitating an urgent re-think of policy, it also had within Treasury the fertile minds that could bring it about. 'Personalities determine the probability of success in reform,' Henry says. 'They dictate its scale and scope, whether it is lasting or temporary. They secure its permanence by constructing a compelling case for change, for why it has to happen now.'[36]

Faster than he could have envisaged, Morgan's moment to help shape the economic destiny of a nation had nearly arrived. The tectonic plates of Australian politics were shifting, in no small part because of the charisma with which Hawke galvanised the Labor Party, such that Morgan and his colleagues in Treasury felt empowered to claim their piece of the action. According to Don Watson, Morgan's old brother-in-arms from La Trobe, 'He would have found a much stuffier culture had he entered Treasury in the seventies – but he got in at a time when all this new talent arrived. The eighties were made for David. It was when his politics were shaped.'[37]

So, too, was his family. After three turbulent years, he and Kelly were married on 5 February 1983. Morgan treated the rite of passage with the utmost reverence, insisting upon the finest church, plus all the flowers they could afford, even if the reception was a more modest family affair in their Red Hill backyard.

While his prolonged advances had paid off, the decision to be married had not been reached without incident. A few weeks earlier, Kelly had discovered she was pregnant with their first child, only to announce that she was heading straight off to Israel on a parliamentary investigation, in the midst of its war with Lebanon. Morgan, little relishing the thought of his expecting wife-to-be in a hard hat and flak jacket, was incandescent. 'I was very, very unimpressed,' he says. 'It seemed an avoidable risk. I made a threat of losing the deposit for getting married, claiming that I would marry someone else if she was not back home in February.'[38]

Her Middle Eastern sortie was a useful testing ground, though, for the types of compromises that would be essential between two career-minded souls striving to make their mark. Kelly stood to be the first woman in the eighty-two years since Federation to give birth as a serving MP, but she feared it would do her no favours to ask for exceptional treatment. The axiom held that women in her situation had to make a choice between motherhood and the political front line, but it was one she was hell-bent on defying.

* * *

With good reason, 1983 is heralded as a seminal year in the making of modern Australia. The buccaneering Alan Bond saw his boat, *Australia II*, become the first successful challenger in America's Cup history, the newly wed Prince Charles and Princess Diana created a hubbub at every tour stop from Ayers Rock (Uluru) to Bondi Beach, and a moribund Liberal administration was kicked out at the ballot box in a Labor landslide.

Where Hawke roused audiences with his hail-fellow-well-met charms, combining sharp political nous with flutters on the horses and a weakness for Cuban cigars, Paul Keating, his choice of treasurer, was less of an open book. They were, famously, from opposite poles of the spectrum: while the consensual Hawke was equal parts Rhodes Scholar and sports fanatic, the adversarial Keating had left school at fourteen and preferred to unwind by listening to Mahler symphonies or collecting French Second Empire clocks. Keating was also, in the words of Labor's Bill Hayden, 'the only bastard tough enough to handle John Stone'.[39]

But perhaps Keating's great asset was that, for all the limits of his formal education, he sopped up information like a sponge, as Morgan would discover first-hand. They had been acquainted before, when Max Walsh, long-time editor of *The Australian Financial Review*, had introduced them at a Canberra restaurant in 1982, but Labor's electoral triumph enabled a far closer collaboration between a minister still finding his feet and a policy wonk in a hurry.

Keating, having held the shadow portfolio for barely three months, could not conceal his anxiety at the vast brief that had fallen into his lap. As Hawke has put it: 'He was extremely apprehensive about being Treasurer. He had an overwhelming reliance, more than most ministers, on experts. He was a great user of ideas from others.'[40] One specialist whom he immediately sought out was Morgan, explaining to him in conversations on the fifth floor of the Treasury his deep respect for the institution and his desire to help forge a mutually reinforcing relationship. It was a charm offensive, to be sure, but his thirst for knowledge was real: almost every Sunday afternoon, he would turn up at Morgan and Kelly's house in the suburb of Red Hill armed with pencil and paper, growing increasingly smitten with the intrinsic elegance of applied economics. 'You only had to tell him something once,'

Morgan says. 'He would know a good idea when he heard one. We just gave him frameworks for analysing the macro-economy and how it worked, or for how the tax system interacted with growth. He was like a kid in a candy store.'[41]

Out of this crash course in how the wheels of Treasury turned, a close friendship was hatched. Morgan and Keating discovered that they had an abundance of overlapping interests, including a shared taste for the antiquarian. Where Morgan enjoyed adding to his rare book collection, Keating indulged a passion for late eighteenth-century furniture. Such quirks would come to be seized upon by the Canberra press gallery as pretensions, as if Keating were trying too hard to be the consummate gentleman *flaneur*, but he always insisted they sprang from his fascination for the art and architecture of the age. Music, likewise, provided common ground, as Morgan and Keating would visit a local music store in Manuka on weekends, seeking out classical and opera records. From May to December 1983, the pair were all but inseparable, uniting in a 'no mountain too high' philosophy to leadership that made them ambitious not only for themselves but for the country. Morgan was an avowed centrist in his economics – 'I was a believer in what worked, that there should be no "isms",' he says – while Keating was still an economic neophyte.

Watson, who by a twist of fate would go from being Morgan's flatmate at university to Keating's chief speechwriter come the nineties, depicts the novice treasurer as a blank slate on whom radical ideas could be projected. 'Paul had not read the General Theory, he didn't know about Keynes,' he says. 'And since he didn't know Keynes, he had no qualms about dismissing him.'[42] Gaps in his knowledge, though, did not dilute his impatience to leave behind the last, lost decade, in which the brittleness of the Australian economy had been laid bare. 'David, behave like there is no time to lose,' he instructed Morgan. 'You just can't run fast enough.'[43]

The mood in Canberra channelled this boldness of spirit. A multiplicity of factors, from the sense of stagnation under Fraser to the enterprise of the Hawke government, from Keating's quick learning to the eagerness of Treasury's young gunslingers to plough ahead with a reform agenda, converged to make 1983 an opportune time for change. Perhaps the most immediate impetus, though, sprang from the '$9.6 billion minute', a document revealing that the projected federal budget deficit for 1983–84 was far more grievous than the $6 billion the Liberals had claimed.

The revised estimate was Morgan's: indeed, he had been called out of a celebration for Kelly's re-election at their Golden Grove home to draft, for Stone's signature, a document declaring that Treasury's best calculation of the deficit on an unchanged policy basis had risen substantially. Hawke, espying a chance to play up the burden upon his administration, used it to express the outrage of a nation. 'It is unbelievable, what we have been faced with,' he said. 'No responsible government can say, "Oh well, there's another $3.6 billion that has been thrown at us, it makes no difference." Of course it makes a difference.'[44] This headline figure of $9.6 billion, for all that it had been arrived at in haste, would serve as a stick with which to beat the Liberal Party for years to come.

Hawke was fierce in his resolve that Labor, unlike in 1975, should not dissolve into disarray, that it would never again lapse into the disastrous fiscal miscalculations that had sunk Whitlam. He made it plain that his government would live or die by its record on the economy; that the overwhelming imperative was to stimulate a recovery that lasted.

Such ideas were central to the National Economic Summit in April, convened by the prime minister as a means of honouring his great election pledge to bring Australia together. It drew an eclectic cross-election of participants, from federal government to local, large employers to small, trade unions to churches. The aim was to create a consensus of view on how best to turn the economy around, with the representatives of the people informed by Treasury expertise to a degree they had never been before. Some scoffed at all this harmony and moderation, with Labor chairman Neville Wran muttering: 'If the public wanted spiritualism, they could join the Hare Krishna.'[45]

It would be Morgan's task to construct Keating's keynote speech, which had to negotiate a deft path between appeasing Labor MPs who wanted to spend their way into recovery and Treasury figures obsessed with slashing the deficit. Barry Hughes, a former academic, produced the first draft, but it was considered too polemical. Keating would recount that he wrote the final version, with Morgan's help, in Sydney, although other accounts weigh their contributions a little differently. According to John Edwards, a Keating staffer and one of his many biographers, 'Morgan spent a weekend working through a new version, which Paul polished.'[46]

The speech served both to establish the coherence of Labor's economic vision and to announce Keating as a star. With his penchant for sharp Italian suits and his capacity for turning on the charm seemingly at will, the thirty-nine-year-old treasurer strode into the House of Representatives Chamber, as one reporter had it, 'like an Academy Award winner on his way to receive an Oscar'.[47] His powers of rhetoric, alas, were not exactly Ciceronian at the time. The delivery was halting and under-powered, the demeanour apprehensive and fidgety. 'It was horrible,' Morgan acknowledges.[48]

Flaws in oratory aside, his address did succeed in the sense of laying out the possibility of a middle ground. Treasury traditionally stuck fast to the old Washington Consensus – the orthodoxy championing free trade and free markets, putting the onus of proof on those who wanted state involvement in enterprise that the private sector conducted perfectly well. But there had been a drift under Stone to a more extreme standpoint, where the preoccupations were to eliminate inflation first and reduce government spending radically. Keating's message to the Summit was that a more balanced view, where, for example, inflation and unemployment could be tackled simultaneously rather than sequentially, should light the way for Australia. 'If we cannot come to an agreement in the state of national emergency that confronts us,' he concluded, by way of warning, 'then we deserve the mediocrity of economic performance to which we have been subjected.'[49]

Keating possessed, as he was seldom shy of admitting, a subtle conception of power and its uses. Nothing showed his keenness to torch the established Treasury rules of engagement quite like his decision to turn up for his first meeting with the secretary without a briefing note or a single advisor, telling Stone, a man fifteen years his senior and a stalwart of the institution since 1954, that he would need to earn his spurs afresh.[50] Ultimately, the chasm between the old and the new was too vast to be bridged. Keating preferred to receive advice from those who kept a healthy distance from Stone's extreme ideology, which Hawke identified as 'somewhere out in Genghis Khan territory'.[51] In the framing of his first Budget, he leant heavily upon Morgan to recommend reforms that would both generate economic growth and equity, thus positioning him as the antidote to Fraser's bequest of a giant deficit.

It came to pass that Morgan frantically drafted the 1983 Budget speech in hospital, as he and Kelly awaited the birth of their first child, with scribblings about job creation and the plight of the disadvantaged scattered to all corners of the delivery room. Still, the breakneck pace of economic events could hardly inure him to the profound sense of grace brought by the arrival of a daughter, Jessica, for whom he had longed.

'It's hard to exaggerate the impact,' he explains. 'When you're a bachelor until thirty-five, you can become very self-centred. Given my parents' experience, I was never going to be a father if I couldn't be confident that I would be around for the duration. Ros had also gone through an ectopic pregnancy, where the doctors said it was almost certain that she would not have children. So, we had both wanted a child, quite badly.'[52]

The juxtaposition of the political and postnatal dramas was deftly captured in a cartoon, by Geoff Pryor of *The Canberra Times*, that depicted Kelly, cradling baby Jessica, glowering at Keating as he accepted plaudits for the Budget, his speech bubble saying simply: 'I can't see what all the fuss is about.'[53]

Such satire was well pitched, with Kelly finding that even
the precious first days with a newborn could be politicised.
The social mores of early eighties Australia being what they
were, she endured a vicious backlash for her decision to
return to work within a week. Bruce Goodluck, a Liberal MP
in Tasmania and a father of five, fulminated on ABC Radio's
Current Affairs: 'She would have been far better thought of
by staying with the beautiful little baby for these few months
that are so important.'[54] Just as Kelly declined the station's
invitation to appear on the program, believing Goodluck's
rant did not dignify a response, Morgan resisted erupting
in uxorious pique. There were, at this moment of incipient
economic transformation, larger fires to fight.

* * *

Since Labor's ascension, a momentum had gathered behind
the idea of controlling the value of the Australian dollar not
through government officials, but the supply and demand
of money within global currency markets. The breakdown
in 1971 of the Bretton Woods system, triggered by Nixon's
severing of the link between the US dollar and gold, had
given Australia twelve years in which to assess the impact of
the floating exchange rates adopted everywhere from Japan
to Belgium. Apocalypse, by and large, had been averted,
hardening the case for Canberra to follow suit. By May, the
Reserve Bank had already equipped Keating with a 'war book'
that explored every conceivable consequence of exposing the
country to the flood tide of international finance.

It was Morgan's brief to construct a paper opposing a float of the currency, while Mike Keating, his counterpart at PM&C, put together one in support. This was an ironic designation of duties: while Morgan advocated a free float, establishing a flexible exchange rate dictated solely by market forces, his opposite number preferred a managed float, allowing the Reserve Bank periodic powers of intervention to steer the dollar in a certain direction. 'David and I were sitting in my office and we agreed to swap,' Mike Keating says, reflecting how they had both grown weary of Stone's rigidity of views. 'The exchange rate was Stone's number one instrument of control. His justification was that he didn't trust politicians to run the economy, and he calculated that if you kept the rate high, it could be a great anti-inflationary device.'[55]

As it turned out, the weight of circumstance would swing the argument in Morgan's favour. By late 1983, Australia was deluged with money from overseas investors attracted by a strengthening dollar, to the point where Hawke perceived no feasible alternative but to float. It was counter-intuitive, he thought, to suppose that Australia, with its relatively limited economic muscle, could fix the rate and expect the rest of the world to validate it. As such, it came to pass that on the morning of 12 December, the markets opened for the first time in decades without a centrally determined price. Stone's words on emerging from the decisive Cabinet meeting were, Hawke alleges, suitably portentous. '"Prime Minister," he said to me, "you'll regret this decision."'[56] Stone, invoking parliamentary privilege, neither confirmed nor denied.[57] Given an opportunity to share his reflections on the period for this book, he refused to comment.

It was a revelation to Morgan and his Treasury peer group that a reform as momentous as the float could be hauled across the line. Its success could, they understood, be the thin end of far-reaching economic liberalisation. 'Once you float, you have nowhere to hide,' Morgan says. 'The world is marking you on the quality of your economic situation daily, hourly. So, we realised that this would bring pressure in other areas. Australia had to be able to take advantage, to achieve a real improvement in competitiveness.'[58]

Keating, whose subsequent dispute with Hawke about which of them deserved greatest credit for this masterstroke would simmer for years, was gleeful at the press conference. He declared that the float would enable foreign speculators to speculate against themselves, rather than the Australian government. Conspicuously, Stone was absent from the announcement. When asked by a reporter if this was because he fundamentally opposed so bold a move, Keating replied: 'Well, there's more than one view in Treasury.'[59]

Innocuous enough on the surface, the comment sparked a furious witch-hunt by Stone. He circulated a memorandum to all senior staff, demanding that anybody who had hatched a contrary view to his own and expressed it to Keating report to his office by close of business that day. Dutifully, Morgan confessed, although he hardly believed it would come as a surprise when they had robustly debated the merits of floating during their Friday drinking sessions. '"John, you know very well indeed my view on this issue," I told him. "I've argued with you about it." "Yes, but you discussed it with the treasurer." I explained to him that Keating had asked me about it a number of times. "But you didn't do a note for file." "John, if I did a note on every conversation I have with Paul, I would be here for the rest of my life. This is a man I see almost every weekend. I try to write notes about Budget deficits and important matters of the moment, but this is entirely impractical.""

Stone digested this information and concluded, stiffly: 'This is very grave.'

'It was at that point,' Morgan acknowledges, 'that I thought my career in Treasury was over.'[60]

The dynamism of Keating's leadership ensured, ultimately, that the reverse was true. While Morgan, as an advocate of freeing up an ossified economy through low tariffs and flexible labour markets, found his star in the ascendant under a young treasurer impatient to build upon the triumph of the float, the outmoded Stone slipped gently towards the margins. By August 1984, he had served notice of his intention to resign as secretary, citing misgivings over public policy – even if such a step owed more, in Paul Kelly's view, to his resolve to throw off the shackles of public service altogether and release 'his long pent-up intellectual passions'.[61] Stone had also tethered his political colours to the mast by emerging in support of Sir Joh Bjelke-Petersen, the long-serving premier of what would, in time, be exposed as an institutionally corrupt Queensland government.

'That highlights the conundrum of his intellectual brilliance versus a lack of judgment,' Morgan argues. 'What possible judgment was there in backing a crook like Petersen?'[62]

An informal advisor to Sir Joh, who investigative journalist Evan Whitton would memorably nickname the 'hillbilly dictator',[63] Stone embraced the National Party's platform of slashing public expenditure and slowing immigration, winning election to the Senate in 1987. 'In a strange sense, I felt good for him,' Morgan reflects. 'One might say that he "came out". For who was the real John Stone? He was much more the politician desperate to be treasurer – that was the job he hankered after. Those whom he was advising were just not up to the job, in his estimation. This way, he could show his true colours: his right-wing ideology, his desire to be in the limelight instead of in the shadows.'[64]

Stone was the first permanent head of a government department to reinvent himself as an MP, but this was a dubious distinction. As Macfarlane, then rising through the ranks at the Reserve Bank, puts it: 'Resigning at fifty-five, then going into politics? That's not what Treasury people do.'[65] No less a figure than Gough Whitlam would express such a transition rather more bluntly. 'He said to me on the phone once,' recalls Don Watson, assuming Whitlam's stentorian voice, '"John Stone: secretary of the Commonwealth Treasury to National Party senator? What a f------ decrescendo."'[66]

CHAPTER 5

Taxing Times

'What is the difference between a taxidermist and a tax collector?' asked Mark Twain in one of his notebooks. 'The taxidermist takes only your skin.'[1] It was an apt statement upon the oppressive fiscal regime in pre-Progressive America, before Theodore Roosevelt turned his fire on the 'malefactors of great wealth', but in Australia the sentiment proved far more enduring. Even in 1984, an antiquated and shambolic tax system saw to it that average workers bore by far the heaviest burden, while the well-to-do submerged their own liabilities at the bottom of Sydney Harbour.

It was a product of the torpor that had crept into the country's economic thinking. The fact that the last tax reform of substance had been in 1942, when state and federal income taxes were consolidated as part of the wartime imperative to raise more revenue, was a sure sign that a moment of reckoning lay ahead. The Asprey Committee, which in 1975 sought to flesh out what an equitable and efficient tax policy might look like, ultimately did little, while Morgan's own calls for indexation had been taken up by the Mathews Report, implemented by the Liberal government for a short while, and then quietly swept into the long grass.

Change, however, was hurtling down the tracks. During the 1984 election campaign, Hawke made a commitment to a tax summit that would explore fundamental change to the injustice of the rules – much to the chagrin of Keating, who could imagine nothing more politically inefficient than drawing up tax options in a public forum. But as Labor retained their mandate to govern, pledging both to provide tax relief to lower-income earners and to smash the tax avoidance industry beloved of the super-rich, the die was cast.

To Morgan, there was no task more central to national reconstruction than a daring and lasting overhaul of the tax model. 'It was shockingly unfair,' he says. 'It had benefited the well-to-do, those who had received sophisticated tax advice. For a start, capital gains were entirely tax-free, such that the fat cats had them running out of their ears. Fringe benefits, likewise, were untaxed, so craftier members of the corporate elite could take company cars or low-interest loans as if they were real income. Even entertainment expenses were deductible without limit. All of this was screwing the average person, under a system where a 60 per cent marginal rate of personal income tax cut in at just 1.6 times weekly earnings.'[2]

Within Treasury, happily, were those with a level of social conscience to make the elimination of such egregious inequality a priority. The triumvirate of Young Turks all understood, to varying degrees, what it meant to scrape by, Morgan having weathered the fallout of his father's ruin, Ted Evans having read economics by night while fixing Queensland telephone lines by day, and Chris Higgins – who by 1984 had been prised back from Paris to Canberra – having required financial grants just to complete his secondary education. Each was marshalled by Bernie Fraser, who stood out among central-casting Treasury types, a country boy whose father had been a labourer on the Snowy Mountains hydroelectric scheme. As such, they were committed, in Morgan's words, to forging 'not just a more economically efficient Australia, but a much fairer Australia'.[3]

Theirs, emphatically, was not an apolitical department. As Morgan would later contentiously tell the makers of *Labor in Power*, the Australian Broadcasting Commission's sumptuous chronicle of the Hawke–Keating period: 'Treasury has always had its own agenda, always will have. The important thing is that Treasury has the discipline to make that agenda consistent, to the maximum extent practicable, with that of the government.'[4]

There was a breathtaking audacity about this era, which by the early stages of Labor's second term had already encompassed the float of the dollar and an approval of the entry of foreign banks, a belated but vital step that would intensify banking competition in Australia and cut costs for consumers. Tax was next on the list for Treasury officers moving up through the gears with their ears pinned back.

Keating, who in 1984 had become the first Australian to win *Euromoney* magazine's finance minister of the year award – an accolade of which he was immensely proud – was a passionate proselytiser for the philosophy behind such change. To this day, in his elegant office in Sydney's Potts Point, furnished with French clocks and candelabras, he has meticulously curated an archive of every document and newspaper report pertinent to the times, so as to safeguard his reputation as a 'big picture' treasurer.

'It had no equal in Australian history, or in that of any OECD member state,' Keating says. 'No one country ever conducted changes on this scale. The policy was the internationalisation of the economy: the rollback of protectionism, the fiscal accommodation of Australia's then emerging current account deficit. We were trying to get blood to the muscles of the economy through the sinews of the financial system, by making it more open and supple. On tax, the challenge was to be able to allocate resources more efficiently than the old system had managed. Operating a policy on that wide a front, and with such direction, meant that Treasury all of a sudden had something to work with and towards. Formerly it had been a policy department in a country without policy. Now there was a policy and, more to the point, there was a government articulating an even grander one than the old Treasury would have done itself.'[5] The Young Turks deserved credit, too, for hatching many of the policy ideas themselves. Asked by Kerry O'Brien whether he had a fully-fledged set of economic reforms in his head when he started, Keating replied: 'No I didn't, but ... I knew how to put electricity in the cables.'[6]

Morgan had reason to believe that his life at this juncture was surging like a flood tide. For all that he doted upon Jessica unconditionally, he had let slip that he would still love to have a son. After a game of doubles tennis at the Lodge with Hawke, one guest in the lounge room pressed him as to his preference. 'I don't care,' he began – intending to add, 'as long as it's a healthy' – only for Hawke to interject, to much mirth, 'as long as it's a boy'. One lunchtime, Kelly invited him to Canberra's Nineteenth Hole restaurant, ordered a glass of champagne, and announced: 'Well, you are going to have your full-forward.'[7] Both of them wept with happiness.

Allied to the joyous flush of fatherhood was Morgan's success in becoming one of Treasury's youngest first assistant secretaries at thirty-six. He had discovered in Keating the same enthusiasm that he harboured for pushing the envelope of reform. Just as Keating was outraged by elements of his inheritance from John Howard, not least the top personal tax rate of 60 per cent – so steep that it was avoided *en masse* – or the fact that dividends were taxed twice, Morgan saw that the feeble tax policy branch set up by Stone, comprising a mere third of one of Treasury's six divisions, was unfit for purpose. 'It was a scandal,' he says. 'How could you have such a tiny amount of resources dedicated to tax?'[8]

Ken Henry, whose long and highly regarded career at the department began in 1984, explains: 'Stone would say that the best tax system is a bad one. A bad system will raise less revenue than a good one. Why is that important? It's the only constraint on government spending that we have. It was such a narrow perspective that I could only conclude he failed to understand the part tax played in how economies and societies functioned.'[9]

To remedy these ills, the new tax division, created and headed by Morgan, was substantially augmented and filled with some of the nimblest intellects available. Henry, who had also been agonising over a job offer from PM&C, would find himself among the first recruits. 'Fresh off my PhD,

I chose Treasury wholly because of David,' he says. 'He was keen, and he knew Richard Manning, my honours work supervisor, having been taught briefly by him at La Trobe. So, he called Manning up. I understand the message was something to the effect of, "Why don't you tell that young colleague of yours to wake up to himself?"'[10]

Viewed from the outside, the rapid if under-the-radar alignment in one place of so much nascent economic talent – including Larry Kamener, who would subsequently lead Boston Consulting Group's global public sector practice, and Martin Parkinson, secretary to the Treasury after Henry and later secretary of the Department of Prime Minister and Cabinet under Malcolm Turnbull and Scott Morrison – was a giveaway that great upheavals were afoot. Sure enough, the story leaked, published by Max Walsh in *The Bulletin* as a cover feature under the headline 'Labor's Secret Tax Plan'.

Reading this with a sinking feeling, Morgan telephoned Walsh, an eminent voice and one of Keating's earliest educators on economics, in a rage. '"Max, why did you write that?" I asked. "This is pretty awkward for me at Treasury." "They've got to expect that, putting a smart guy like you in charge of tax reform," he shrugged. "They must have big plans."'[11] It was a chastening lesson in the need for circumspection around journalists.

More than this, it was a cause for delay in the reform itself. 'There was a witch-hunt about who had spoken to Max,' Morgan recalls. 'It wasn't carried out very virulently or forensically, but it was embarrassing, both for me and for the team, because we had to put our pens down until after the '84 election.'[12]

A clarity was forming, though, on the reform that Treasury most wanted to haul across the line: namely, the introduction of a huge consumption tax of 12.5 per cent on all goods and services, accompanied by major reforms to both personal income tax and company tax. Ideologically, the broad-based consumption tax was an affront to elements of the Labor caucus, since the lowest earners stood to pay more on their purchases while benefiting relatively little from the tax cut. And yet the patent inadequacy of Australia's direct taxation structure, which haemorrhaged money by encouraging a culture of rampant avoidance and minimisation, stirred a compelling case for change. There ensued a 'blood pact', as Paul Kelly has described: a potent fusion of political energy and bureaucratic expertise, with Keating and his most senior Treasury advisors grasping a once-in-a-generation opportunity to revamp Australia's ramshackle tax arrangements.[13]

* * *

The morning after the 1984 election, when Hawke's gamble to build on the Labor honeymoon backfired with a reduced majority, the heavy lifting began in earnest. From a standing start, the underpinnings of the Australian tax code essentially had to be reinvented in five months, ready for crystallising in a white paper that would be debated at the tax summit in July 1985. It was a Herculean enterprise, for which Morgan needed to commandeer the ground-floor Treasury training complex, next to the cafeteria, as a war room. 'The bunker', those who toiled within its walls dubbed it, with good reason.

Seven days and seven nights a week, the place thrummed with industry, as the officers involved ate there, slept there, even brought their children there to rest on mattresses wedged under desks.

For Parkinson, it was a dizzying time. Morgan had cornered him during one Friday-night happy hour to be told, as a fait accompli: 'You're on the team.'

'I'm not interested,' he said. 'I know nothing about public finance.'

'Well,' Morgan shot back, unmoved, 'here's your chance to learn.'[14]

It was a choice Parkinson would not regret. 'I would go and fetch my son from day care, and there would be a little camp bed where he could sit around and eat a ton of pizza or charcoal chicken and chips. The effort was titanic, and it would be hard to think of any other time in the past fifty years where such a collection of talent worked together on the same issue. That group generated three secretaries to the Treasury, in Ted Evans, Ken Henry and myself. We cleaned out the area that would have been the bar, and we turned it into one where we survived purely on junk food and adrenalin – as well as coffee you could stand your spoon up in.'[15] Parkinson's work would help earn him a coveted scholarship to Princeton, to pursue his PhD under the instruction of Ben Bernanke, later chairman of the US Federal Reserve.

One factor in Parkinson's initial hesitancy about plunging into this environment was that he had regarded Morgan, who could still project the machismo of the ex-footballer, as a 'testosterone-around-the-ankles type'. Bernie Fraser, having been blessed as secretary with a far more equable temperament than his predecessor Stone, would observe the same trait: 'David was effective at working with those above him on the ladder, but not so much with those below. He was slightly less focused on those people.'[16] To Parkinson, a tender twenty-six years old when enlisted into the crack squad on tax and just a couple of years removed from his masters studies, Morgan's dervish-like energy, coordinating the grunt work behind one of the most consequential reforms in the history of Federation, was overwhelming at times. Whether in philosophical argument or mathematical modelling, he discovered that there was seldom much margin for error.

'You had to be intellectually and emotionally robust to survive,' he reflects. 'There were times when David had a sharp tongue. He had very high standards about how quickly he expected people to think on their feet. If you didn't meet them, he could be dismissive. He could let the pursuit of the objective override the engagement of the individual.'[17]

Parkinson glimpsed Morgan's wired intensity at closer quarters than most – not least when, for one inter-departmental football match, he was given the dubious distinction of umpiring. 'David was playing against people of nowhere near the standard he had reached, but he was just a yard too slow,' he says. 'He infringed on one opponent, so I awarded the other player a free kick. He subjected me to a character assessment and I gave a 50-metre penalty against him. This happened a couple of times – he was raging and ordered me after the game to report to his office. "You'll never get to Princeton," he ranted. "I'm going to cancel your scholarship." There was steam coming out of his ears, because he had that first recognition that he was no longer the person he thought he was.'[18]

The crucial moderating influence, in Parkinson's eyes, was Evans. Where Morgan's uncompromising rigour left him ill disposed to suffer fools gladly, Evans, as deputy secretary, was a softer-edged soul, pensive and strangely imperturbable.[19] 'Ted was strategic, David a little more charge-ahead. Ted tempered David, bringing extra empathy, that vital sense of how others might be feeling. The combination of the two was much better than either of them alone.'[20]

Over the years, the pair had grown exceptionally close. Evans had been best man at Morgan's wedding, even pulling up the car on their drive to the ceremony to crack open a beer and ask the groom, 'Are you sure you want to go through with this?' On another occasion, Morgan, deeply concerned with the perspectives of others on his character, pressed his friend over a bottle of red wine at the Canberra Hotel on what he truly thought of him. 'Quite some time later, I finished giving my opinion, and we left the place in silence,' Evans says. 'The next afternoon, I was at home working in the garden, and David turned up unannounced with a notebook in his hand, saying, "Do you mind if we go through that again?"'[21]

A freeing up of Treasury's rigidly stratified pecking order, one bequeathed by Stone, had bred a lively jostling for prominence among the 'ginger group'. For all that Morgan, Evans and Higgins were the tightest of trios, almost fraternal, the introduction of a man of Keating's meritocratic zeal – determined, by his own admission, to dismantle the 'crusty old boys' network' – added an extra layer to the dynamic. 'They felt, in this new order, somehow out of their comfort stations,' Keating reflects. 'Suddenly they could make their way with the treasurer of the day, an option denied to them by the Stone style. The chance was there, but there was a worry. It was edgy.'[22]

One night, Morgan took Keating into the bunker so that he could see for himself the round-the-clock assiduousness of the tax brigade, complete with all the detritus of prefabricated beds and discarded takeaways. Theirs was more than a purely collegial relationship. Since Keating had moved for family reasons from his Blaxland electorate home to Canberra, he and his wife, Annita, lived just two blocks from the Morgan– Kelly household in Red Hill. The four of them had shared a fortieth birthday dinner in Sydney for Keating, who was also godfather to the newborn Ben. At the Keatings' home in Beagle Street, the treasurer would hold forth on his obsession with budgerigar breeding while Morgan tested the latest stereo systems they had bought together.

But it was public policy that united them as powerfully as anything extracurricular. In particular, the broad-based consumption tax struck Keating as potentially the glorious centrepiece of Labor's work. Years of mediocrity and inertia in Australian policy-making could, he and Morgan reasoned, be swept away by a seismic piece of legislation that caught out the tax-avoiders, offered a fair go for the average Joe, and saved the government's reformist credentials for posterity. As such, they would present the endgame to members of the tax team in the language of a crusade.

'That's how we felt, too,' Henry says. 'Did we bother to ask ourselves whether it was appropriate for Treasury officials to behave in this way? I didn't, personally. It was just fantastic to be engaged with something so important, with so much energy, knowing how ineffective the department had been in the past.'[23] Henry even kept a record of how ferociously he and his fellow bunker-dwellers were working in the early months of 1985, and it averaged 100 hours per week. 'We were at a level where we were not rewarded for overtime, but I calculated that if I had been one level lower in the public service, I would have received an amount in excess of my annual salary. We were very conscious of working twice or three times as hard as those elsewhere at Treasury, but it did not cause resentment – quite the opposite. Others were envious of us, which spoke volumes about the quality of the group.'[24]

Beyond the confines of this bureaucratic lair, it was Morgan's task to sell the masterplan to a sceptical outside community. The trade unions would not make life easy for the government, demanding as they were an attractive set of numbers for their membership, while Keating drove his 'tax cart', as he called it, headlong into some vehement voter opposition. 'Consumption taxes reinforce inequality', read one typical protest placard.

In February 1985, as part of the Australian Tax Research Foundation's 'Changing the Tax Mix' conference at Monash University, Morgan delivered a paper designed to assuage the fears. Entitled *An Agenda for Tax Reform*, it advocated imposing a consumption tax 'on the broadest possible base', as well as substantial personal and company tax reform, and argued that 'in Australia, the difficulty of achieving tax reform is less one of appropriate diagnosis than of implementation'.[25] There needed, he suggested, to be a reframing of the terms of debate around tax, to move beyond the ghoulish focus on every way that certain slices of society might suffer short-term setbacks to an awareness of the profound national benefits in the long run. He was careful to clarify that these were personal views, not necessarily supported by the treasurer, but his speech provided, as *The Australian Financial Review* noted at the time, an 'indication of the direction that the government's review is taking' as well as signalling a 'renewed attack on tax evasion and avoidance'.[26] It had been a kite-flying exercise, designed to test whether Treasury's preferred tax solution could draw the requisite support, but it had worked.

Keating had seen and heard enough to be convinced of the righteousness of the cause. He would spend the next few weeks hammering at Hawke's door, twisting his arm repeatedly in a desperate attempt to win prime ministerial approval. A line of fracture was starting to appear, not just between the consensus-loving Hawke and his bull-headed treasurer, but between the departments that worked for them. Where Morgan and the rest of Treasury's top brass were positively evangelical about the consumption tax, Bob Hogg, Hawke's senior advisor, was counselling him to drop the idea. Neville Wran also spoke for many in the party he chaired by arguing that a tax on bread, meat, fruit and vegetables was anathema to everything for which Labor should stand.

Come the evening of 7 March, though, it appeared as if Hawke had been won over. A memorandum written by Morgan, after a lively day's talks at the Lodge, recorded the prime minister's view that tax reform had to be substantial and that a 'broad-based consumption tax was therefore necessary – subject to the ability to ensure that low-income groups were not worse off'.[27]

Soon after, Hawke rowed back on such certainty, in what would become an endless pattern of prevarication. Morgan likened it to playing a grand final, thinking you had won, only to be told you had to do it all again the following Saturday. In this time, Keating, contemptuous of such vacillating, was believed to have coined the caustic nickname for Hawke of 'Old Jellyback'. He would deny it, insisting that Hawke's 'Manichean court' had fitted him up and that Peter Walsh, Labor's take-no-prisoners finance minister, had first used it.

There are theories, kept alive to this day, for why Hawke's mind was not fully engaged in the task at hand. For a start, he was embroiled in his first crisis on the foreign policy front, after it emerged he had kept quiet about an American ballistic missile test program that involved rockets landing just 225 kilometres off the Tasmanian coast. The intensity of public backlash to this revelation – one that 'cast doubt', according to an editorial in *The Age*, 'on the political strength and stability of the Hawke government' – encouraged Keating to present tax reform as a perfect way for an embattled administration to show it could still act decisively.[28] But another, far more personal trauma was at play.

Back in August 1984, Hawke had discovered, to his horror, that his daughter Rosslyn was addicted to heroin. The news shattered him to the extent that he broke down in tears in front of the Malaysian prime minister. Hawke would maintain that the anguish did not prevent him from making appropriate judgments on the country's behalf, although Keating suspected otherwise, claiming in conversations with Kerry O'Brien that depression had engulfed him for years afterwards. He cited as support a 1985 article in *The Sydney Morning Herald* by writer Blanche d'Alpuget, who later married Hawke after they had conducted a relationship for almost twenty years.[29] 'My overwhelming impression was of a lack of vitality, that he was vanishing,' d'Alpuget said. 'Going to talk to him for the first time in three years, I expected the old zing and was taken aback by its absence – one that seemed both poignant and shocking.'[30] Morgan, who saw glimpses of these tensions, reflects: 'Hawke was knocked around. Paul used to claim to me that he never recovered from it, that he never got his mojo back.'[31]

As an autumnal gloom gathered over Canberra, prospects of a tax revolution looked precarious. Hawke was alternating between cautious support and anxious backsliding, the Business Council of Australia did not like the notion of losing a free pass on tax-deductible four-hour lunches, while the ACTU pressed hard for substantial tax relief to present a more palatable package to blue-collar workers. Keating seemed increasingly besieged.

'I said to Paul at one stage, "Mate, I'll understand if this is all getting too hard,"' Morgan recalls. '"Is Treasury still behind it?" he asked. I reassured him that it was. "Well, that's the thing that keeps me running with it."'[32] It was a potent demonstration of his conviction, as expressed in one of the more famous Keating lines, that good policy was good politics.

The treasurer conveyed to Cabinet a view that he had carried with him since his election as an MP sixteen years earlier: namely, that a 50 per cent marginal tax rate for the majority of wage-earners was unsustainable. With this in mind, he argued, tax reform was not simply optional, but mandatory. Unveiling to them a white paper 414 pages long, he said: 'The Prime Minister and I have taken this more seriously, put more time into it, had more discussions over it than any other issue. And that includes economic policy in '83, the float, or anything else. What you have before you is the most comprehensive, conscientious effort we are capable of presenting. We've worn ourselves out over it.'[33] Equally frazzled were Morgan and his team, who after burning the midnight oil in the bunker had produced three bullets for Keating to fire: options A, B and C.

The political equation was that A would prove unacceptable to business, as it did little to slash the top rate of tax, and that B would be rejected by the unions due to its regressive impact. This left option C, a label that seeped deep into the lexicon of the era – as shorthand for the most ambitious, least adulterated consumption tax – as the one choice for which the government could plausibly mobilise agreement.

The lines drawn, Keating extolled the virtues of the favoured option C with astounding vigour. For two-and-a-half bruising days, he assailed Cabinet members with statistics, theatrics, charm, rage, intellect, impatience, and the full artillery of his splenetic language. 'It was,' says Morgan, 'the most remarkable Cabinet room performance I have ever seen.'[34]

Keating smiles at the memory. 'Oh, I had the big skates on,' he says. 'I had swords everywhere. It was like a scene from *Ben Hur*. There was so much vehement opposition, and I was so persuasive but so aggressive at the same time. You need to manage the power in those situations. Australia will probably never see a scene like it again. I'm not sure its kind has been evident in an OECD Cabinet in the postwar years. No country, not Britain, not Germany, has taken on a reform program like it, done with such gusto and élan. To be part of that was to be part of something truly special.'[35]

At his right arm were Morgan, Evans, Greg Smith, a key advisor specialising in company tax changes, and Chris Higgins, by common consent the finest macro-economic mind that Treasury possessed. High stakes evidently warranted high-grade input. The progress from the absolutism of Stone's day, when the unequivocal Treasury position was the secretary's alone, could be measured in light years.

'Treasury officials were brought to the centre of power in a way they had never been before,' Keating explains. 'Plus, the prize was on the table. It wasn't some prize that might be grasped in twenty years' time, or that was a glint in someone's eye – it was there in front of them. They were engaged in the political process. They were part of the weaponry.'[36]

All day and all night the debate raged, as Keating, who had his ducks in a row, shot down any objections with a measured, disdainful flourish. In one charged exchange, Peter Walsh pressed him on why he had nominated 49 per cent as the top rate of income tax. Keating, using unconventional logic for a Labor minister, answered that it was to make a philosophical point that the state received less than half your income. 'I believe in rendering to Caesar the things that are Caesar's,' he said. 'But if you let Caesar confiscate the revenue of the country in his dictate, then you'll always have an economy limping along.'[37] At every turn, Keating remained mindful of how each grandee-led inquiry into taxation in Australia, from Asprey to Mathews, had eventually just dissolved into the ether. This chapter, he declared, would have a different ending.

At around 1.30 am on Monday – the sparring had started on a Saturday – Gareth Evans, minister for resources and energy, rested his glasses wearily on the table and said: 'I've been listening to this argument for two days, waiting for the hole to be punched in it, and none of you has been able to.'[38] Taking this cue, Keating gathered up his reams of paper to leave. Stewart West, a prominent voice on Labor's left, told him that there was still no majority in the package's favour. 'But Stewart,' he shot back, 'do you think you have a majority to stop me walking out of the door with a decision?'[39] With that, he bolted into the night, his Treasury adjutants in tow.

Bleary-eyed but euphoric, Morgan, Evans and Bernie Fraser headed back to the treasurer's office to pop the champagne. They felt that they had just borne witness to a pivotal moment in the economic history of the nation. Even the normally deadpan Evans avowed that it had been the toughest, tensest political duel he could recall.[40] All the doubters had apparently been thwarted by the blend of Treasury's bureaucratic heft and Keating's *coup de théâtre*. While the looming summit was a reminder that any changes were still far from being legislated, there was a tangible joy at having moved a 'monster proposal', to use Keating's term, past Cabinet. 'It showed that it was not all for nought,' Morgan says. 'It proved that if you put in enough intellectual muscle, and enough eye-wateringly hard work, anything was possible.'[41]

* * *

It took only one day of the summit for the mood to come crashing back to earth. The spectacle of 30,000 aggrieved farmers outside the House of Representatives, bearing posters with such salty messages as 'The drover's dog is a big bitch', encapsulated the trials that lay ahead. Steering the tax cart through Cabinet was one thing, but manoeuvring it beyond a plethora of sectional interests was quite another. Extensive polling had already illustrated that it was electoral kryptonite for Labor. The mutinous atmosphere on the Parliament House lawns, flooded with the largest demonstration Canberra had seen, was mirrored inside the chamber, where for six long, spirit-sapping hours delegates thundered against perceived flaws in the consumption tax. A typically extreme Sir Joh Bjelke-Petersen – 'demented', according to Hawke – denounced it as the 'dead hand of socialism'.[42] Keating shrugged off the detractors, saying that they were merely trying to 'get the dirty water off their chests'.[43] The drama was splashed over newspaper front pages across the land, as fierce political combat emphasised the real-life urgency of the issues for all Australians.

To succeed, Keating needed the backing of both business and the unions. Neither, it turned out, was prepared to make the leap. Bob White, president of the Business Council, declared that his body did not endorse approaches A, B or C. Bill Kelty, Morgan's former rival for top student honours at La Trobe and one of the country's chief powerbrokers as secretary of the ACTU, said the union movement would have no truck with a consumption tax until it had digested its own commissioned study on the likely fallout. That research, when published two days later, would prove a damp squib, concluding that the government's preferred shift from direct to indirect taxes could take place 'without any undue or adverse macro-economic effects'.[44]

It was Keating's instinct to hold firm against the naysayers, but Hawke was becoming unsettled. From the unbroken chorus of hostility, he inferred a message that Labor was perhaps grievously harming its chances at the next election. With that thought he decided, in an astonishing piece of late-night backroom dealing, to pull the rug from underneath his treasurer's feet.

Kelty was staying at the Canberra International Hotel, having endured a third straight day of gruelling summitry, when Hawke showed up at the door. 'What's happening?' Simon Crean, the ACTU president, asked. 'Where's Paul?'

'I'll be talking to him later,' Hawke said, evasively. 'I just want to know what your position is.'

'Bob, you know what it is,' Kelty replied. 'We can't accept option C.'[45]

Soon after, Morgan, sitting down for a meal at around 10 pm, received a call at home from John Short, a reporter for *The Sydney Morning Herald*. Short informed him Geoff Walsh, Hawke's press secretary, was briefing the gallery that a deal had been struck, that the consumption tax was dead in the water, and that the government would instead press ahead – as the ACTU had wanted all along – with a limited extension of the existing tax base. It was enough to make Morgan catch his breath. 'I told Short that he had to be mistaken, that I had been with the treasurer just forty-five minutes earlier and he would be sure to have heard of it. I was incredulous.'[46]

Daylight brought the sinking realisation that it was true. Hawke jettisoned option C, on the justification that it lacked a sufficient cross-section of support, while behind closed doors Keating gnashed his teeth at the prime minister's 'ratting'.[47] In public, he strived to keep up a united front, thanking Hawke at a post-summit press conference out of a sense of political duty, while ruefully acknowledging that his tax cart had 'crossed the line – but with one wheel off'.[48] Keating could be forgiven for feeling let down. For months he had soaked up the theoretical and practical subtleties of tax reform, criss-crossing Australia to convince nervous constituencies of the merits of great change, and at a stroke this colossal endeavour was unstitched.

Kelty, at least, found a seam of dark humour in it all. During the summit, Keating had cautioned the assembled leaders that there would be no 'magic pudding' to satisfy everyone. At its culmination, Kelty could think of no more fitting gift for the beaten treasurer than a copy of Norman Lindsay's *The Magic Pudding*, signed by each member of the ACTU executive.[49]

It was testament to Keating's irrepressible nature that his reaction to so scalding a setback was not despairing, but sanguine. He viewed the consumption tax, on which he had all but staked his political reputation, less as a gutted shell than as a noble project that could yet be salvaged. For all that he felt betrayed and abandoned by Hawke, he saw how tax reform was a cause with inexorable momentum.

Sure enough, on 20 September 1985, after excruciating recalculations at the Treasury coalface, a thinned-out but still hugely significant raft of changes to the Australian tax architecture won Cabinet's blessing: a fringe benefits tax, a capital gains tax, elimination of deductions for entertainment, taxation of gold mining, a foreign tax credit system, not to mention full dividend imputation, thus creating the revenue capacity for Keating's longed-for slashing of the top marginal rate from 60 to 49 per cent.

The sense of triumph was tempered by a nadir in relations between prime minister and treasurer. Keating deeply resented Hawke's absence from the crucial Cabinet talks to attend a state celebration in Papua New Guinea, and let him know as much with some choice invective. 'We had implemented the decisions broadly agreed at the tax summit, but there was then another battle,' Morgan says. 'Hawke went missing for that final four-day debate in Cabinet, and Keating thought he had been left to get rolled.'[50]

As Keating wrote in a livid note on his newspaper clippings: 'The envious little bastard did everything to destroy it.' Hawke, for his part, has dismissed such accusations as a 'pathetic rewriting of history'.[51]

Few who had experienced the convulsions and power plays that defined 1985 would forget them in a hurry. When Morgan looked back at his year, he realised that there were only four days of 365 that he had not worked.

The balancing act required in his family life was elaborate, not least because Kelly was in a critical phase of her own career. She would recoil from presumptuous headlines in Australian women's magazines that pigeonholed her as a parent first and a politician second. Nine days after giving birth to Ben, she had taken him with her to Sydney Opera House for Labor's campaign launch. Throughout the next exhausting year, Ben and Jessica spent no shortage of time at Parliament House as the first children born to a serving MP. Occasionally, Kelly would receive letters from women who alleged she could not sympathise with their concerns, when she had her mother helping out with childcare, as well as a cavalcade of nannies. She struck back in *The Canberra*

Times, saying: 'I know what it is to subsist on minimum sleep for eight months, to race a child into casualty on Sunday afternoon, to try to fit everything into the day.'[52]

Both she and Morgan knew what it meant to run hard for what they wanted. In many ways, this restless striving was the spirit of the age in the nation's capital. Keating, in particular, would function according to what he termed the 'Road Runner principle – run fast enough for a great change, you will get it. Look over your shoulder once, and you're dead meat.'[53] It was a feeling that underpinned his impatience with Hawke, whose leadership struck him as far too ponderous and deferential, and the passage of over thirty years has done nothing to dilute it. 'If all people are led, if the governing party has direction, then this provides energy to the bureaucratic process,' Keating says, forcefully. 'You pick up adherents.'[54]

Morgan, unashamedly, was one of those adherents, whose come-rain-or-shine absorption in the tax exercise was a product of their attachment to the minister's cult of personality. At the IMF, Morgan had enjoyed limited success in his quest to strengthen the economies of struggling nations, with the exception of South Korea. In his home country, by contrast, where Keating had restored Treasury not just to relevance, but to a pre-eminent role in the crafting of policy, Morgan and his associates were thrust to the heart of the game. As Bill Kelty puts it: 'Keating was the great peacetime treasurer of Australia, without a doubt. He did what Labor hadn't always done, in that he won over Treasury. Once Stone went, he got the intellect of the department on side and he harnessed it. He did smart things, of which David was a very significant part.'[55]

History is likely to judge their work kindly. The sweep of reforms unleashed by the end of 1985, which justified Treasury's gargantuan labours despite the roadblock of the summit, changed the behaviour of the country's taxpayers irrevocably. Gone was the patchwork quilt of a system that enabled the super-rich to regard tax as a matter of personal discretion, and in its place was one that went a long way to treating all forms of income equally, compelling even business magnates to honour the same rules that bound the vast majority of Australians. Alarmism spread that swathes of Sydney restaurants would shut down, now that their pinstriped clientele had to declare a liquid lunch not as a legitimate company expense but as a taxable fringe benefit, and yet trade held firm. Keating goes as far as to argue that the present-day design of Australian taxation is essentially the same as he bequeathed, with John Howard's turn-of-the-millennium goods and services tax bolted on.[56] For him and his loyal Treasury henchmen, it would stand as a stirring accomplishment. The more immediate question, though, was what on earth they intended to do as an encore.

CHAPTER 6

Hawks Versus Doves

Nobody on Australia's political scene has rivalled Paul Keating for a lacerating tongue, or for using the power of diction to expose uncomfortable truths. It was long before he derided the Senate as 'unrepresentative swill', or likened the parliamentary performance of John Hewson, a favourite adversary, to 'being flogged with a warm lettuce', that he uttered perhaps his most momentous line not at the dispatch box, but in the kitchen.

The improbable setting was the Kismet Function Centre, in Melbourne's outer northern suburbs, where Labor backbencher Neil O'Keefe had enlisted Keating to speak at a breakfast fundraiser. In the circumstances, the treasurer could be forgiven for appearing distracted. The day before, on 13 May 1986, the government and Treasury alike had received a ghastly awakening through the latest balance of payments figures, illustrating a deficit of $1,476 million.

'I took one look at them and thought, We're stuffed,' Morgan says.[1] Diminishing returns on the mainstays of Australian export business – wheat, iron ore, coal, zinc – had combined with rising prices for the most popular imported goods, such as colour televisions and video recorders, to create a terms of trade crisis.

Keating was booked for an interview that morning on talkback radio with John Laws, of Sydney's 2GB station, but the only telephone he could find was next to a swinging canteen door. It was here, on a call set to a soundtrack of clattering trays laden with coffee and croissants, that he told Laws, in a remark as arresting as it was unrehearsed, that Australia was at risk of becoming a 'banana republic'.

Not a politician who normally tended towards self-doubt, he would later concede to Morgan that perhaps he had gone too far.[2]

The comment set markets ablaze as if flung from a flamethrower. When it flashed up on the Reuters news ticker at lunchtime, dealers took it as an immediate cue to sell. By close of trading, the currency had collapsed, from a high of almost 75 US cents just two days earlier to 70, the largest ever Australian dollar devaluation in a twenty-four-hour period.[3] Speculators, still conscious of the economic mayhem that had marked the Whitlam years, were inherently sceptical of Labor and needed little nudging for another bout of jitters. Keating's outburst was also picked up with a cold dread in Beijing, where Hawke was in the middle of a diplomatic visit to China. To be told that his treasurer had just tossed a grenade at Australia's very perception of itself, at a time when he had a sequence of tightly scheduled appearances at state functions and panda sanctuaries over 9000 kilometres away, was less than ideal.

But where Hawke found his authority questioned, Keating scanned the newspaper coverage with a certain relief. Far from depicting his broadside as cavalier or misjudged, a leader in *The Australian Financial Review* called it a 'rare and refreshing piece of clarity from a Treasurer'.[4] At last, or so the sentiment went, there was an awareness at the highest levels of power about the scale of problems the country faced. For all the strides made in modernising taxation, and liberalising the financial system, the government could not yet say the same of the macro-economic sphere. On this front, Australia had still to emerge out of the darkness and into the light.

Keating was fond of delineating a 'J-curve', a Treasury graph that suggested an initial slump in fortunes would be followed by a sustained and emphatic upswing. But such a prognosis was difficult to believe, when, one bleak Monday in July, a teetering dollar fell off a cliff. Markets, shaken for weeks by plunging commodity prices and Keating's stark warning that Australia was struggling to pay its way in the world, unravelled to force the dollar to a then historic low of 57 cents against the US, a nosedive curbed only by a relaxation of foreign investment rules. Peter Walsh, over at the Department of Finance, would disclose that he was closer to despair that night than at any other point in his political life.[5]

Morgan's reaction at Treasury was more collected: had the government not funnelled all its energy into the mammoth tax reform enterprise, he recognised, there might have been a stronger impetus to find the right remedies.[6] Besides, at this moment of reckoning, there was little to be gained from agonising over past sins of omission. The 1986 Budget, due on 19 August, was the perfect platform for Labor to show that it was acting to correct unfinished fiscal business.

So pressing, indeed, was the need for boldness that talks about the headline figure on deficit reduction went to the wire. Morgan was at Keating's house on a Sunday afternoon and expressed concern that cutting the deficit to $5 billion would be deemed by foreign exchange markets as too lily-livered a reaction to the 'banana republic' furore. 'Mate, this isn't a helpful comment, but I think we need a three in front of it,' I told Paul. '"I think you're right," he responded, immediately. So, we stopped the presses.'[7]

In the space of a single meeting the next day, involving just four people – Hawke, Keating, Morgan and a representative from the prime minister's office – a far more palatable prediction of $3.5 billion was established. For all the risks that an unprecedented interruption of the print run would leak, there were no backroom whispers beyond those present, and the Budget was received with an enthusiasm seldom reserved for the cold detail of financial statements. Far from being the 'horror' many had anticipated, it was credited with striking the rare balance of being both economically responsible and politically honest.[8]

The view outside Australia was more jaundiced. Come September, Moody's rating agency in New York had decided that the country – whose inflation rate of nine per cent had risen far in excess of other first-world nations – was living beyond its means. For the first time since ratings began in 1962, its coveted AAA credit score was revised downwards to AA1, with immediate ramifications both for borrowing terms and for the markets to which Australia had access.

'This is a sad, sad day,' Jim Carlton, the shadow treasurer, thundered. 'The government will never be forgiven for tarnishing Australia's proudest symbol of international credit worthiness.'[9]

His assessment was a touch melodramatic. Largely, Labor could afford to shrug it off as a psychological wound, given that the rating from Standard & Poor's, the only rival to Moody's and the market leader in sovereign debt ranking, held firm at AAA. But the downgrade offered a powerful signal to the government that if it presumed it could sit pretty on the progress over tax and financial deregulation, it was sorely mistaken. If it hoped to persuade a dubious outside world that the country had turned a corner, then its deficit had to be brought under control. 'It was high-wire stuff,' Morgan says. 'We had played our cards on financial deregulation and tax reform, but we still didn't have the confidence of domestic or global markets.'

Keating has described the huge subsequent heave to balance the books as a 'long-hand' option.[10] Slashing the deficit by $1.5 billion, let alone eradicating it and ultimately moving to substantial surplus, was not an undertaking accomplished by short, sharp shocks, but by years of painstaking, line-by-line graft, searching for every conceivable saving. Hundreds of decisions would accumulate as Cabinet's Expenditure Review Committee (ERC) sat for marathon sessions, all of them highly charged as ministers baulked at having money for their departments taken away. Susan Ryan, the education minister, would talk of 'almost physical blows' raining down, disclosing that she had 'never been in such an aggressive environment'.[11]

Morgan, who by now had been promoted to first assistant secretary in charge of general financial and economic policy, sat at Keating's right hand for these gruelling round-tables. He could be unapologetically hawkish in outlook, always advocating the toughest option, regardless of political niceties.

'David would always try to push the system to the limit,' Keating says. 'Inside Cabinet, I had a better idea of what the traffic would bear. A treasurer, as Bernie Fraser once put it, has to be a wise prince, feeling the forces at the same time as guiding the policies. At first, David belonged to the school who believed that you gave the political system certain imperatives, which would then be taken up or not. The better way is not just to provide tablets from the mount, but to garner the confidence of ministers to adopt them.'[12]

For Morgan, a powerful motivation was to ensure that Stone's gloomy prophecy that Australia, as soon as it developed a decent tax system, would just raise a colossal sum of money and spend it all, did not come true. The theory, first proposed by British economists Alan Peacock and Jack Wiseman in the early sixties, that government spending was like a ratchet – in that once increased, it could never be wound back – was there to be disproved.[13] By December 1986, the fastidious pruning of outlays was starting to bear fruit. The dollar had shot back up to 67 US cents, a six-month high, while interest rates dropped. Although Labor took merciless flak for certain decisions, not least the lifting of a three-year ban on uranium sales to France, all for a paltry saving of $70 million, Keating remained convinced that he was plotting the correct course.

There would come a time, many years later, when the treasurer found himself bracketed with Tony Blair, who credited Keating as a 'role model' and as an originator of the centrist politics – the so-called 'Third Way' – that inspired his reinvention of Labour in Britain.[14] But where the two were aligned in their relish for bold policy-making, they diverged sharply in their working practices. Indeed, Keating claims to have been told by one source at Westminster that Blair would not spend one hour sifting through budgetary minutiae, still less ten hours a day for ten weeks a year.[15] In Canberra, such work was critical, and it was work to which Morgan's talent for cutting complex economic argument down to the bone was well suited. Some of his minutes, Keating would reflect, were so elegant that he wanted to frame them.[16]

'David had a prodigious capacity for work – he was conscientious, perfectionist,' Keating says. 'The ERC would often meet until eleven at night and then insist on a fresh submission, around certain agreed principles or programs. Somehow, David would churn this around overnight. For the biggest matters, I would drive from my place to his place, to see how he was going. Would it be ready for lodgement at 8 am, one hour before Cabinet met? Invariably it would, and it was always a very fine piece. Very few are called upon to do this kind of work, and very few can do it. He would do this month in, month out, when the most significant discussions were taking place.'[17]

By 1987, the sheer spadework of sifting through every fiscal detail, from science to social security, trade to foreign affairs, had in Keating's words left those involved 'like stunned mullets'.[18] His particular relentlessness gave Labor an advantage at the polls in July, though, as he forced opposition leader John Howard into a humiliating admission of a $540 million mistake in a Liberal tax plan that had taken two years to draw up. Keating made little secret of his delight at leaving his lifelong adversary 'in fiscal tatters at a critical moment in the nation's economic history'.[19] But even as Labor toasted a historic third term, the economy was not yet in a state where the government could bring out the bunting.

True, the deficit had been dismantled, down from an unsustainable four per cent of gross domestic product (GDP) to a meagre $27 million, the best outcome for seventeen years. All the delicate and hard-won trimmings to spending had ensured, Keating said, in a September Budget delayed by the election, that Australia had 'turned the corner'. Not that all observers were convinced, as Melbourne cartoonist Geoff 'Jeff' Hook suggested in an artwork that juxtaposed a man reading about 'Keating's Balanced Budget' with his wife loading shopping into a car whose number plate read simply: 'Skint'.[20]

Since 1983, there had been 820,000 new jobs created, and yet inflation was still running at over eight per cent. Even graver, though, was the maelstrom stirred up by the stock market crash of Black Monday, 19 October 1987, the largest one-day Wall Street wipe-out on record. Where the Dow Jones tumbled by 23 per cent, Sydney's All Ordinaries index, among the first to open in the aftermath of this New York nosedive, had a quarter of its value erased. Robert Holmes à Court, then Australia's richest man, watched $440 million dissolve from his fortune in twenty-four hours, while Rupert Murdoch, by his own admission, 'nearly went broke' despite his burgeoning media empire, and was forced to mortgage his Manhattan apartment.

In the month that followed this unravelling, Keating and Morgan, meeting for one of their regular Sunday tête-à-têtes, came to a crucial realisation. 'We were sitting on these mean little wire chairs in my garden,' Morgan recalls. 'The shade had come halfway over. I had just been appointed deputy secretary, in charge of monetary policy, and I mentioned my view that monetary conditions had been relaxed too far. "I think you're right," Paul said. We concluded that money was too cheap.'[21]

Tremors from the markets' implosion had spread far and wide. The Basel Committee on Banking Supervision believed that it portended another thirties-style calamity, while the US Federal Reserve embarked upon a massive injection of liquidity to help a volatile economy settle down. In Australia, fears of a recession were equally acute, as Bob Johnston, governor of the Reserve Bank, decided against a hike in interest rates that he might, in a less feverish financial climate, have approved.

But far from hurtling into an abyss, the country juddered over the crash as if it were a mere pothole. As 1988, the bicentennial of the First Fleet's arrival, dawned amid a blaze of fireworks across Sydney Harbour, Morgan was one of the few at Treasury to fret that interest rates were low – dangerously low.

At first glance, the nation appeared galvanised by a new-found prosperity. Property prices were surging, a crowd of two million lined Sydney's foreshores for an Australia Day flotilla of tall ships, and the Queen was poised to open

Brisbane's staging of World Expo 88. The revelries concealed deeper economic fault-lines, though. Close to fifteen years of high single-digit inflation had encouraged almost an acceptance that consumers' diminishing purchasing power, allied to high unemployment, was the natural state of affairs. Morgan moved early to the view that the trend could only be bucked by the prescription of some unpleasant medicine.

Mindful of how the 1987 stock crisis had not produced the global recession that so many had forecast, he kept Treasury alive to the need to tighten monetary policy. He sensed that the economy was running too hot, that the surge in income and investment was making it increasingly difficult for the government to adjust Australia's balance of payments on current account and to limit the accumulation of foreign debt. Morgan wrote in a minute to Keating on 30 March, ahead of a long and vigorous debate with the Reserve Bank about the merits of tightening policy: 'As you are well aware, the primary objective is to ensure that progress in correcting our external imbalance proceeds as rapidly as practicable. You indicated earlier that the pace of domestic demand was too fast to be consistent with sustained improvement in net exports.'[22]

A battle was taking shape within Treasury between the hawks and the doves. Bernie Fraser, as secretary, belonged firmly to the dovish camp, uneasy about any agitation within his own bureaucracy for more draconian action to force an economic cool-down. An impeccably measured man, known for his hushed voice, scrupulous restraint, and his willingness to tolerate dissenting voices to a degree unthinkable under Stone, he felt that there was a place for compassion in the department. 'Monetary policy, particularly on its own, won't solve things,' he told *The Australian*. 'You might hammer people into submission by jacking up interest rates, but after a time the unemployment consequences will be such that you have to relent and come back to the same starting point. You haven't made any progress.'[23]

Morgan, undeterred, took a different tack. With most OECD countries having disinflated during the early eighties, Australia was almost alone with its entrenched high inflation. Morgan was persuaded there could be no remedy but to make interest rates, however briefly, punishingly high. By March 1988, his message was explicit, even if it was couched in careful diplomatic code. 'We think the time has come for a firming in financial conditions,' he said in his formal note to Keating. 'The tightening we have in mind is marginal, rather than a big hit – the sound of a harp, not a blunderbuss.'[24]

It was more a matter of judgment than principle. Although Fraser claims that Morgan, whose flamboyance made him a polar opposite as a personality, leant naturally towards a 'dramatic style, overkill, the big splash', this was not quite the full story. Morgan, even at the age of forty-one, carried his childhood scars.

'The period was personally agonising,' Morgan says. 'I had experienced at first hand the pain of a family having its home repossessed by the bank.' He understood only too well, from his position to influence policy, that he was endorsing the type of strong-arm tactics that would subject many Australians to a similar torment. With power, as Keating was fond of emphasising, came untold leverage. Move on the bridge by an inch and you can shift the country by a mile.

'Frankly, it was gut wrenching. But so, too, was persistently high unemployment.' In his hard-headed calculation, the issue resolved itself into one of ends and means, where the longed-for elimination of high inflation – with all its corrosive effects upon the employment picture – would be justified by short-term suffering.

Keating perceived the same necessity to keep the boom in check, telling Morgan on a flight to see the Reserve Bank in Sydney that he wanted policy hardened. With cash rates elevated from 10.3 per cent at the start of 1988 to 11.5 in April, Australia became the first country to accept that the post-crash status quo, of leaving monetary conditions accommodating, was not working.

For Morgan, there was still scope for more of a 'king hit'. 'We may need to move further before too much longer,' he argued to Keating. 'We cannot afford the risk of letting the economy overheat. There is a real possibility of that happening if recent measures do not have a fairly quick impact.'[25] These were exceptional times, in which the traditional wisdom that monetary policy operated with at least a twelve-month lag went out of the window. Morgan was unshakeable in his view that a rapid response, not a softly-softly approach, was the order of the day. The official projections by the Joint Economic Forecasting Group supported his sense of restlessness, warning in July: 'On the basis of present policy settings, prospective domestic demand growth and inflationary pressures are much stronger than desirable.'[26]

As deputy secretary, Morgan had acquired extra security clearance to access the most sensitive information available. At vital moments, he would even take Cabinet papers home

Morgan's acting career takes flight. Here he is standing to the right, playing the dastardly Spider McGlurk, in an episode of the TV series *The Ten Again*.

Above left: Morgan starred in thirty-nine half-hour episodes of *The Magic Boomerang*, assuming the lead role of Tom Thumbleton.
Right: Courtesy of his mother's connections at a Melbourne photographic studio, Morgan found himself in demand as a child model in newspaper adverts.

Morgan in his La Trobe University football kit, 1969. He kicked 175 goals for the season in the Panton Hill League, comfortably a competition record.

Right: Morgan with Sir
Rohan Delacombe, governor
of Victoria, at his Rhodes
Scholarship interview, 1971.

Above: Morgan interviewing
John Gorton, prime minister
of Australia, for his La Trobe
honours thesis, 1970.

Right: Morgan in his office at
Federal Treasury, Canberra,
early 1972.

Above: The morning after Morgan's thirtieth birthday party, 1977, in Washington DC, where he worked for the International Monetary Fund.

Above right: Morgan in central London, 1974, soon after he had embarked on graduate study at the London School of Economics.

Morgan with his bride, Ros Kelly, at their wedding celebration in Red Hill, Canberra, 1983. There was no honeymoon as Kelly, a Labor MP, had to go straight into campaigning mode for that year's election.

Morgan and Kelly with Paul Keating and his wife, Annita, in Keating's Parliament House office, just moments after his successful leadership challenge against Bob Hawke, 1991.

Morgan, Keating, Ted Evans (secretary of the Treasury, left) and Bernie Fraser (governor of the Reserve Bank, right) sharing a joke at Morgan's forty-fifth birthday party, 1992.

Left: Morgan on the cover of *Australian Business* in 1983 alongside, left to right, Mike Keating, Geoffrey Yeend, Ian Castles and John Stone.

Right: Morgan (here again on the cover of *Australian Business*, in 1985) spearheaded the mammoth mid-eighties tax reform exercise. In Keating's words, he was the 'principal engine'.

Cartoon by Geoff Pryor of *The Canberra Times*, 1983, juxtaposing Kelly and baby Jessica with Keating delivering his first Budget. Morgan wrote the Budget speech on the day his daughter was born, in a delivery suite strewn with briefing notes.

Morgan, Kelly, Jessica and newborn son, Benjamin, 1984. Within days of Ben's birth, Kelly was back in election mode once more.

The Morgan family at their Red Hill home, early 1990. Morgan had recently made the move from Treasury to Westpac.

with him at night, much to the surprise of Kelly, who had not long since been made minister for defence, science and personnel. It was strictly against rules, even if he was fastidious about carrying such documents in a locked Samsonite briefcase. 'Ros would ask, "How did you get those?"' he says. '"You're just a bureaucrat. I'm a minister, and even I can't see them."'[27]

Time was of the essence, but Morgan had to be wary about pressing Keating too hard to turn the monetary screw. For one thing, there were concerns about the implications for the exchange rate, with higher interest rates likely to pull up the dollar and perhaps damage Australia's trading competitiveness. Plus, it was the 1988 Budget, confirming as it did the country's largest ever surplus of $5.5 billion, just three years on from a $5.7 billion deficit, that dominated Keating's thinking. Intensely proud of the achievement, he declared: 'This is the Budget that brings home the bacon. This is the one that brings the whole game together from 1983 onwards.'[28] Quite deliberately, given that his designs on Hawke's job as prime minister were by now an open secret, he expressed it in the language of a last will and testament.

But beneath the glowing headlines – 'The Beer's on Paul', trumpeted *The Sydney Morning Herald*, in reference to a cut in beer excise – lurked a mounting sense of trouble.[29] For in this Budget, despite its assurance that Australians had worn the worst of economic adversity, was an admission that imports, even after a 15 per cent bounce in the terms of trade, would continue outpacing exports.

As such, Morgan waited barely a fortnight before lighting the monetary fuse. On 7 September, he minuted Keating, with an unusual sharpness in tone: 'Over the last three years, there has been a tendency, within the "official family" and more generally, to underestimate the strength of demand and inflation. If more could not have been done on the fiscal and wages fronts, it could be argued that monetary policy has been somewhat looser, on average, than appropriate.'[30] The note had the recommendation of Chris Higgins, an important signal that the most senior of Treasury's three deputies was siding with the hawks. Ted Evans did not endorse the minute, apparently disliking the bluntness of its wording.

Keating, it turned out, liked it even less. Having been handed the message ten minutes before the latest discussions with the Reserve Bank, he gave Morgan a fearful dressing-down in front of those present, including Bernie Fraser and Bob Johnston. While Keating had a tongue that could strip wallpaper when the mood took him, once saying of Andrew Peacock that the Liberals ought to 'put him down like a faithful old dog', these barbs tended to be saved for political opponents. It was unusual, as Paul Kelly observed in a 1989 article dissecting the row, for him to turn so witheringly on a Treasury official.[31] But he loathed having his good sense called into question.

Doubling down on the outburst in writing, Keating said: 'David, I find the tone and content of this note very annoying. The whole message is unnecessary. It is trying to prove a case in a strident way for a strategy to which I am already publicly and privately committed. I said in the Budget speech that demand must be kept under control and that monetary policy must play its vital balancing role. I wrote those words myself, knowing precisely what they mean.'[32] Bristling,

Keating inferred from Morgan's pointed language that he was being accused of unnecessary delays in lifting interest rates. In a reassertion of his authority, he stressed that while he was open to further increases, they would happen only at his discretion.

With a certain chutzpah, undaunted by the treasurer's face-to-face challenge, Morgan had returned to Canberra and penned his own jocular version of what he imagined would be Keating's reply. The paraphrasing, according to Paul Kelly, went roughly as follows: 'Thank you for the tough advice. On mature reflection, I realise you are correct and we could have done much more. I have made the mistake of listening to wimps for too long.'[33]

It was a joke meant for the most limited circulation. Keating, at least, saw the funny side, recalling it with his Treasury boys amid much laughter during IMF meetings in Berlin in October. But it did not require Inspector Clouseau to work out the 'wimps' to whom Morgan could have been alluding. One was Fraser, by now outnumbered as a dove, who took the remark as an affront. Almost thirty years on, he has not forgotten it, although Morgan has since insisted that it was less a direct attack than a tongue-in-cheek aside. Defending his reluctance to ramp up rates to the hilt, Fraser says: 'I'm one of those pragmatic people – "wimpish", in David's eyes, on some policy matters, but very concerned to ensure that economic reforms aren't pushed ahead without regard for social consequences.'[34]

A scorched-earth interest rate policy did, as Fraser feared, have a savage effect on the community beyond the capital's panelled chambers. The hawks had won the day, their arguments driving the cash rate to 15 per cent by November, 16 the following February, and an extraordinary 18 by May 1989. It was at this point, and with palpable suddenness, that the bubble of the country's 'roaring eighties' popped. 'You could actually feel it,' Don Russell, Keating's long-time principal advisor, would reflect. 'Something snapped.'[35] Home ownership, the great Australian dream of the postwar generation, was threatening to come apart at the seams. 'Paul,' asked one protestor's sign, in a jab at Keating's part in all this, 'can you afford 60 per cent of your income for your mortgage?'

The treasurer, true to form, had little time for the detractors. Conscious that there was no more divisive topic of national conversation in 1989 than interest rates, he joked in a speech at Sydney's Menzies Hotel: 'I guarantee that if you walk into any pet shop in Australia, the resident galah will be talking about micro-economic policy.'[36] He poured scorn on calls for relief schemes to soften the blow of such sky-high rates, deriding them as 'embroidery' and 'economic ratbaggery'.

This was the essence of Keating's adversarial style. His broadsides spoke less of his commitment to monetary tightening at its most brutal than of his steadfast view that a government should set a policy and stick to it. The contentious question is whether the driving of interest rates to these levels, as advocated by Morgan and his fellow hawks, led directly to Australia's early nineties recession – the one, as Keating would infamously put it, that 'we had to have'.

Ian Macfarlane, who carved a decorated twenty-eight-year career at the Reserve Bank, has cast doubt on this theory. In his Boyer Lectures in 2006, he argued that by 1989, nobody at Treasury or the RBA was seriously querying the need to raise the rates. With the economy having built such a boiling head of steam from late 1987, there were few plausible alternatives. While the high-water mark of an 18 per cent cash rate might seem astronomical in retrospect, it was not, Macfarlane pointed out, without precedent. After all, short-term rates had touched 19 per cent at the end of 1985 and 21 in April 1982.

The difference this time was that mortgage rates had been deregulated, magnifying the impact on the average household. There could be no denying the scale of the economic contraction that ensued in 1990, with bankruptcies, business collapses and negative equity galore. But the lasting benefit, in Macfarlane's analysis, was that inflationary expectations were definitively reduced, falling from a consistent high of 10 per cent throughout the eighties to under five after 1991.[37] Once the distress and the disquiet eased, Australia could at last call itself a low-inflation economy.

* * *

Looking back can sometimes bring a false romanticism. 'So we beat on, boats against the current, borne back ceaselessly into the past,' as the closing lines to *The Great Gatsby* remind us.[38] Australia could do far worse, though, than to remember how its Treasury was in the eighties a repository of intellect and experience, harnessing both in the forging of effective public policy. In her *Quarterly Essay* on this theme in 2015, 'Political Amnesia: How We Forgot How to Govern', veteran journalist Laura Tingle traces the steady erosion since the Hawke–Keating era of the country's bureaucratic class, and of knowledge as an essential powerbase.[39] Today, the image of Keating's *cri de coeur* to his troops after the 1983 election – 'I want a strong Treasury, it's an important national institution' – is receding from collective memory.[40]

A book by Chris Bowen, about those whom he regards as Australia's twelve most notable treasurers, reinforces the point. Bowen, himself the treasurer for the last three months of Kevin Rudd's Labor government, writes Treasury itself almost entirely out of the picture. Referring to twenty-six consecutive years of economic growth since 1990, an unparalleled achievement, he says: 'Credit can be claimed by many people: Prime Ministers and Treasurers, world-class financial regulators, prudent bankers, visionary mining executives, hardworking employers and, to some degree, Lady Luck.'[41] Nowhere here is the role of Treasury, which furnished the full force of its expertise throughout the breakneck eighties reforms that underpinned more recent success, even acknowledged. Instead, running through the book is an idea that the institution evolved solely under the tutelage of successive treasurers.

'Give me a break – it was much more the other way,' Morgan says. 'Treasury never gets to tell its side of the story. Governments are broader than politicians alone. I want to call this out, to speak up for a silent treasure. For as long as Treasury is belittled in its role, its withering on the vine, slow but cumulatively devastating, will go largely unremarked, unlamented and unfixed.'[42] It is a Westminster tradition that the minister is the face of policy, while the bureaucrats beaver thanklessly in the shadows. 'That applies only to a point,' Morgan argues. 'An institution such as Treasury is vitally important to the proper functioning of democracy, the economy and society. It needs to be respected.'[43]

What its key figures from the eighties whirlwind fear is that it now finds itself in terminal decline. While Treasury translated more of its agenda into policy under Keating than in all the preceding postwar years combined, it has since been emasculated by cutbacks. Towards the end of Julia Gillard's administration, the denuding of expertise became so severe, with sixty-two redundancies from 2012 to 2014 at Treasury alone, that the median length of a public-service career shrank to just nine years.[44] The ramifications of this neglect, or at the very least the failure to esteem the strength of the bureaucratic machine, are profound. 'It is not just about politicisation,' Tingle observes. 'It is a result of politicians failing to value and preserve our institutions.'[45]

One explanation for the bureaucracy being bled dry, Ken Henry volunteers, is that the perceived epicentre of power in Australia has shifted. This change has its roots, paradoxically, in the very period when Canberra felt, in Morgan's words, 'like the only place to be'.[46] Henry, drawing on almost a decade as secretary to the Treasury, from 2001 to 2011, explains: 'Many of the market-liberalising reforms of which David was a part opened up extraordinary private-sector opportunities for those well trained in economics. In my time, hundreds left to take up lucrative positions that simply didn't exist in the early eighties. It has become difficult to entice those excelling at university in Sydney or Melbourne to consider a career in Canberra. Equally, there is just not the mountain of policy reform to conquer any longer. The loss of so many high-calibre people will, I predict, turn out to be costly for Australia.'[47]

Singapore, by contrast, has scrupulously sought to attract the finest talent by remunerating its civil servants with the same lavishness they could expect in banking or finance, thus staunching the 'brain drain'.

A solution, in Australia's case, will require far more than an adjustment of recompense. In 2016, Peter Varghese, the retiring head of the Department of Foreign Affairs and Trade, expressed his fears that the once-exalted standing of public servants was under dire threat as the political climate grew ever more impatient and short-termist. 'The public service has lost depth when it comes to policy thinking,' he said. 'I fear that the combination of a relentless news cycle, social media that can often distort the centre of gravity of a policy issue, and the technology of instant connectedness, has weakened our capacity to reflect.'[48]

Increasingly, the lines of distinction between the political and bureaucratic systems have become blurred. Tony Abbott took the decision in 2014 to sack Martin Parkinson as the nation's top civil servant, while Scott Morrison chose four years later to appoint his own chief of staff as secretary to the Treasury: a decision condemned in *The Sydney Morning Herald* as 'the flouting of convention and good governance'.[49] Demonstrably, the once cast-iron status of the Australian Public Service (APS) as an apolitical body, free from government interference and concerned only with imparting frank and fearless advice, can no longer be guaranteed.

It is amid this rising sense of alarm that Morgan has made a submission to an independent review of the APS, pressing for a restoration of its original purpose. 'To be responsive is to deal with the issues of the day,' he says. 'To be responsible is to nurture capabilities that equip the country to deal with long-term challenges. Today's public service is very responsive, but is it responsible?'[50] Just as crucial, he argues, is that the APS becomes independent again, if it ever hopes to empower its staff and regain its place as a coveted destination for the best graduates. The environment, inescapably, has shifted, with public servants now jostling to make themselves heard above a panoply of think tanks, special advisors, lobby groups and NGOs. But if Australia continues on the path of devaluing its experts, Morgan warns, then it risks the destruction of a priceless national asset.

History cannot simply be rewound. Any suggestion, for example, that the country needs to unearth another treasurer in the daredevil mould of Keating feels glib. Instead, any recapturing of the public service's grandeur rests more upon an understanding that the quantum leaps of the eighties were, in essence, a collaborative creation. As Morgan said in a speech at Keating's seventieth birthday party in 2014: 'Did you achieve all of this single-handedly, Paul? Of course not. It was done in combination with a select group of talented, ambitious and dedicated people.'[51]

For all that Keating has waged a tit-for-tat battle with Hawke about who deserved the greater plaudits as the architect of reform, he acknowledges that he formed part of an ornate tapestry at Treasury. 'In economic policy, Australia had only ever moved incrementally under Liberal or Coalition control,' he says. 'All of a sudden, there was a government moving it on in leaps and bounds. It was my wish that Treasury responded to this policy opportunity, which it did in a very substantial way, largely because of the quality of officers at the top. After my "banana republic" remark, Cabinet decided to embark upon the biggest fiscal consolidation in the history of the OECD. Outlays went from 29.5 per cent in 1986 of GDP to 23.5 by 1990. Six percentage points: for any country, that is massive.'[52]

From Morgan, Keating remembers an unwavering commitment to the task, not to mention an uncommon flair for conceptualising blizzards of technical detail for ministers' benefit. 'David was the officer most charged with the burden of these responsibilities. Somebody had not just to coordinate the process, but to guide it, and he did.'[53]

Testimonies to the energy of these times are as abundant as they are effusive. Ian Macfarlane, for example, is hardly a figure given to grandiose or unguarded statements. In his decade at the helm of the Reserve Bank, he granted not a single newspaper interview. But he identifies this phase at Treasury, without hesitation, as 'the golden period'. The decisive factor, in his view, was Keating's art of inspiring loyalty, of imbuing the department with a power over policy to which it could never have aspired under the yoke of Stone. Call it a cult of personality, perhaps, but the relationship was symbiotic. 'Treasury worshipped Keating, which itself was most unusual,' Macfarlane says. 'Usually you just treat the treasurer as some political appointee. They got so much done, though, both in the tax system and in returning the Budget to surplus. We have never had anything nearly as good.'[54]

* * *

Professionally, it seemed logical for Morgan to keep riding the wave. Still in his early forties, within reach of the secretaryship, he derived what he called unparalleled 'psychic income' from being in the vanguard of such a sweeping economic transformation.[55] Channelling his acting skills of old, he even presented a Treasury recruitment video, entitled 'Making a Difference', to encourage some of Australia's most gifted students to follow suit. The same rush, he understood, would prove hard to replicate elsewhere, even though more lucrative job offers regularly passed across his desk.

Competition for talent between the public and private sectors was a hallmark of the era, with Morgan arguing that the bureaucracy needed to offer more attractive salaries to prevent the finest young graduates from being prised away for a fatter cheque. Equally, he felt there was a gap in Treasury's intellectual armoury about how private enterprise truly behaved. 'It tended to revere analytical excellence but to disparage what it frequently termed "managerialism",' he explains.

These factors coloured his thinking towards his own position. While far from persuaded about the merits of turning away from Treasury, he knew that if he ever did jump across the public–private divide – at a level high enough to tempt him – he would need the type of business qualification that complemented his academic credentials. One option presented itself more vividly than all others: a short but immersive course at Harvard Business School, known less by its scholastic content than by its lofty promise to mould demonstrable leaders into future global executives.

Sure enough, come February 1989, Morgan was swapping the committee rooms of Canberra for the graceful stateliness of Cambridge, Massachusetts. It was an interlude designed to last just thirteen weeks, and yet it would recast his life in ways he had scarcely dared envisage.

CHAPTER 7

The Cancer of Hubris

Those chosen for Harvard's fast track to executive empowerment lived in near-identikit apartments. Bedrooms at Baker Hall, the Business School's hulking campus by the Charles River, were little more than the size of ship cabins, intended to force the resident 'living group' into a more generous communal space that doubled as an intellectual salon, where prospective captains of industry could augment their studies through the robust exchange of ideas. That was the theory, at any rate.

Morgan tended to find that he absorbed the more lasting lessons from such seasoned, hard-boiled US business leaders as Gene McGrath, who defied a bruising upbringing in public housing to become the long-serving chief executive of Consolidated Edison, an energy company of such clout that it long held a virtual monopoly over gas and electrical supply in New York. 'An unflashy character, he would tell me, "Business is actually quite simple,"' Morgan reflects. '"Take the right decision for the long term, not the short term. Do the right thing, not the political thing.'"[1]

This was not the modesty of message Morgan had anticipated, having crossed the Pacific to join the Advanced Management Program (AMP). A purist on all forms of higher education, he expected to approach the private sector with the same sophistication of analysis that was his stock in trade as an economist. Instead, he encountered Harvard's beloved case-study method, one he was conditioned to regard as ad hoc, arbitrary and lacking in rigour. Where were the frameworks, the neat conceptual rubrics?

A Sunday evening conversation with one of his professors, after many hours' toil at the Baker Library, disabused him of this presumption. 'David,' said Theodore Levitt, a man acclaimed as the global guru of modern marketing – despite reputedly never having read a book on the subject before he started teaching – 'there are no analytical foundations of business.'

The purpose of this bespoke Harvard training has long been to lay out a path to leadership. Since its inception in 1945, the AMP has enticed ambitious executive climbers on the cusp of assuming heavier responsibilities. But in Morgan's class of 1989 it was also a form of consolation prize, a halfway house for those aspiring to greater glories.

This was partly true of his own circumstances: it had been tacitly agreed within Treasury that Chris Higgins would succeed Bernie Fraser, off to take the reins at the Reserve Bank, as secretary, which left Morgan confronting a stick-or-twist decision on his professional future. He had received many expressions of private-sector interest and Harvard's promise to demystify this parallel universe would give him both the time and insight needed to judge the merits of a move.

'It was part of a deal, saying, "David, what do you want to do?"' he explains. 'I was forty-one. I recognised that if I was going to make the leap, I had to do it soon. Plus, I had felt distinctly uneasy, ever since my earliest days at Treasury in 1972, that I knew very little about how the private sector operated. We made all this tax policy assuming – rather than understanding – how the private sector would respond. This was not just a shortcoming of Treasury, but of most of the discipline of economics at the time.'

For all that the Harvard route multiplied Morgan's options, it was not initially received with raptures at home, with Kelly facing three months with two small children to care for and a complex ministerial portfolio to master. A dinner party in Red Hill with their close friends Jill and Peter Wilenski, who had just been appointed Australia's ambassador to the United Nations, brought matters to a head. Kelly, listening to the three others chat animatedly about their American adventures to come, rose slowly to her feet and, in a scene never witnessed in their marriage before or since, threw the fish supper at her husband. 'I was exhausted,' she says. 'I didn't believe that there had been any concession to me, either to have babies or to have time off. I felt left out. So, one night, at our tiny square dinner table, I thought, I've had enough of this. Everybody was shocked. They had never seen me lose my cool.'[2]

Over time, such resistance was tempered. Morgan's immersion at Harvard was, in his words, 'life changing', fundamentally reshaping the prism through which he viewed the perfect business leader. Such a person, he had assumed, was invariably the smartest in the room, to the point where he began the AMP still anxious that he had not studied for a Master of Business Administration. But through living in the pockets of 159 fellow CEOs-in-waiting, he found these misgivings were assuaged.

'In the dying days of the course, I looked around to see who I thought might make CEO and who wouldn't – and I surprised myself,' he says. 'They weren't necessarily the brightest guys. They tended to be those who were good with people, decent human beings with ambition and a track record of execution. It broadened my model of leadership.'[3] While most had enrolled coveting the top job, overtly or otherwise, there was no finishing school for crafting the optimum candidate.

Morgan returned to Canberra with a growing conviction that his public-service career had run its course. Higgins' appointment as secretary was rubber-stamped in September 1989, and there was a nagging suspicion that Kelly's likely next move to a Cabinet role would be incompatible with his own as the second most powerful figure at Treasury.

'We both knew we had pushed the envelope as far as we could,' Kelly explains. 'It wasn't the money. We didn't have goals to have a waterfront home in Sydney. But David has always had a hankering to explore, even if the problem with any shift to the private sector was that we would no longer be able to live in the same city.'[4]

Two distinct offers had materialised: the first to join a Melbourne brokerage, the second to enter the wealth management division at Westpac, then Australia's second largest bank by market capitalisation.[5] Initially, Morgan leant towards the Melbourne option, before receiving some inimitably blunt advice from his friend and confidant Paul Keating – 'I told David that I believed he was an institutional person, that he would be much better off at Westpac than he would as an elevated broker.'[6]

Morgan headed off with Kelly on a parliamentary delegation to Geneva, for a telecommunications conference, where the crisp Swiss air brought clarity to a vexed decision. One morning, he broke it to Kelly, fresh off an early-morning lakeside walk, that his mind was set on Westpac.

The kudos was undeniable. Westpac revelled in a reputation as the oldest company in Australia, a constant of national life since 1817, when Joseph Hyde Potts, a porter and servant, walked into the solitary branch of the Bank of New South Wales as its first employee, agreeing to be paid £25 a year so long as he slept on the premises. Its proudest moments were stitched like red threads into the canvas of history: it was Lachlan Macquarie, last autocratic governor of New South Wales, who saw in this institution a chance for a private economy to flourish in an era when Australia itself was virtually a state-owned enterprise, and it was Alfred Davidson, the bank's general manager in the thirties, who forced – contrary to the prevailing mood – a devaluation of the Australian pound to mitigate the ravages of the Great Depression.

And yet in the eighties, buoyed by a flood tide of liquidity and enamoured of the notion of being the country's global bank, its leaders overreached themselves. Westpac, as it became known after a 1982 merger with the Commercial Bank of Australia, succumbed, in its restless burst of poorly thought through asset building, to what Morgan would later call the 'cancer of hubris'.

Desperate to expand beyond its Australasian base, Westpac threw vast bounties at such heedless buccaneers as George Herscu, who created US shopping malls of an extravagance to match his personal taste. Where the bank liked to imagine that it was taking the best of Australia to the world, Herscu, an enduring emblem of eighties greed, was opening his latest outlet in Cincinnati as the band played 'Tie Me Kangaroo Down, Sport'.[7]

If this backdrop of misguided and excessive lending threatened to complicate Morgan's move to Westpac, so too did the cosiness of the corporate culture he would encounter. He recalled a conversation some years earlier with Sir Bede Callaghan, former head of Commonwealth Banking Corporation, who had described how banks' usual criteria for hiring in the sixties would extend little further than looks, personality and sporting prowess.[8] The upshot was a monochromatic profile to the workforce: reactionary, often right-wing, overwhelmingly male, where a fresh recruit from secondary school could all but expect a job for life, on a prescribed path from teller through to retail manager, and where the premium lay on attracting the 'bonzer bloke' rather than the brightest mind.

'These were oligopolies, primarily run by the staff, for the staff,' Morgan says. 'Historically they set rules in rural areas that you could never poach another bank's customer. They would devote huge amounts of time refining the details of their pension schemes, working out what car they could have, even what parking space. When we deregulated the financial system, there was some real decision-making power at last placed back in the hands of the banks, but parts of the old guard remained.'[9]

Morgan received some frank advice from James Wolfensohn, later a 'force of nature' as president of the World Bank but then running a boutique investment bank in New York, about his Westpac plan.[10] 'They will find you very threatening there,' Wolfensohn told him. 'Ignore the politics. Just put your head down and do a really good job.'[11]

It was sage counsel, but easier to give than to act upon. The very act of appointing Morgan was mired in strife within Westpac, as managing director Stuart Fowler expressed doubts about embracing a senior bureaucrat known for his closeness to Keating and his marriage to Kelly, whose Labor politics were anathema to the bank's ultra-conservative establishment.[12]

Impressions of the bank, from both outside and inside, were of a boys' club. Just ask Helen Lynch, the first woman to assume real seniority at Westpac. 'I was an outsider, no question,' she recalls. 'I found, when I left Queensland for the Sydney headquarters on a huge promotion, that I couldn't take all the cliques on. I made some significant statements: I told them, for example, that I could not be on a selection panel unless it had other women involved. But I let other things go, lest people muttered of me, "Oh, she's that aggressive feminist from Brisbane." I had to learn how to play the game, to stand up for myself only when it was a matter of integrity and principle. David felt this insidious discrimination, too. External people were not welcome, but tolerated.'[13]

The homogeneity of the place was extraordinary: of Westpac's seven-strong executive committee in 1989, only one member, Peter Wilson, had been to university.[14] Sir Robert Norman, whose own career at the bank spanned fifty-six years, including thirteen as its leader, stuck fast to a view that the institution alone could provide all the education an aspiring general manager required.[15] To him, the idea of a public servant with three academic degrees – let alone one with the most intimate ties to Labor – gatecrashing the monolith that was Westpac seemed too much to bear. It took chairman Sir Eric Neal, who had built a reputation for toughness as head of construction giant Boral, to recognise that Morgan's connections to government, coupled with his deep economic learning, could prove invaluable.

The wrench that Morgan felt at leaving Treasury was powerful. It had defined his career for almost two decades, ever since he first strode in for his cadetship, full of the audacity of youth, to request a one-on-one meeting with then secretary Sir Richard Randall, whom he all but instructed to read his honours thesis. Ted Evans, his friend and confidant throughout these years, and later secretary himself, had by 1989 left to become executive director of the IMF but faxed a tribute from Washington. 'You will always be a Treasury man, just as you have always been a consummate performer on any stage,' it read. Evans added, drily: 'An old IMF colleague once complimented us at Treasury on progressing David's "descent from the trees". His untimely departure cuts short that process and we are obliged to leave to Westpac the difficult process of turning grass into lawn.'[16]

Morgan's pangs about his departure from public service were writ large in the remarks he gave at his farewell dinner that December. His exit had, he acknowledged, given him sleepless nights. He said, 'I've never left a marriage, but I imagine it must involve the same deep-seated agony. I realise the private sector is held in some contempt in this room, and by ex-Treasury people who have gone there to essentially presentational roles. This job, it is fair to say, represents a far greater challenge, and I leave with the intention of giving Westpac the same loyalty I have shown here. Thank you for the privilege.'[17]

As soon as Morgan was implanted into Westpac, he felt like an 'artificial kidney that the host body was constantly trying to reject'. His detractors' label for him, 'Chifley's Revenge' – a nod to former Labor prime minister Ben Chifley, who had a referendum in the late forties to nationalise the Australian banking industry – whispered through the corridors. Even before his formal start date, he turned up at the 1989 Christmas party to be greeted by a well-watered Sir Robert, who slurred, with nary a hint of irony or sarcasm, that there was no room for 'socialists' like him at Westpac. A mortified chairman offered his apologies on the bank's behalf.

Still, Morgan hardly did much to shake the charge of socialist sympathising when he enticed Garry Weaven, his old sparring partner at La Trobe, the son of a lorry driver and a union man to his bones, to follow him to the bank. An advantage of his Treasury training was a capacity for predicting how the financial system would evolve, and he was quick to call a key change in the composition of Australians' household savings, where money was increasingly shifting from bank deposits to superannuation. Weaven, as a prime architect of the country's superannuation revolution, could ensure that Westpac was best poised to exploit this trend, but his appointment was nothing if not provocative. 'For an outsider to bring in somebody from a union background?' says Andrew Cornell, then of *The Australian Financial Review* and a keen chronicler of Morgan's transition into banking. 'You can see why the clubby Westpac world would go off its nut about that.'[18]

Morgan was making the leap across the public–private fence with gale-force gusto. His first office, at Endeavour House on Pitt Street, was down the hill from Westpac's headquarters in Martin Place, but he refused to be detached from the heart of the action, soon requesting that he be based at the main building. Unlike Jim Goldman, whose imminent retirement promised to propel him to the summit of the wealth section, Morgan attended Fowler's 7.15 am coffee meetings with the executive committee.[19]

Aware that he was perceived as the rogue scholar, he formed a view of early nineties Westpac as arrogant, hubristic and obstinately anti-intellectual. He was taken aback by the haphazard nature of much of the bank's bookkeeping. Some years later, he wrote a note, intended for limited circulation, on the lack of discipline and detail he found upon his arrival. 'There were no files to speak of,' Morgan observed. 'Major decisions were taken on the basis of what I thought was quite flimsy analysis and documentation. Many were taken without any at all.'[20] He advocated the use of management consultants to comb through the chaos, only to hear the common reply: 'What do we need them for? They just take your watch and hand it back to you, telling you the time.'[21]

One evening, Kelly – who, after Labor's March 1990 election win, held a sweeping government remit as minister for arts, sport, environment, tourism and territories – accompanied Morgan to a typically lavish boat party at The Spit, for her introduction to his fellow executives. 'You can't stay at Westpac,' she told him as they left. 'Those people are not good enough to get the bank out of its difficulties.'[22]

While Morgan agreed, privately, about the delusions of adequacy among certain colleagues, he did not see the same reason for abandoning course. He intuited that the storm looming over Westpac could provide opportunities to prove his worth that would be unthinkable in more placid waters.

Bad debts were accumulating month by month, to an extent that neither the bank's prudential regulator nor external auditors had envisaged, and yet Westpac Financial Services Group (WFSG), the realm over which Morgan would soon preside, remained essentially untouched.

Its success as the only major division to meet its forecasts helped ensure, by October 1990, a seamless transition from Goldman to Morgan, who was also channelling his acting background to give exuberant speeches about WFSG's feats and aspirations on the road. His profile rose, fuelling both restless personal aspiration and a resolve to make his section of the business an example to emulate. Experts from Boston Consulting Group were brought in to enhance its status as the fastest growing area of Westpac, as Morgan relentlessly emphasised his belief in the importance of integrity, commitment and *esprit de corps* in depoliticising the culture.

* * *

No best-laid plans, though, could account for the twisted capriciousness of fate. On the evening of 3 December 1990, Morgan received a telephone call that would hold any thought of Westpac in abeyance. It was Veronica Goldrick, a Canberra physician well known to Morgan and Kelly, ringing to say that Chris Higgins had died. It was a shock too grievous for those who knew him to absorb properly. He was just forty-seven years old. Passionate about his running – his personal best for a marathon was a remarkable two hours, forty-six minutes – Higgins had been advised by doctors aware of his heart condition not to overdo it, but after a 3000 metre race at the Australian Institute of Sport he collapsed and could not be revived. At the funeral, Morgan, a pallbearer, was inconsolable. The two had drunk together, dreamt together and had collaborated in shaping an electrifying economic period. 'Wunder', they had nicknamed Higgins at Treasury, for his lightning intelligence, after the German *wunderkind*.

'I don't want to paint Chris as too good to be true, because he wasn't,' Morgan says. 'But there was nothing ostentatious about him. He was unshowy, unpolitical, a true meritocrat. Rather than having to be the guy who took all the credit, he just wanted the right outcome.'[23]

Keating, under whose command the two of them worked, was similarly shattered by the loss. He changed the wording of his normally boisterous speech to the National Press Club the next evening, telling journalists: 'This game is all about whether you want to be a participant or a voyeur. Chris Higgins was a participant.'[24]

If ever Morgan needed another reason to heed Keating's urgings, over several years of breakneck reform, to make each moment count, then here it was. The passing of Higgins, far too young, was a warning of life's cruelties and of the pitilessness with which time ticked on. It came with a suddenness, too, to create an unexpected void within Treasury. Higgins had served as secretary for barely fifteen months, having given a grimly portentous promise: 'David, I'm not going to be here forever. I'll give you whatever you want.' In the saddest of circumstances, the job for which Morgan had once busily auditioned was available. Keating, deploying a trademark blend of charm and cajoling, offered Morgan the role of secretary to the Treasury, knowing full well that he had committed to Westpac for the long term. 'It's like a former fiancée who comes back after you've married someone else,' Morgan said, wryly.

All through the Australia Day weekend of 1991, Morgan wrestled with the conundrum, finally choosing to stay where he was. 'You've made the right decision,' Keating said, matter-of-factly.

'You bastard,' Morgan shot back, albeit good-naturedly. 'You've been trying to talk me into the other option for four days.'

'I know. But this way, you can be king of the big league, leading the private sector in Australia, as opposed to king of the little league here.' Time has not tempered that verdict. 'David had the intellectual equipment to be secretary to the Treasury,' Keating argues. 'But I think he took the right path.'[25]

Not that he appreciated it at first, given how strongly Westpac's management viewed him as a threat. 'The academic', many called him, less than flatteringly. Frank Conroy, who rose to the level of chief operating officer – in effect, CEO-designate – in 1991, mooted an alliance with the Australian Mutual Provident Society (AMP), which would hold a 15 per cent stake in Westpac and thus help staunch the haemorrhaging of money. Morgan, however, interpreted this as a flimsy pretext for AMP to exit banking gracefully and for Westpac to give up on life insurance. At a board meeting in Melbourne, Conroy's plan looked sure to sail through without objection, until Sir Eric Neal asked if there were any further comments. Morgan took his cue to make his displeasure plain.

'While I said that I could support a genuine strategic alliance, I stressed that this was nothing of the kind,' he reflects. A major problem for financial institutions around the world, he argued, was a 'them and us' tension between the wealth arm and the bank arm, which the sale of Westpac Life, then a crown jewel under his control, was only likely to exacerbate. 'I portrayed it as it was, a ridiculous sell-out, and convinced the bulk of the board to reject it.'[26]

As he left in a hurry to fly to Europe, he sensed that he had won the day, even using a conference address in London to highlight the wisdom of Westpac's decision to grow a life insurance company from within. But he was wrong: his absence was used to reconvene the board and overturn the earlier decision, while the chairman compounded Morgan's indignity by saying that he was to play no part in implementing the AMP tie-up, as he so vehemently opposed it.

Even though Morgan later made Conroy see sense, explaining that he could hardly be expected to run the Westpac side of the joint venture without any say in negotiations, he grew frustrated by the perpetual politicking.

One antidote was the emergence of a key ally at board level, in the quiet, self-assured form of John Uhrig. The pair had met once before, in the Trans Australian Airlines lounge at Sydney, when Morgan was first contemplating a step away from Treasury. He knew Uhrig by reputation and admired him. Uhrig had chaired a committee of inquiry that recommended reducing tariff protection, despite the fact that he was a direct beneficiary of existing protection as chief executive of Adelaide's Simpson Holdings, a white goods manufacturer. This laudable stance cut against the grain of attitudes in the business community. Westpac had dealt with Uhrig already, when he oversaw their purchase of a defence service home loans scheme from the government, and soon invited him to become a director. From the outset, he was supportive of Morgan, strongly backing him over his rejection of the AMP deal and identifying in him qualities that could take him far. But where Keating's credo had always been to seize opportunity with a breathless intensity, Uhrig preached the virtue of patience. 'I saw David, from day one, as a person with a wonderful career in front of him,' he says. 'I told him, though, that he had to be recognised for what he did well, rather than what he said well. He listened intently and behaved accordingly.'[27]

A chance for Morgan to demonstrate that he could match rhetoric with reform arose, unexpectedly, in New Zealand. Having been assigned by Conroy, in late 1991, to head up Westpac's Asia-Pacific operations, he recognised that his best hope of making a blueprint for the bank's future lay across the Tasman. New Zealand had slid into recession earlier than Australia, and arguably more deeply. As such, the cycles of crisis enveloping Westpac, from bad debts to merchant banking subsidiary problems, tended to be manifested in Auckland before they reached the Australian franchise.

From Morgan's perspective, it was close to an ideal scenario: not only could he remove himself from the vipers' nest of internal politics in Sydney, but he could effectively use New Zealand as his testing ground for change. 'The problem with these banks is that they are big ocean liners, with lots of moving parts,' he explains. 'It can be hard to work out cause and effect. But in New Zealand, just one-sixth the size of Australia, you could pull the lever and see what happened. The country was smaller, nimbler, less political. It was a model that distilled the issues of a more complex world.'[28]

Although successes on the Kiwi front redounded to Morgan's credit, they could not mask the bank's wider malaise. Come May 1992, Westpac announced a $1.6 billion loss, then the largest ever recorded by an Australian corporation. All of the bank's exotic sidelines – its experiments in trading gold bullion, buying commodity bond dealers' licences, positioning itself as the seventh largest lender in the US even though it had no source of comparative advantage – had reduced it to a castle built on sand. Brian Johnson, a respected equity analyst in Australia since 1987, says: 'Westpac had essentially lost 120 years of shareholder funds in one quarter, because they were just too big in everything they did.'[29] The consequences of a contracting property market were calamitous, with half of Westpac's problem loans earning no money. In October 1992, Sir Eric Neal and four other directors resigned *en masse* as Uhrig took over as chairman. Uhrig also demanded the resignations of all remaining non-executive directors, but was rebuffed.

'It really was dramatically difficult,' Uhrig says. 'There was a strong feeling in the community that we could not survive as an independent organisation.'[30] The delusions of grandeur that had fuelled an expansionist rush now threatened to sink Westpac altogether. Facing a yawning hole in the balance sheet created by $2.2 billion worth of commercial property write-downs, the bank opted for a deeply discounted, three-for-ten rights issue at three dollars a share, but it failed. Credit Suisse First Boston, which had underwritten the issue, was left holding $883 million in unsold shares, having not managed to dispose of any during a one-day tender offer. Westpac, a victim of its own cupidity, teetered on the precipice.

Worse, the barbarians were at the gate. Billionaire media mogul Kerry Packer, in tandem with his fearsome American lieutenant, Al 'Chainsaw' Dunlap, chose his moment to pounce, acquiring a 10 per cent stake for $500 million to make him the second-largest shareholder. Immediately, Packer, fresh from a polo trip to Argentina – not to mention cash-rich from asset sales that had turned his company, Consolidated Press, into a $2 billion investment house – cut a swathe through the Westpac hierarchy. At the first board meeting that he and Dunlap attended, on 17 December, the knives were out. Within hours, Conroy, who had dutifully wished Packer a happy fifty-fifth birthday, was summoned by Uhrig to the twenty-eighth-floor boardroom at Martin Place and told to resign.[31] It was a dramatic defenestration, but Packer had made his mind up in a flash.

'He had come to a view at a pre-Christmas party, when he saw Conroy glad-handing and back-slapping all these complete third-raters who were part of his history at the bank,' Morgan says. 'Packer, who wasn't particularly educated but who had acute business acumen, said, "This guy hasn't got the balls to get rid of these people, and he's not good enough to attract new talent."'[32]

It was merely a precursor to the mayhem that followed. The bull-headed Dunlap, whom British financier Sir James Goldsmith had once dubbed 'Rambo in pinstripes', decided that he wanted Uhrig gone, too. It was part of his bloodthirsty New Jersey style that if a company could not be turned around within twelve months, then it was not worth bothering. While this reflected a crass indifference to local sensitivities, Packer himself, a titan of Australian business if a neophyte in banking, was not showing much sureness of touch either. On a visit to Westpac's Avalon Beach branch in Sydney's northern suburbs, he thumbed through the brochures on the shelves and called Morgan, enraged. 'These are bloody hopeless,' he said. 'They need to be rewritten.' Rob McLean, a McKinsey consultant whom Morgan had enlisted in New Zealand, recalls the episode with amusement: 'It was a tumultuous time, with so much uncertainty, and Packer somehow thought that David's forte was going to be rewriting term deposit brochures.'[33]

The interlude was as bizarre as it was abbreviated. No sooner had the Packer–Dunlap duo set about a slash-and-burn exercise at Westpac than they walked away in a fit of pique. On 14 January, their first meeting as directors was marked by an ultimatum to replace Uhrig with former Reserve

Bank governor Bob Johnston. The night before, Packer had circulated a note to the board to this effect, and he appeared confident he had the numbers to roll Uhrig. But Uhrig, in typically forthright style, responded by calling for a vote of confidence that soon changed the mood. First to speak was Peter Ritchie, former CEO of McDonald's Australia, who said, gravely: 'This is not the right way to go, Kerry.' Next came Peter Baillieu, who, in spite of his marriage to Edwina Hordern, Packer's cousin, also expressed disapproval. It quickly dawned upon the two raiders at the table that they had overplayed their hand. 'Al, we're out of here,' Packer told Dunlap, as both stalked out of the room, continuing a furious row as they rode down in the lift.[34] Such was the wild hurry in which they left, they forget that they had left some of their board papers behind. Among them was a purely vindictive 'dirt file' that Packer had prepared on Uhrig. The only person ever to read this file was Reg Barrett, Westpac's legal counsel and later Supreme Court judge in New South Wales, who assured Uhrig he had no undue cause for concern.

Morgan had been scheduled to have dinner with Packer that evening, at the tycoon's Bellevue Hill home. Ever since he had attended a lunch at Packer's Park Street headquarters, in his role as head of Asia-Pacific, he had become a primary point of contact, and he sensed that he was being assessed for higher responsibilities. At 5 pm, he was sitting in his office wondering anxiously if the arrangement still stood, when Packer rang. 'Mate, why don't we postpone dinner for a while,' he said. 'It might not be good for your career to go ahead with it.' The message was cordial, but Morgan had seen enough over a giddying few weeks to conclude that

Westpac had been reprieved by Packer's retreat. A lunch with Dunlap, a man since found guilty of massive accounting fraud and barred from serving as an officer of any publicly traded corporation, had flagged the dangers all too clearly. 'He was infected by self-obsession, probably the vainest person I've ever met,' Morgan wrote subsequently. 'I could not countenance letting Australia's first company fall into the hands of this vile and untalented individual.'[35]

As the dominoes fell, Morgan's stock rose. Shortly before Conroy's exit, he had been assigned control of retail, small business and commercial banking, not to mention wealth management, technology and operations: a brief effectively encompassing two-thirds of Westpac. The promotion – conveyed via a brief telephone call, in which Morgan was told to cancel a trip to Fiji – was a response to the imprint he had left in New Zealand, although he has since interpreted the move perhaps as less an act of munificence on Conroy's part than that of a CEO under extreme pressure to enact the board's wishes.[36]

Either way, the trade press lapped up the tale of his warp-speed rise. In a generous profile, which included an interview with Morgan, *The Australian Financial Review* noted that his rate of progress had, in a little under three years, been 'nothing short of breathtaking'.[37] The coverage raised eyebrows at Westpac: indeed, shortly after the interview, Conroy had called his office to say, 'David, this is not going to help you.'[38] But such was the tempest engulfing Westpac, with Uhrig under pressure to find a leader who would repair the community's shattered confidence, a tilt at the vacant chief executive's post did not seem out of the question.

Uhrig, however, had other ideas. For all Morgan's vaulting ambition, the chairman knew that a beleaguered Westpac needed a name that would impress capital and equity markets. To that end, he sanctioned a search that spanned the entire English-speaking world. Cutting short a fishing holiday on Kangaroo Island, he flew to Los Angeles to interview the man who would quickly emerge as the outstanding candidate to haul Westpac out of the mire.

Bob Joss, having launched his career as a White House fellow at the US Treasury, had grown renowned for his subtle analytical skills during twenty-two years at Wells Fargo, as well as for an unpretentious leadership style borne of a spell as a bank teller while he put himself through university. At Uhrig's invitation, Joss spent several days at the Park Hyatt in Sydney, with unfettered access to Westpac accounts, but he stressed that he wanted some time back home in California before deciding whether to commit. A worried Uhrig was left, at the annual general meeting, to confront the wrath of 5000 furious shareholders without any succession plan in place.[39]

When Joss finally agreed, thirty days after the first contact was made, to take the reins as CEO, Morgan absorbed the news with some ruefulness. 'David was very disappointed when the board chose Joss,' says Paul Keating, whose counsel he often sought at such moments. 'I sense he thought they might have chosen him then. He used to get worked up about these issues, but I reminded him that agitation would only end up being in inverse proportion to his progress. If you are less agitated, you will go faster – and more smoothly.'[40]

By the same token, Uhrig used all his straight-dealing to encourage Morgan towards a sanguine view. 'Most pages of the *Financial Review* were printed on the back of Westpac's shortcomings,' he says. 'What we were about to deal with had to be something that the public across the country could believe was possible. To appoint somebody who didn't have the widest experience at the very top of a bank wouldn't have got us there. David accepted the situation, with regret. I tried to assure him that his time would come.'[41] Maturity, ultimately, brought realisation that it was too much, too soon. Morgan concedes: 'To think I was ready then was just pure fantasy on my part.'[42]

With his remit vastly enlarged by the retail move, the markets reacted auspiciously, Westpac's share price improving. With six chief general managers answering to him and a division that had the best scope for profit growth, Morgan drastically revised ambitions for the bottom line, which he expected to show at least $341 million of improvement by September 1993. 'Westpac had never had that kind of stretch before,' says McLean, who had been retained from McKinsey as a senior advisor. 'It required meticulous care in both planning and execution.'[43]

All Christmas and New Year leave was cancelled as Morgan, in an echo of the day-and-night graft he had championed in the Treasury's tax bunker, strived for fresh ways to place the bank on a firmer footing.

An underlying failing of Westpac was that it had reacted so inappropriately to the challenge of financial deregulation. In the eighties, Morgan had conveyed to successive treasurers, first Howard and then Keating, his belief that a deregulated environment could produce a truly world-class banking system in Australia. But when at last the revolution came,

Westpac fluffed its lines. As opposed to nurturing the retail bank, its core business, it embarked upon an orgy of grabbing whatever assets it could, out of a misplaced conviction that bigger meant better. Elsewhere, National Australia Bank (NAB) was illustrating what was possible with a modicum of restraint, astutely deciding to keep credit conditions tight during the property boom and resisting diversification into areas where it lacked expertise. Ironically, Conroy, within days of confirming a once unthinkable Westpac loss, scoffed at such an approach as 'strategically sterile'.[44] 'It was an idiotic remark,' Morgan says. 'He later had the decency to call his counterpart at NAB to apologise.'

In 1993, the effects of the two banks' contrasting philosophies were mirrored in the numbers, with Westpac finding that its overall expense base was almost $500 million greater than NAB's. The diagnosis was grim, and the treatment necessarily severe. 'The bank was in a parlous situation,' McLean says. 'We said to the board: "This truly looks bad. You have to get out of the US, where you're losing money and have no cause to be. You have to do a work-out on all your non-performing loans. Plus, you have to transform your retail franchise into a profit machine, to give the kinds of returns that investors expect."'[45]

One oddity of Westpac's make-up lay in its preference for hiving off huge power to the states. From Queensland to Western Australia, these state offices were laws unto themselves, miniature fiefdoms that ran their own human resources, their own public relations, and where anybody on the outside needed express permission just to visit. All were run by near-untouchable executives who tended to resent external interference. 'Crown princes', Morgan called them, and made it his priority, metaphorically at least, to lop their heads off. 'Under their influence, there had essentially been six Westpacs, not one,' he says. 'So, I abolished their positions, and the bureaucracy around them. People would say, "Don't do it. They'll get you before you get them."'[46]

Trudy Vonhoff, then working for Bill Brewer, who had Queensland as his domain, recalls the swiftness with which the sackings were carried out. 'Nowadays, there has to be HR in place, where you make a call, arrange a meeting, explain it face-to-face,' she says. 'But David fired my boss by fax. I pulled the message off the machine myself.'[47]

The backlash was fierce: the deposed princes, affronted at being offered lowlier alternative employment, thought that if they resigned from Westpac altogether, they could strike a blow that would force Morgan out. It was a miscalculation: the dismantling of the state citadels, a process unthinkable against a calmer and more stable backdrop, continued unabated.

Few could dispute the strength of the business case. The retail bank was bloated and chronically overstaffed, with personnel costs consuming 55 per cent of Westpac's total expenses, but Morgan believed it was nothing some brutal streamlining would not cure. By 1994, he had overseen the culling of almost 5000 jobs. For this, he was depicted in some quarters as a ruthless hatchet man – 'Dr Death' was one nickname. 'Bob Shearer, one of my HR guys, was in tears as we were putting through involuntary redundancies,' says Morgan. But he was unrepentant about forcing through stringent measures he saw as central to the bank's revival.

'Taking out 5000 people was unprecedented, but we had to do it to make the other 15,000 jobs safe. Those were the facts.'[48]

Morgan relayed this message with a bracing, sometimes disconcerting starkness. He had grown to detest the cliquey culture that endured in parts of Westpac, where adversaries plotted against each other like Elizabethan courtiers. Tom Saar, among the McKinsey experts assigned to the retail recovery program, says: 'My most vivid memory was David telling his top team that behaviour needed to change, especially the back-stabbing and gossiping. He said, "If I hear of it happening from this day forward, then you are out. That includes if you did it yesterday and I hear about it tomorrow." You could hear a pin drop – and ten throats gulp.'[49]

For all his aversion to underhand scheming, Morgan did grasp the need for a certain political astuteness, after experiencing at first hand the cost of careless talk. Come September 1994, Westpac was facing pressure to raise the variable interest rate on mortgages to buttress its profits, even though there had been no rate change by the Reserve Bank. Instinct told Morgan to resist, but internal forces at Westpac pushed him to fall in line.

Pat Handley, the chief financial officer, agitated for a rate hike that proceeded despite vehement government criticism. Morgan, knowing that he had erred by supporting a decision he thought would be 'reputationally terrible' for the bank, compounded his mistake by claiming to the press that he was responsible for it. 'I was shuttling between meetings in Darwin, when a *Financial Review* reporter called to ask how it had happened,' he says. 'I admitted, off the cuff, that I had to take accountability. Then it got written up on the front page as if I was the sole author. I guess you could say I took one for the team.'[50]

In the five years since attending his first Harvard lecture, Morgan had learned enough about the machinations of corporate politics to last a lifetime. Having felt a connectedness and a kinship at Treasury, he long harboured a sense of being a lone wolf at Westpac, shunned for his academic approach. But he was compelled to examine his own deficiencies closely, too. As Daniel Kahneman, the Nobel Prize–winning author of *Thinking, Fast and Slow*, put it: 'I look for ways of changing my mind. I have been shifting positions all my life.' Kahneman contended that the person who never changed their mind never learned, a pitfall that Morgan was hell-bent on avoiding.

Helen Lynch, who as a company lifer saw how much Morgan needed to adapt to thrive in Westpac's world, suggested that he should submit to rigorous, 360-degree executive development under Stephen Drotter, a noted authority on leadership. The review was based on anonymous comments from colleagues; the results rocked Morgan back on his feet.

Some said that he was too tough on people, others that he could seem excessively self-interested. Although his first reaction was shock, followed by denial and anger, Morgan resolved to make the adjustment, moving away from the command-and-control style to which he had become accustomed with men such as John Stone and Paul Keating.

'David started to read a lot of books, to surround himself with people who had skills different from his,' Lynch says. 'It took him a while to get it – longer than it should have done – but get it he did.'[51] It was an ability that Joss, too, would come to admire. 'I would say his most remarkable quality was to improve and learn,' he argues. 'He would actually change. You would see him, within a matter of days and weeks, modifying his thoughts and behaviour. Not many people do that.'[52]

The stresses involved in such change had not been without a personal toll. The two-city, two-career life pattern, where Morgan would leave on the first flight out of Canberra at 6 am on Monday and not return from Sydney until 7 pm on Friday, was proving unsustainable for his young family.

His son Ben, now eight, was clearly missing a steady paternal presence. 'Every morning I would leave him at his new school, Canberra Boys' Grammar, crying his eyes out,' says Kelly, who in 1994 was fighting her own battle in the 'sports rorts affair', as opposition MPs demanded to know whether $30 million of sports grants were unduly benefiting those in marginal Labor seats. 'Then I would go to parliament to face Question Time. I was a nervous wreck.'[53]

All the joy that she had experienced through the sport brief, as Sydney won the rights to host the 2000 Olympic Games amid riotous celebrations in Monte Carlo, evaporated as shock jocks such as John Laws – 'particularly vile', in her words – subjected her to character assassinations. Morgan, while powerless to prevent it, seethed at such treatment.

'The thoughts I had towards one particular journalist were quite violent,' he says. 'It is a horrendous situation when the person you love is under attack.'[54]

By February 1994, Kelly had resigned as a minister, and eleven months later gave up her seat to step away from political life. It was a heavy sacrifice of a prize that she had spent the better part of her life chasing, but it was conducive to a less rootless existence.

By making a permanent home in Sydney, Morgan regained his attachment to areas of his children's lives in which he felt he had missed out. The challenge of assimilating into Westpac, and then dealing with the fallout as it flirted with oblivion, had burdened him like nothing before. A life without commuting, which had only ever been a means to an end, would restore crucial equilibrium. For his turbulent journey through a troubled bank was about to gather pace.

CHAPTER 8

Culture Shock

As a foreign element implanted into the Westpac body politic, Bob Joss was a leader who cut against the grain. Understated, cerebral, averse to flamboyant public pronouncements and scrupulous about keeping fit, he brought a convivial Californian air at odds with the *ancien régime*, which had been characterised by insularity and largesse. 'Bob was very West Coast,' says Ann Sherry, who joined the bank in 1994 to help reshape its culture. She would eventually become one of the most influential women in Australia.[1] 'When he spoke to people about the business, he would sit on a stool with his legs crossed. He almost needed a guitar.'[2]

Sometimes, the hiring of Americans to fight financial fires in a foreign market could go awry. George Trumbull, for example, prised from US insurance giant Cigma to take charge at AMP, was in many eyes a bombastic headbanger, who once fist-pumped the air and declared that he was 'king of the world'.[3] Against this yardstick, Joss, Australia's first $1-million-a-year banker, was a study in moderation.

'He was the first person I ever heard say, "You never do one thing at a time,"' recalls Edna Carew, author of *Westpac: The Bank that Broke the Bank*, the definitive account of the early nineties turmoil. 'If he was on his exercise bike, he would be reading the papers and watching the TV news. The average Westpac guy, by comparison, looked pretty well fed. They would indulge in lavish lunches, even in-house. Joss's view was: "What the Dickens? Wine and port? This is ridiculous. Get rid of all that. Save costs."'[4]

On this front, he was squarely aligned with Morgan, who had already sliced through the retail bank's bloated expenses with the sharpest blade, a move since heralded as the 'centrepiece' of Westpac's recovery from its near-death experience.[5] The parallels between the pair were self-evident: both had plied a path from public service, and both placed a premium upon intellectual capital in banking. Ernie Arbuckle, a former chairman of Wells Fargo during Joss's era, had sought to weave the closest links between the company and Stanford Business School, which he had steered to prominence in the sixties. It is to this seat of learning that Joss, holder of an MBA and PhD from Stanford, has since returned as dean emeritus.

In an interview at his office in Palo Alto, a leafy focal point of Silicon Valley, Joss identifies the scholarly dimension that he shared with Morgan as a rich area of common ground. 'In some ways, David and I were the extrovert versus the introvert,' he says. 'But we each had training in graduate-level economics and we approached problems with the same intellectual rigour.'[6]

Any recriminations that Morgan felt at losing out to Joss for the CEO position soon dissolved. Indeed, as George

Parker, distinguished professor of finance at Stanford and a fixture at the university since 1973, argues, unsolicited, during conversation with Joss: 'The friendship that David has with Bob is quite extraordinary, because they had the potential to be terribly rivalrous. Instead, they became professional partners, in a kind of mentor–protégé relationship.'[7]

It was one of Joss's first observations in Australia that turned out to be perhaps the most telling. At his inaugural town hall meeting, glimpsing only the serried ranks of men in suits, he asked: 'Where are the women?'

The query, which would seep into national business folklore, reflected the extent to which Westpac had slipped behind the arc of progress elsewhere. At the time Joss departed Wells Fargo, almost 60 per cent of its branches in the US were run by women. From this environment, he says, the transition to Westpac, where the proportion was closer to five per cent, 'felt like going back in time'.[8] The anachronism was not one he could tolerate much longer. As such, he looked to Sherry, who had already made waves at Australia's Office of the Status of Women and as part of an all-female crew in the Sydney to Hobart Yacht Race, to begin oiling the wheels of change.

Sherry was confronted with attitudes towards women that ranged from dated to downright toxic. Although anti-discrimination legislation had been passed in the seventies, areas of Westpac, the trading floor in particular, were infected with a chauvinism to suggest that it did not apply. 'Even in 1994, women would be getting dildos, wind-up vaginas on their desks as Christmas "gifts",' she says. 'Sexually explicit toys were the standard. The men would go to the Hellfire

Club in Sydney, where people would be tied to a wheel and publicly flayed. They had meetings there. We are talking senior executives.'[9]

To counter the debauchery, which belonged more in a scene from *The Wolf of Wall Street* than in a modern bank desperate to rehabilitate its image, Sherry introduced rudimentary sexual harassment training, requiring all employees to sign a legal document to show that they had understood. While a potent deterrent, her action still did not weed out all transgressors. 'The guy running the dealing room at the time was notorious for bad behaviour, and at the Christmas party he dropped his pants,' she recalls. 'I told him that he needed to pack his desk. He came back with his lawyer, and I said, "See you in court." That is what it takes to change a culture.'[10]

Morgan readily endorsed Sherry's hardline stance. When he switched roles at Westpac to take charge of the institutional bank in 1995, Sherry was among the first people he approached, asking her to be his HR chief.

If Sherry was the lightning rod for the women's disaffection, then the issue of paid maternity leave became the battlefront on which they could make their voices heard. In the mid-nineties, the subject of women returning to work after having a baby was a loaded one in Australia. The historical strength of the male breadwinner model, coupled with arguments that the costs of child rearing should be borne primarily by parents and not by industry, created a recipe for political strife. Sherry's answer was to redefine the equation in terms of commercial logic. In 1995, a mere 32 per cent of Westpac's female staff were heading back to their jobs after maternity leave, a figure that there was a compelling business case for improving. Noel Purcell, then responsible for handling the bank's relationships with its investors, says: 'We had to show why it was value-enhancing, and we worked out that if we could get a 10 per cent rise in the return-to-work rate for female staff, then it would pay for itself.'[11]

Through his skill for intellectualising problems, Morgan would pursue what he called a 'sweet spot – a solution that was both the right thing to do and also good for business'.[12] Supporting the predicament of working mothers offered the perfect platform, enabling Westpac to set a standard for the rest of corporate Australia to emulate. Within two years of its maternity pay scheme coming into force, 53 per cent of women resumed work post-childbirth, as the bank carved out a position as their employer of choice in the industry.

For Morgan, this was not purely a matter of hard numbers. Kelly, after all, had been the very inverse of a stay-at-home mother, taking Jessica into parliament and Ben out on the campaign trail when both were babies. 'David had a lot of influence at home on the women front,' says Helen Lynch, who studied his evolution as an executive at close quarters. 'Ros was an extremely successful politician, a minister in the Keating government, no less. Most senior men at the bank did not have a wife with her own career. His daughter, Jessica, was a force, too. David was thinking along the lines of, What kinds of opportunities do I want Jessica to have?'[13]

By degrees, the rusted-on Westpac ways were being stripped off. To accelerate this trend, Morgan made a point of surrounding himself with those who had not climbed up the bank thanks to the old 'jobs for life' system. Women, especially, were elevated to positions unheard of just a decade earlier: while Sherry did all she could to stamp out sexism and misogyny in the workplace, Alex Holcomb, a graduate of Wharton Business School in Philadelphia, was enlisted as Morgan's head of strategy. The appointments were not tokenistic or designed to hit any set quotas, but to furnish his section of the company with abilities distinct from his own. Conscious that there was nothing to be gained from an inner sanctum comprised solely of acolytes, he leant towards those who would challenge his point of view.

Phil Chronican, who had followed Morgan from the retail transformation, says: 'Ann and David, for instance, were entirely different personalities. She was far more naturally gregarious, but he recognised that she brought to the table valuable qualities. This was a real strength of his business leadership, because you don't see that often. Leaders tend to have people around them who act like them and think like them. But David refused to do that.'[14]

***

The irony was that Morgan had baulked initially at running the institutional bank, regarding it as a dismal demotion. During a self-development exercise in 1995, he wrote: 'The shift from retail was a bombshell. I realised how decisions are made that you have no control over. I was shattered, shocked, hurt and disappointed.'[15]

He interpreted the switch as a ruse by Stuart Hornery – then Westpac's largest shareholder as chairman of Lendlease, the multinational construction group that had taken over the

Kerry Packer stake – to sideline him from any plans to find a successor to Joss. 'Hornery wanted me out of retail, because he felt that I was keeping Lendlease at bay,' says Morgan, who had learned a lesson about the dangers of alienating an influential board member. 'I should have been more politically sensitive.'[16]

So corrosive was the dynamic with Hornery that Morgan initiated a come-to-Jesus meeting between the two of them, in an effort to temper the mutual loathing. Hornery explained how the reasons for his hostility were twofold: first, he claimed, Morgan had obstructed his moves to appoint Lendlease executives to senior roles in the retail recovery program. To an extent, this was true: Morgan did not deem the mooted candidates to be of sufficient calibre and perceived anybody from Lendlease, which was also in the mortgage business, as de facto competitors likely to be used as internal spies. But Hornery's second objection, based on allegations from one aggrieved woman whom Morgan had fired from the retail bank, was vigorously contested. Her version of the facts, Morgan demonstrated with documents at the table, was wildly at variance with reality.

From his unpleasant jousts with Hornery, a man he saw as 'talented but utterly unscrupulous and very vain', he came to appreciate the importance of not having a Rasputin in one's camp. Hornery's conspicuous agenda to control Westpac made it almost impossible, according to Morgan, for him to have an open and trusted dialogue with the bank's board. One visible manifestation was the misadventure of Westpac's $100 million mortgage-processing centre in Adelaide, without any of the normal close scrutiny such a grand project would normally have received. While such centres were common in the US, essentially the administrative back office for all mortgage processes, they were poorly suited to the Australian model.

In this period of flux, Morgan was bombarded with enough outside perspectives on his character to trigger an intense bout of self-questioning. As well as receiving guidance from Rosemary Grieve, an executive consultant, Morgan chose to digest more anonymous testimony from across the company as part of an exhaustive performance review that examined every facet of how he behaved. Although he had commissioned most of the critiques himself, many were, in short, devastating. If being manoeuvred out of retail had seemed a retrograde step in his eyes, then some blistering assessments from his own colleagues gave the sucker punch.

'The American firm that conducted it read to me verbatim for two days,' he reflects. 'A few things were like stomach blows. For example, our top forty people had all been asked to describe their best experiences with their bosses. I said that mine was with Bob Joss, but this was seen by two people as shamelessly sycophantic. Then one figure on the board claimed that I had gone into a funk at an institutional lunch, just because the guest speaker – who was hopeless, despite having my approval – had made me look bad.'[17]

While these remarks cut him to the quick, they were equally unpalatable to Kelly, who had resigned from parliament only weeks earlier, in part to adjust to the demands that Westpac life was imposing upon the family.

'I showed her the report and she broke down crying,' Morgan reflects. 'She looked at it and said, "You'll never be CEO." I had been so focused on this massive job rescuing the bank that I had done it to the exclusion of any smart or empathetic thinking about those around me. I had been somewhere between naïve and grossly negligent in not tending to relationships more. That would be a fair charge.'[18]

Compounding the distress for Kelly was the trauma of her parliamentary exit, marked by creative if stinging headlines involving whiteboards, after it emerged that she had worked out the sports grants that proved her undoing on a giant whiteboard in her office. 'I had been through a horror with the sports stuff,' she says. 'So, I was already drained, and then this report illustrated, essentially, that David was a policy wonk who was not great at managing people. In a way, that's why he was so good at Treasury, but it was no skill base to be a CEO. He had to change – and I have never met anybody his age who could change so dramatically.'[19]

In his determination to change how he came across, Morgan remembered a piece of advice offered by Harry Price, the 'old-school wise guy' he had made chief executive of Westpac New Zealand. 'David, never assume that people understand your motives for doing what you do,' Price told him. 'You need to tell them.'[20]

Equally, he made a concerted effort to give those reporting to him his unfiltered attention. The temptation, across days divided meticulously into segments, was to wrap up each encounter with a briskness that limited much human engagement with the person across his desk. 'One hurtful comment,' he concedes, 'was that at gatherings, I would often be looking over someone's shoulder to see if anybody more important was in the room. But in that pressured period, it was probably true.'[21]

Finding a remedy would become a running theme of his sessions with Rosemary Grieve. Karen Miller, who started work as Morgan's executive assistant in 1995, says: 'David had an empathy problem – he couldn't seem to understand other points of view. Rosemary was good for him, though, being quite soft, but quite strong. Over time he became much more aware of his behaviour and how it affected other people.'[22] Emotional intelligence, or EQ, psychologists call the ability to gauge the signals of those around us. It is this that Grieve would work to instil in Morgan, even if Ann Sherry casts doubt on any subject's capacity for acquiring a gift that many possess naturally. 'You can't learn it,' she argues. 'It's not a learned skill.'[23] Joss, though, saw plenty in Morgan's responses to counter such an argument. 'He had this big appetite for feedback,' Joss says. 'Some people don't – they don't want to hear it. But it was easy to give it to David, because he was so receptive and you could see him work with it.'[24]

There was one final lesson to be gleaned from this personal reckoning. An instinct that Morgan had long indulged, given his penchant for public performance, was to speak candidly to journalists. It was a habit that had landed him in trouble just four months after joining Westpac, when Robert Hadler of *The Australian* called for what he assumed was an off-the-record chat, a breezy catch-up. Instead, the conversation was reproduced in the newspaper, including sensitive details of a proposed merger between ANZ Banking Group and the National Mutual Life Association of Australasia – as well as references to Morgan's potential conflict of interest as a 'former senior government advisor with detailed knowledge of the prudential problems involved in regulating banking and insurance companies'.[25] 'Risks for Westpac Man', ran the awkward headline, which forced the bank to issue a correction. 'It was my naïveté, and I never spoke to the guy again,' Morgan reflects. 'Actually, I did. I phoned him up and ripped the crap out of him.'[26]

Still, though, he was disposed to offer a ready quote, or to cooperate with trade publication articles that carried the less-than-subliminal sense that he was a CEO-in-waiting. 'A tendency that David had at the time, because he could see Joss was not going to be there forever, was for external self-promotion,' Lynch says. 'That was not the culture of the bank. John Uhrig would ask me, "Why is David getting himself in the paper all the time?" I replied, "You have to tell him that unless he stops, he is not going to be in the running for the top job."'[27] Uhrig informed Morgan, soberly, that he should not speak to the media if he did not have a concrete message to impart or he did not want his words to be published. Plus, the chairman cautioned, any such communication should be firmly in the interests of the bank, not his own.[28] Such advice was, as Ian Macfarlane noted at the Reserve Bank, swiftly heeded. 'To my surprise, David pulled right back from that,' he says. 'He wasn't cultivating the press any longer. He showed great restraint and good sense.'[29]

If this marked a pivotal juncture in his maturing as an executive, then so, too, did the discovery that the institutional portfolio – a prize that he had viewed at first as akin to a wooden spoon – could burnish his expertise. With Westpac's operations across Asia and New Zealand bolted on to his brief, he gained, after his years in retail, a more fine-grained understanding of the bank's many layers. Through an alliance with Standard Chartered Bank to improve service for Asian customers, the acquisition of Trust Bank New Zealand to add 10 per cent market share across the Tasman, and the hiring of Citigroup's highly regarded Mike Hawker to head the financial markets team, the institutional bank burgeoned in the mid-nineties to become Westpac's strongest-performing division.

'I know that David had taken his shift to Institutional as this big, crushing blow, but he rolled up his sleeves,' Joss says. 'This work was all about sophisticated transactions and large corporate finance. David had both the intellectual horsepower and the macro-economic training to be on top of it.'[30]

By 1996, Joss had decided that it was time for a different kind of reshuffle. At Wells Fargo, he had grown accustomed to the American hub-and-spoke model of leadership, where the CEO dealt individually with their direct reports. In the Australian system, which imposed weightier checks and balances on the most powerful figures and placed greater faith in the value of collaboration, this worked less effectively. As such, Joss saw fit to appoint, essentially, three co-deputy CEOs in Morgan, Pat Handley and John Morschel, Hornery's former second-in-command at Lendlease. The move, while not publicly spelt out, was intended as a clearer demarcation of the executive pecking order and as a first tentative draft of a succession plan. Joss, naturally, wished to give no such impression beyond this closed circle.

'I was never a believer in saying, for instance, "I'm going to work for three more years and then so-and-so will take over,"' he explains. 'When you are in a major leadership role, you want to have in your mind that you are there forever.'[31]

But the jockeying for position stirred by his shake-up was unmistakeable. Morgan's wariness of Handley was well established, as attested by his private admission in 1995 that their relationship was 'catastrophic'.[32] With Morschel, who had taken over as chief officer in Morgan's old realm of retail, the ambience was far more cordial on the surface, even if an intensifying rivalry bubbled beneath. As Morgan puts it: 'There was never any open animosity, but we were fierce head-to-head competitors.'[33]

Before long, the lines of this power struggle became increasingly evident. Morschel was represented in sections of the press as the favourite to replace Joss – 'the heir apparent', *The Age* called him – but come the winter of 1997 there were signs he may have overplayed his hand.[34] On 14 August, a board meeting was convened to help lift the uncertainty, and yet within barely a fortnight Morschel had left the bank as an executive, while Joss agreed, albeit without a formal contract, to a minimum three-year extension that would take him to the age of sixty. 'There was some speculation that Morschel may have tried to force the issue before Bob was ready to leave,' Morgan explains.

While Morschel's exit promised to smooth the path to the hotseat for which Morgan hungered, Joss's renewed commitment threatened another substantial delay. If this caused Morgan some anxiety, he at least had the counsel of a Canberra confidant, a certain Paul Keating, on which to fall back. 'David was especially disappointed when the board reappointed Joss for a second term,' Keating says. 'But I told him I would be very surprised if Joss served the full term. I said: "Americans are like homing pigeons. They all go back in the end."'[35]

Keating offered a sage and soothing voice, and so did Joss himself. Morgan, after all, was far from marginalised: he had a seat on the board, he had been granted one million unhurdled share options, and he had received an assurance from John Uhrig that the board would, when the time came, look for an insider to carry the flame after Joss. All of these gestures were indications, Joss insisted, of Westpac's confidence in him. He also threw in one telling piece of advice: 'Be yourself more.'[36]

For all that Morgan had been poleaxed by some of the searing character appraisals from his colleagues, he kept seeking them in relentless volume, sticking fast to the idea that it was a 'gift' to see himself as others saw him. But Joss, a man quite comfortable in his own skin, cautioned him against adjusting in too calculating a fashion for the benefit of observers. 'You cannot change yourself too much, or make this wholesale personality transplant,' Joss argues. 'But you can be yourself with more skill.'[37]

* * *

Morgan's moment would arrive a good deal sooner than he expected. It is a story never before told that in late 1998, Westpac was actively exploring the possibility of a merger with Commonwealth Bank (CBA), a sizeable economic shift that would reduce the 'Big Four' Australian banks, also including ANZ and NAB, to a 'Big Three'. 'There were some powerful reasons for doing so, with so much overlap and duplication between banks,' Joss says. 'If you could put two of the Big Four together, you could add tremendous benefit for your shareholders and still do a great job for your customers.'[38]

The critical day was 1 October 1998: with a federal election due, members of the two parties were poised to announce a deal at the Lodge, whether or not they had the express approval of then prime minister John Howard. But a sticking point arose when advice was received that chances of the deal being approved might be assisted by having an Australian in charge of the combined entity. Accordingly, it was decided that David Murray, CBA's chief executive, would be CEO, and Uhrig chairman. Joss was to be merely vice-chairman in charge of restructuring. 'Bob was pretty hurt by that,' Morgan reflects. 'It was a staggeringly incompetent decision.'[39]

Joss, for his part, asks: 'Would the politics have tolerated a non-Australian in that role? It was a sensitive subject at the time. I would probably have to be out to make a deal like this happen, to get the other party across the line.'[40]

In the end, this vision of a Westpac–CBA 'superbank', one that would hold 38 per cent of all the retail deposits in Australia, never took wing.[41] The agreement was all but sealed when CBA announced that they would not accept Morgan and Handley staying on as executive directors, demanding either that both be removed or that CBA be free to add two of their own. With that proviso, the deal disintegrated, the feuding sides poles apart on how such a behemoth of a bank should be constituted.

There was also, inescapably, a rupture between Joss and the Westpac board, even without a consummation of the mega-merger. Uhrig's willingness to accept the accession of Murray to the overall CEO position above him had stunned Joss, to the extent that he was ready to contemplate a move elsewhere. Overtures had begun, in particular, from Barclays in London, but he and his wife, Betty's two children were both newly married and living in California, and the homeland started to exert the emotional pull that Keating had envisaged. 'We thought, Do we want to retire in Australia at sixty-five?' Joss says. 'We had a sense of being tugged back.'[42]

Joss would be leaving behind a bank in far more robust health than the one he inherited. In 1993, he had confronted a company on its knees, humiliated by a loss larger than its shareholders' funds. As Uhrig acknowledges: 'It really doesn't get much worse than that.'[43] And yet in six years under Joss's stewardship, Westpac had not merely weathered the tempest but thrived, finding itself $1.3 billion in the black by 1999 and with a share price hovering between $10 and $11, up from $2.85 on the day he had started. A more progressive, female-friendly culture held sway, while the once-endemic politicking had been cut back almost to an irreducible minimum. 'Westpac recruited an experienced, thoughtful banker, with the ability to act decisively rather than brutally,' *The Sydney Morning Herald* judged. 'Joss was a builder, not a wrecker.'[44]

In Morgan, who had meshed disparate skills across all spheres of the bank, an heir presumptive had been found.

Fresh off a short summer break, Morgan discovered early in February 1999 that he was to be only the twenty-third chief executive of Westpac in its 182-year history. In a sense, it was a precious surprise, given the mellowing of his habit for 'managing upwards' – as one colleague acidly expressed it at the time – and his acceptance that Joss appeared to be settling in for a longer haul.[45] 'When the edge was taken off the ferocity of my ambition, my chances of getting the job improved,' Morgan says. 'If ambition is too over-the-top, too naked, it gets resented. You're seen as too sharp-elbowed, too out for yourself. Mine began to moderate once I had digested all the harsh peer reviews and got over the hurt of my own ineptitude.'[46]

It reflected the seamlessness of the handover that Morgan's appointment was confirmed simultaneously with Joss's departure, but the announcement still gave the markets the jitters. Joss had been a stable and successful hand on the tiller, while Morgan remained a relative unknown in the eyes of the investor community, which threatened the type of uncertainty that shareholders detested. As such, the share price was subdued, as reporters cast around for theories as to why Joss was walking away from his Westpac work midstream. Had he stalked off in high dudgeon? Had Morgan engineered a coup?

The truth is possibly best captured by financial journalist Andrew Cornell, who contends that six years of hauling Westpac back from the cliff edge had shaped Morgan into the outstanding candidate. Amid the traumas of 1993, he had still encountered pockets of resentment as the resident bureaucrat, but with the banking seas becalmed by 1999, he was the natural choice to take the helm. 'Over time, David grew into a far more rounded leader, as opposed to just a smart one,' Cornell says. 'When I first met him, he still had a very theoretical understanding of what was going on. Straight out of Treasury, he was accustomed to looking at banks as regulated entities that had to be told what to do. But the reality of life on the ground was vastly different.'[47]

Just one day before his rise to CEO was broadcast, Morgan delivered that year's Chris Higgins Memorial Lecture, named in honour of his late and much-lamented friend, to the Economic Society of Australia in Canberra. He was careful not to take questions afterwards, lest the story leak out early, but the speech offered a distillation of some vital learnings that had led up to this auspicious juncture in his life: the dangers of devaluing the federal bureaucracy, the importance of business-friendly economic policy, the value of a dynamic and entrepreneurial private sector to the success of a nation. 'It seems clear to me that high-quality public policy is too important – and too difficult to secure – to be left to politicians and bureaucrats,' he told the audience that evening. 'If we leave the task solely to government, as the velocity of economic change accelerates, we will inevitably move too slowly.'[48]

Not even twenty-four hours later, Morgan would be handed keys to an office from which he could turn his words into deeds. The sense of responsibility was solemn, the rush of anticipation close to overwhelming. There was room for reflection, too. Having grown up frightened of whether or not his father would be able to pay the rent, he was about to ascend to one of the highest-profile and best remunerated posts in the land. If Morgan's elevation was a statement upon his abilities, then it was also a statement upon his times. Without the fight against cronyism that had been a hallmark of his Treasury adventures, a leader in Morgan's mould would barely have crossed the threshold at Westpac, once Australia's starchiest and most stubbornly conservative bank.

'David Morgan, CEO of Westpac?' said Paul Keating, in a subsequent speech. 'A technocrat, the husband of a Labor minister? That would simply not have been possible before we opened up the Australian economy.'[49]

Luck, likewise, plays its part at these moments. As Morgan has put it: 'Any chief executive of a major company who denies the role of luck is either dishonest or delusional.'[50] Such CEO positions are rarefied, available infrequently, and coveted by just about everybody in the organisation. Any route to the pointy end of the pyramid must, by extension, rely to some degree on good fortune. Morgan was fond of an analogy of the waves rolling in at Bondi Beach: one needed luck for there to be any good waves at all, but one also had to be skilled and ready to catch them. Once caught, those waves needed to be ridden all the way to the shore.

CHAPTER 9

Risk and Resilience

There is seldom a smooth line between prosperity and popularity. For banks, perhaps uniquely among society's core institutions, a healthy bottom line gives no guarantee that they will be loved, liked or even grudgingly respected.

In December 2017, a decade after the collapse of the US subprime mortgage market started a spiral towards a global financial crisis, then prime minister Malcolm Turnbull conceded that a royal commission was the only means of restoring faith in the Australian banking industry.

Amid the pre-millennial angst of 1999, with banks nervous about whether their computer systems would survive the Y2K bug expected to arise from the century date change, this image problem was no less acute. For Westpac, perceptions could be poisonous, with the bank's internal reforms and its comeback from near-extinction having done little to endear it in the eye of the beholder. 'The community hated us,' Morgan acknowledges. 'None of our constituents seemed to trust us. They thought our profits were too high, that our service was ordinary at best, that some of our fees were egregious and unfair. They still saw us, essentially, as a cosy oligopoly.'[1]

The flaws in the external face of the company were mirrored in diminished staff morale. Banks' annual reports would, by nature, try to give even the gravest shortcomings the rosiest tint, but Westpac's 1999 instalment was candid in admitting that employee satisfaction had sunk into the bottom quartile just two years earlier.[2]

Noel Purcell, until 1996 the head of operations in North Asia, discovered as much for himself when he returned home from Tokyo to Sydney. Westpac's overarching philosophy in the nineties, of shrinking to survive, had created a damaging dissonance between its historic place as a pillar of Australia and its modern incarnation as a bank that slashed jobs and services while amassing vast profits. Public anger spilled out on to the streets, stoked not just by a spate of rural branch closures but by Westpac's sideline as a custodian of the controversial Jabiluka site in the Northern Territory, which mined uranium on Aboriginal lands. 'I just couldn't believe what I came back to,' Purcell says. 'Staff wouldn't even wear their uniforms on public transport for fear of being abused.'[3]

Morgan was passionate about purging any such negative connotations, sending a note to his executive team that spelt out how he had barely slept in the six weeks since learning of his accession to CEO. 'Most people,' he wrote, 'spend their entire professional lives without getting close to the opportunity we have to create a truly world-class, truly great Australasian company.'[4] Leading and motivating Westpac's 32,000 people more powerfully became, from the outset, a key plank of his rationale, as he emphasised the importance of taking pride in one's work and of behaving in a way that gave no cause for cynicism or ethical concern.

In his twenty-seventh-floor office at Martin Place, with views of Sydney Opera House and the Botanical Gardens, he was discovering that a major bank CEO's division of labour represented almost an exact reversal of his former duties at Treasury. In Canberra, he had been accustomed to devoting 80 per cent of his time to finding policy solutions and the remaining 20 to persuading the government to throw its weight behind them. This time, perhaps 20 per cent of his energy was expended on plotting the right course of action and 80 on convincing a small army of staff to follow his lead.

If there had been a criticism of the Bob Joss era, it was that the disavowal of the 'old cardigan brigade', as Phil Chronican labelled the Westpac warhorses, had encouraged too drastic a lurch in the other direction. A burst of external American hires, including Drew Tanzman in retail and Mary Carryer in consumer marketing, had sown, in Morgan's view, a certain concern among insiders that they 'may not have been competing on a level playing field'.[5] In response, he made it an article of faith of his tenure that Westpac, in everything it did, should strive for equilibrium, instead of careening to extremes. He likened it to the armada principle of banking, where, in the delicate task of meeting the needs of all the core constituencies, from staff to shareholders, customers to the community, the speed of the fleet tended to be governed by the slowest ship.

The conundrum for Westpac was encapsulated in the first half-year results issued under his command, in May 1999, where a record net profit of $679 million was offset by dwindling customer satisfaction. For all its reach and renown, the company was struggling to sell more than one product to each of its seven million customers, the worst cross-selling rate in Australia and lamentable by the standards of the world's better-performing banks.[6] The market was unimpressed, with Westpac underperforming the All Industrials Index by two per cent and its peer group by nine per cent.

Such problems were far from terminal, given the reliable influx of money from housing, credit cards and funds management. But the wider scepticism offered a reminder, even after the strides taken under Joss, of how much progress still needed to be made. Indeed, as Morgan put it at the results announcement, there was 'greater urgency' to complete the 'unfinished business' left over from his predecessor's reign.[7] He stressed, too, that he wanted to hear the unvarnished truth about every corner of the business. To this end, he dramatically upgraded the discussion forums with Westpac's top 2500 people, devoting around twenty days per year to meeting them, up to 400 at a time, across the country to ensure that he was appraised of any problem or grievance.[8]

Emphasis was shifting, fundamentally, from the expression of a grand strategy for the bank's next phase to the raw, often unglamorous graft of bringing it to fruition. It was a task to which Morgan, with his natural punctiliousness, was well matched.

Execution was the watchword, even if this simple concept formed a lacuna in the business literature of the time. There was, Morgan believed passionately, a world of difference between knowing what to do and making it happen. Helen Lynch, a key ally in his reshaping of the retail bank, was inclined to agree. 'Bob Joss was the person deciding the strategy, but strategy is the easy part,' she says. 'It is the execution that is hard. If people subscribe to that view, then it would be David who saved the bank.'[9]

As the first of his four chiefs of staff in the CEO's role, Trudy Vonhoff would see this consuming preoccupation with detail at close quarters. 'His perfectionism was off the charts,' she says. 'No matter who or what he was engaged with, he saw it as a failure if he was not 100 per cent "on". This applied from the tiniest procedural point, such as a piece of lost paper, to the deepest conversation about a deal.'[10]

The temptation for any freshly minted chief executive was to chase the splashiest, most headline-grabbing deal possible, thus defying the doubters in one fell swoop. For Morgan, the Australian division of Bankers Trust (BT), the US wealth and investment banking giant subsumed into Deutsche Bank in 1998, offered itself as an alluring potential acquisition after only three months in the job. The jackpot on the table was tantalising: Westpac, with a single mighty bound, could vault above AMP to the summit of the wealth league, bringing $62 billion in funds under its management.

Inevitably, there was fierce competition, as both NAB and CBA kept their eyes firmly on the same prize. Morgan, though, was eager to outflank his rivals, eventually reaching an agreement in principle to buy BT for $2.2 billion – a gigantic enough sum to stir unease among some shareholders, but still far below Deutsche's asking price of $3 billion. Come the evening of 2 June, all that remained to be done, as the two parties convened on the fifteenth floor of BT's Chifley Tower offices in Sydney, was for Westpac and

BT's would-be wealth arm to convince each other that they were the right fit.

Morgan was joined in the room by just two people: BT's Ian Martin, who had worked under him at Treasury on financial deregulation, and chief executive Rob Ferguson, a man not shy of admitting he had a 'bit of brashness'.[11] Soon enough, the ambience assumed a certain *froideur*, as Ferguson, sensing he was speaking from a position of strength, became defensive about the BT culture, demanding that his company should retain an exceedingly high degree of independence and warning that his clients would pull their money out if the integration went awry.[12] The tactic made Morgan bristle, and he grew anxious that hubris and a warped sense of autonomy had infected his prospective business partners.

'What came through was their arrogance,' he says. 'They thought they were doing us a favour, failing to understand that contemporary wealth managers really needed to tie up with distribution to a customer base. Never mind strategic logic, they wanted outrageous money. Ian had just received a $10 million bonus and insisted lavish remuneration for his people continued.'[13] Weary of these outlandish terms, Morgan wound up the meeting at around 11 pm and made the short walk back to his desk at Martin Place. The night air brought clarity to his thinking, as he left a note for his executives that he had serious misgivings about the lack of compatibility.

By morning, key lieutenant Pat Handley, Morgan's bullish CFO, remained gung-ho about the deal. Morgan, recounting the awkward discussions of the previous evening, eventually peeled him off the ceiling. Just before 3 pm, he called Clive

Smith, Deutsche's chairman, to break the news that they no longer had a buyer for their most sought-after business. A tie-up he had so keenly pursued was, after a few hours' summit talks, dead in the water.

Chronican, speaking for many within Westpac, was glad of it. 'The right thing to do was to walk away,' he says. 'My own view is that they should never have gone so far down the line. A large factor was Pat, who never saw a bank he didn't want to buy. They were stretching the valuation much too far when David pulled the plug. It was with a sigh of relief from most of us that he did so.'[14]

In a litmus test of his substance as a CEO, Morgan had shown that he was inherently risk-averse. In mergers and acquisitions, he knew, deals often ended up benefiting the seller far more than the buyer. Here, the carrot of a glitzy, market-shaking deal had been dangled, and he was content to let it slide. On the one hand, this was a sign that even the most enticing acquisition could be sabotaged by a cultural clash. But on the other, it gave an insight into how Morgan viewed the essence of leadership, where a CEO was defined by the chances he took and also by the chances he turned down.

* * *

As Australia hurtled towards the dawn of the next millennium, preparations were underway for an event that would give the nation its greatest global showcase. The 2000 Sydney Olympics, prefigured in pyrotechnic splendour at the city's New Year's Eve fireworks, were mere months away.

Mammoth in scale, eye-watering in budget, they represented, according to French newspaper *L'Équipe*, 'Australia's road to recognition in the eyes of the world'.[15]

Morgan had been a close observer at each stage of the Games' gestation. Kelly had been sports minister in 1993; Morgan had been standing beside her in Monaco when it was announced that Sydney had beaten Beijing by just two votes to be chosen as hosts. 'We had received a tip-off after the ballot,' he recalls. 'Sure enough, we won.'[16]

Six years on, he found himself thrust into the Olympic frame once more, with Westpac designated as the occasion's official bank and partner. For all that the year 2000 presented complications for the banking industry, as Morgan forswore New Year revelries to resolve any glitches from the Y2K virus – one of technology's strangest false alarms, as it transpired – it also offered, for Westpac in particular, a historic moment.

As well as supporting an Olympic job opportunity program, with forty-seven Australian athletes employed across the business, Westpac also directly sponsored the country's outstanding gold medal prospects: Ian Thorpe, the teenage swimming prodigy setting world records for fun; Susie O'Neill, dubbed 'Madame Butterfly' for her brilliance at the stroke; not to mention the 'Oarsome Foursome', the men's rowing quartet already anointed Olympic champions in Barcelona and Atlanta.[17]

Having lavished around $50 million on sponsorship, Westpac needed to put in almost the same amount again to leverage the rights. Given the projection and prestige attached to any corporate involvement in the Games, these were not sums that caused Morgan to lose much sleep. 'It was the best $100 million on marketing the bank had ever spent,' he argues. 'It was a phenomenal experience for our staff, many of whom volunteered to be a part of it. Employee commitment went through the roof.'[18]

Westpac's customers were equally enamoured, from the minute Cathy Freeman ran up four flights of stairs, crossed a shallow pond and lit a ring of fire that ignited the Olympic cauldron. Ten days later, Morgan interrupted a speech to the bank's leading institutional clients so that they could all watch Freeman, resplendent in her green, gold and silver body suit, claim the most emotional victory over 400 metres, the first Olympic gold medal by an Aboriginal sprinter.

The raptures that greeted her victory, in front of 112,000 at Stadium Australia in Homebush, encapsulated the spirit of a Games that did more than any to convert the Olympic ideals of peace, fraternity and noble contest into dazzling twenty-first-century form. On the eve of the closing ceremony, Juan Antonio Samaranch, president of the International Olympic Committee, told Morgan in a private meeting that he would be heralding Sydney 2000 as the 'best Games ever'.[19] In his closing address as the curtain fell, Samaranch was true to his word, while commentators clamoured to agree. 'I invite you,' wrote American author Bill Bryson in *The Sydney Morning Herald*, with forgivable flourish, 'to suggest a more successful event anywhere in the peacetime history of mankind.'[20]

Tellingly, this wave of Olympic euphoria, electrifying as it was, still could not dilute the sense of discipline that typified Morgan's managerial style. Mid-Games, there were advanced talks for Westpac to merge with the Development Bank of Singapore (DBS), so as to deepen its Asian footprint. Several DBS executives were flown to Sydney to attend Olympic events, with Jack Tai, the bank's American CFO, spotted in earnest conversation with Handley, his Westpac counterpart, during a basketball match. The mooted merger had been painted in the Singaporean press as a 'win-win', with relatively low risk: Westpac, having curbed the expansionist excesses of the eighties, had minimal exposure elsewhere in Asia, while DBS was treating Australia effectively as virgin territory.[21]

But Ann Sherry, by this time CEO of the Bank of Melbourne, a Westpac subsidiary, reflects how she spotted warnings that the arrangement would never work. 'The Olympics were a distraction, because no one was really looking at what was going on,' she says. 'We booked a data room in the Westpac building to try to thrash things out. The Singaporeans were very formal, above-board, but some of our guys showed no cultural sensitivity, throwing their weight around. It didn't help, either, that a couple of our directors had a deep distrust of state-owned Asian enterprise. We played the thing out to its logical extreme, but ultimately, the two banks were just a bad fit.'[22]

Morgan had his own reasons, quite apart from the cultural tensions, for considering the move ill advised. Leon Davis, elected to the board just a year earlier, had been a vociferous opponent of any relationship with DBS, adamant that it did not represent good value for Westpac and threatening to resign. As a former metallurgist who had cut his teeth in the mining industry, rising through the ranks at Rio Tinto, Davis was a straight dealer accustomed to giving his views in the bluntest language. 'I always felt that a deputy chairman's role was not worth a bucket of warm spit,' he says, quoting John Nance Garner's famous line on being US vice-president to Lyndon Johnson. 'I didn't like the deal and I wasn't going to participate. I told the board that they would be doing it without my support, that I would find something else to do. That made them think pretty seriously.'[23]

After much deliberation, Morgan backed out of the DBS negotiations, not over a cost dispute or even over concerns that Westpac would be a subordinate partner, but because he feared the potential loss of both Davis and John Uhrig, the chairman whose counsel he deeply valued, would be too great a sacrifice. He was disappointed, though, with Davis for how he had handled the affair. 'Leon came into my office shortly afterwards,' he recalls. '"Look, this just isn't working," he said. "I'm trying to build bridges with you, but you're not meeting me halfway." And I wasn't.'[24]

In later years, Morgan saw sense in the advice of Colin Powell, the four-star general turned US secretary of state, to 'get mad – and then get over it'.[25] There was a recognition that most petty grievances, if left to fester, would prove corrosive for the individuals and the company alike. Courtesy of an intervention by the wives of the two feuding executives, the pair was reconciled over dinner and plentiful wine at Davis's apartment in France, in what they would come to call their 'Paris Accord'. Morgan held Davis's wealth of boardroom experience in high regard, even coining the phrase 'the Davis Doctrine', to capture his various succinct points.

Davis, appointed to follow Uhrig as chairman in December 2000, smiles at the reminder. 'One of my sayings was that there could be nothing worse in an organisation than a hard-working fool. You would rather have a lazy fool than a diligent one who really screws things up. I had no such worries with David – he was both conscientious and highly intelligent. That's a major asset.'[26]

Despite the occasional flashpoint, their personalities married up neatly in propelling Westpac through the next phase of change. Where Morgan had the skills to adapt his behaviour to suit the circumstance, Davis, a tough operator, had the requisite ruthlessness to weed out ineffectual board members. 'When I joined, there were still a lot of old right-wingers who didn't read their board papers, slept through meetings,' Davis says. 'Uhrig actually apologised for what he left me with, explaining that he didn't want any more aggravation. So, we cleaned a few people out.'[27]

The relationship between any CEO and chairman could, Morgan had come to grasp, be pivotal: a priceless commodity if nurtured correctly, but a serious corporate liability if neglected. Uhrig had been the most dependable ally to Morgan and Bob Joss alike, credited since the latter's departure with shepherding Westpac through the stormiest of seas – 'Without him, I don't know whether the bank would have survived,' argues Noel Purcell.[28] The same dynamic did not always hold firm elsewhere; at ANZ, for instance, the strain between John McFarlane, the Scottish chief executive who had joined from Standard Chartered in 1997, and his chairman, Charles Goode, was well known to their peers. 'John was a guitar-playing man, a bit of a hippie on the quiet,' Davis says. 'But

Charles also wanted to be a figure in the community, which put the pair of them in conflict. They didn't get on. The same problem has been mirrored in Australia more widely: where does the governor-general fit vis-à-vis the prime minister, as chief executive of the country? It was a danger that David and I were very conscious of avoiding.'[29]

Morgan, for his part, developed a clear set of qualities to look out for in a chairman: namely, somebody who did not strive to be a de facto CEO, who was not covetous of the CEO's profile or remuneration, and who, ideally, had already performed the same role, thus gaining a precious understanding of the singular pressures that it brought. It was fortuitous, then, that the role of Uhrig's successor had fallen to Davis and not to his opponent in the vote, John Morschel.[30] Davis, mindful of the awkwardness between them, does not demur. 'They would have clashed,' he says. 'Morschel was seeking his place in the sun.'[31]

For all the exhilaration of CEO life, for all the accoutrements and lofty public profile, there are plenty of elements that can be suffocating for the unwary. One that Morgan struggled at first to conquer was the remorseless examination of his every move. Both at Treasury and in his greener Westpac days, he had fallen foul of journalists with unguarded asides, but he learned quickly as leader of a global top-20 bank that he could never let his defences down.

'The scrutiny by the media, by politicians, by regulators, by investors, by the board, by your team, by your employees, by your customers is unrelenting,' he explains. 'It makes for a loneliness in the job – not that you can ever acknowledge this. You are being paid up to $10 million a year and you complain about your lot? So, you strap on this armour. You might just have made the most finely balanced, 51/49 decision, but you have to present it as if it was a complete no-brainer.'[32]

Morgan made a point of hiring David Lording, who had worked with Kelly in the early nineties on heading off several media scrapes, as his communications chief, identifying potential banana skins in interviews and polishing the bank's official response to the toughest question until it gleamed. The approach was not always watertight: when pressed on why the DBS deal had fallen over, Morgan had to give a polite 'no comment' out of corporate confidentiality, sidestepping the jarring cultural differences that had led to its undoing.

The task of maintaining a smooth façade for the outside world was exhausting, not least because Morgan had few confidants with whom he could raise it openly. He believed, much as Kelly was far better versed than most in the extreme pressures of managing a huge portfolio, that her advice was unlikely to be strictly impartial. 'Spouses are never dispassionate,' he says. 'They care for you so much, they end up going completely overboard.'[33]

As such, it would often fall to Trudy Vonhoff, as head of his office, to tie up every possible loose end to ensure that the stresses did not spill over excessively into his home life. 'Friday nights were the worst for me,' she says. 'I'm not sure I ever escaped before 10 pm. David liked to have everything in his head sorted for the weekend.'[34] At this stage of a week, even somebody of Morgan's abundant energy tended to be running on fumes. Annette Davis, Leon's wife, once lamented to Kelly: 'All we get at the end of it are the wrung-out rags.'[35] Or, as Kelly herself put it, she felt rather like a boxer's corner-man, patching up the fighter to put him back in the ring come Monday morning.

It was against this background that Morgan found it difficult, at first, to listen to complaints from employees about overwork. 'He couldn't talk to anybody about work–life balance,' Vonhoff reflects, 'because he didn't have one.'[36]

* * *

Balanced or not, work and life were about to collide in the most traumatic fashion. A little before the Easter weekend of 2001, Kelly opened a letter from her local hospital: a routine mammogram had shown up an area of concern. Surprised but not shaken, she returned to her specialist to be informed she needed a biopsy. While she tried to present a stoic face at the theatre that evening, her sister's look of dread at learning of her treatment told a different story.

At her appointment the next day, oncologist Dr Paul Crea took her aside and uttered the words that confirmed her deepest fear: 'You have cancer. We've got it quite early, and we're planning to operate as soon as we can.'[37] In one ghastly instant, all the diary items to which she had attached such significance – the presentations and the parties – became the most trifling fripperies. Her mind in a whirl, she leapt in the car and drove straight to her husband's office, pulling him out of a meeting and ordering him to the downstairs lobby to talk.

If her sister's reaction had conveyed a silent terror, then Morgan's was far more overtly pained. 'Some meetings are seared on your memory,' he says. 'This was one of those.

I remember sitting on the couch and bursting into tears. She was rather braver than I was about it.'[38]

And yet even upon the couple's most shattering moment, an odd shaft of light intruded. Their son, Ben, asked to sit down because his mother had something serious to announce, responded to the cancer diagnosis as only a sixteen-year-old could. 'I thought,' he said, visibly relaxing, 'you were going to tell me that you and Dad were splitting up.'[39]

Kelly underwent surgery in the first week of May, discovering with delight that she did not require a mastectomy. The ensuing worry was unbearable, to the point where she demanded David call Dr Crea himself to see if the pathology tests were clear. The news was encouraging: the tumour itself was low-grade, and her cancer had not spread to the lymph nodes. Overjoyed, Morgan left work early to join her, bearing a bottle of the finest champagne.

Somehow, under the most glowering cloud, their lives had to preserve a semblance of order. At his half-yearly results speech the following morning, few in the audience had any inkling, as Morgan dissected every slice of the bank's $924 million net profit, of the weight of personal anxiety that had just been lifted.[40]

Of the exotic perks particular to leaders of the largest banks, perhaps the most glittering was an invitation to the annual Microsoft CEO Summit in Seattle, conceived in 1997 by Bill Gates to give the highest-level global executives a platform to share their experiences. Morgan received his first such golden ticket in 2001, within weeks of Kelly's ordeal. To all but a chosen few – the guest-list was limited to ninety-nine, on a once-only basis – the occasion was cloaked in secrecy, with the identities of invitees suggested only by the registration numbers of private jets landing at Boeing Field. It promised an invaluable talking shop: Warren Buffett, the investor extraordinaire who typically rivalled Gates for the title of world's richest man, was a regular, along with Jack Welch, nicknamed 'Neutron Jack' for firing over 100,000 employees at General Electric but a CEO who had swelled the company's value forty times over during his twenty years in charge. Welch's severance package in 2001, worth $537 million, remains the most lucrative in corporate history.[41]

One relative newcomer to this gilded gathering was Jamie Dimon, the vibrant, fast-talking, ferociously bright chief executive of Bank One in Chicago. Whenever Morgan had asked competitors about who were considered the finest banking executives in the world, Dimon's name had often cropped up. Furnished with the quicksilver instincts befitting a Baker Scholar from Harvard Business School, Dimon was not afraid of ruffling feathers. He had hit the headlines for an acrimonious parting from Sandy Weill, who had hired him at American Express but then fired him at Citigroup in 1998, prompting a vow that he would never work for anyone else again. 'He's very smart, very sophisticated, but he doesn't play the game,' Bill Daley, Dimon's long-time associate and later White House chief of staff to Barack Obama, told *Vanity Fair*.[42]

Morgan, intrigued and impressed by Dimon's reputation, made a beeline for him on the boat ride across Lake Washington to Gates' house. 'We struck up an instant rapport,' he says, as the two found much symmetry in their thinking, from the need for discipline on mergers and acquisitions to the importance of subordinates feeling safe to challenge the CEO. By the time they repaired to the boat's bar, a friendship was sealed. 'There was another person who tried to join in, but we were having too much fun and froze him out,' Morgan recalls. 'This was Rajat Gupta, then CEO of McKinsey. Gupta was later jailed for two years for insider trading.'[43]

Dimon has since claimed his place as a titan of Wall Street, a figure of such giant renown in banking that Annie Leibowitz has taken his magazine portraits, while Francis Ford Coppola has expressed interest in weaving his character into film. As chairman and CEO of J.P. Morgan Chase (JPMC), America's biggest bank, since 2006, he sits atop an institution holding US$3 trillion in assets and $1.7 trillion in deposits.[44] Although a Democrat by political persuasion, he was approached by Donald Trump in 2016 to serve as Treasury secretary, a role he politely declined before it fell to Steven Mnuchin, formerly of Goldman Sachs. While his stature as the outstanding CEO of his time is now axiomatic within the banking sector, the range of his ability was far from common knowledge in 2001, when he and Morgan were introduced.

In a rare interview, in his office on New York's Park Avenue, Dimon reflects on a relationship that has strengthened ever since. 'At the end of the boat ride, David told me, "Hey, we've got to stick together" – and we have,' he says.[45]

One intriguing parallel that they discovered in their pasts was an estrangement from a former mentor: where Dimon fell out spectacularly with Weill, who had backed him straight out of Harvard, Morgan had endured his own quarrels at Treasury with John Stone, a man he had once revered.

Paul Keating, for all the vital qualities that he ascribed to Morgan in their years working together, remembers how his friend and colleague 'had a bit of a vulnerability as a hero-worshipper'.[46] It would seem a fair charge, based on Morgan's initial dealings with Stone, who at the time was a towering authority within the Australian bureaucracy and whose favour, out of professional necessity, Morgan had keenly sought. But rapid political change, coupled with Stone's intransigent attitudes, would end up driving a wedge between them. Dimon discovered, through his battles with Weill, how even the closest bonds could come apart. 'Now I urge people not to look for mentors,' he explains. 'There is a bit of a misconception with mentors, in that just because you are getting advice from someone, it doesn't mean that it is the *right* advice. You need advice from lots of people. I've learned how to handle certain things from many people – not just from one person.'[47]

The stardust so liberally sprinkled over Gates' gatherings could, Morgan realised, wear off quickly. Proximity to the icons of business bred an understanding that many were mere mortals, flawed and fallible, exceptional in their fields but often ordinary in others. Preconceptions of their power and charisma did not always hold true. Sir Richard Branson, for example, who as founder of the Virgin Group had perfected a certain hail-fellow-well-met charm with his droll quips and open-necked shirts, was, in Morgan's judgment, 'very nervous' within the confines of the Microsoft Summit.[48]

Among all the luminaries who assembled each May in Seattle, one to whom Morgan was naturally drawn was Buffett, by common consent the shrewdest investor of modern times, worth over $110 billion in 2018, despite giving almost half his fortune to charity. Such sums conceal an extreme frugality in his day-to-day routine: Buffett, who lives in the same house in Omaha, Nebraska, that he bought in 1958 for $30,000, was depicted in a 2017 documentary counting his nickels and dimes each morning, depending on what type of hamburger he fancied at the nearby drive-through McDonald's.[49] A self-confessed creature of habit, he was equally stubborn in his views on how banks operated. 'Banking,' as he once put it, 'is very good business if you don't do anything dumb.' After a presentation that Morgan delivered at the 2004 CEO Summit, Buffett appeared to see somebody who would resist any moments of rashness, telling him: 'David, you won't screw it up.'[50]

An avoidance of risk had been hardwired in Morgan's psyche since childhood. It had informed any number of life choices, from his abandonment of acting in favour of a university place to his decision, as Westpac CEO, to walk away from a $2.2 billion price tag for BT. With Dimon, he shared both a basic conservatism that formed the foundation of banking and an acute appreciation of the flipside of risk.

Banks, far more highly geared than other companies, function on an approximate ratio of 10 per cent equity to 90 per cent debt, which can leave an extraordinarily fine line between risk and recklessness. James Gorman, who, like Morgan, had been brought up in the suburb of Glen Iris before his rise to become head of Morgan Stanley, the world's second-largest investment banking house, explored this theme in a speech at Melbourne University in 2015. 'Managers have a much greater capacity in banks to create downside than upside,' he argued.[51] Where risk-taking might be a highly desirable impulse in those launching high-tech start-ups, bank CEOs tend to be better advised erring on the side of caution.

'People have funny misconceptions about taking risks,' Dimon explains. 'Sometimes, just by the very nature of your job, you are taking risks. As a bank, if I make you a loan, that's proprietary risk. I have made a decision: I am going to do this. But I think that in the better companies, you spend much more time working out whether you can survive the worst-case scenario, rather than just the day-to-day risk management decisions.'[52]

While Morgan had applied this principle diligently in rejecting a tie-up with BT, the opportunity was to resurface, three years later, in circumstances that he least expected. As the winter of 2002 closed in, he took a surprise phone call from Barry Griswell, CEO of Principal, the Iowa-based financial services group into whose hands BT had fallen after being offloaded by Deutsche. Griswell would not confirm to Morgan's office what he was calling about but insisted on being put through. 'I know this is highly unusual,' he began, 'but would you come down to my hotel for a one-on-one discussion? I don't want you to tell a soul that we're meeting.'[53]

His curiosity piqued, Morgan headed straight for the Intercontinental on Macquarie Street, where Griswell spilled forth about the very problems he had prophesied for Westpac in 1999. There was an instant rapport between the two. BT, Griswell claimed, was too remote and high-handed for Principal to cope with any longer. He was serious about selling and prepared to thrash out a realistic price. In the most unlikely twist, a deal that had been dismissed as unfeasible was back in play, with executives from both sides arranging to meet in Chicago on 5 June. The location was chosen for anonymity: Westpac had no other business being in the Midwest, while Principal flew in their senior team from Des Moines by company jet.

With the essential elements of a deal all settled, subject to sale and purchase agreements, Morgan left it to David Clarke, his head of wealth, to resolve the fine print. Soon enough, some familiar roadblocks sprung up, as Clarke despaired that BT were too inflexible as negotiators, advising colleagues that Westpac would be better off going it alone. By this stage, though, Morgan was of a mind not to let the deal vanish into the ether.

More often than not, critical junctures in a CEO's career flow from an immense collaborative effort, but this was one case where his personal intervention resurrected a seemingly lost cause. He saw, for a start, how much sense a deal made: Westpac had a huge number of baby-boomers among its customers, many with wealth management needs, to whom a far superior service could be tailored. Given that Westpac had just bought Sagitta Rothschild for $323 million, as well as taking a 51 per cent stake in Hastings for $36 million, the acquisition of BT promised to cement the bank among Australia's premier wealth players. 'I knew Principal was very highly motivated to sell,' Morgan says. 'So, there was a great deal to be done by us. I wanted this to happen – very badly.'[54]

As he played his full hand, the soundings from the US were hardly encouraging. 'David, it's dead,' Griswell said. It was an answer Morgan refused to accept, imploring his opposite number to give the talks one last push. After all else had failed, any hope of salvaging the deal hinged solely upon the rapport between the two CEOs. Now that he had gone so far, the BT prize was one on which Morgan was staking his entire reputation.

A last-ditch summit was set for 11 August 2002, at the Ritz-Carlton on Laguna Beach, just south of Los Angeles. It was a blazing hot Sunday, with swimming trunks more the order of the day than business suits. In his head, Morgan, accompanied in California by legal counsel Ilana Atlas, had a clear idea of how much he would consider paying Principal for BT: US$1.25 billion ideally, $1.5 billion at a push. Griswell and Morgan went alone to a back room of the hotel. It took some time-honoured thespian skill, then, for Morgan to keep a straight face when Griswell, sensing that this was their last chance, uttered the words '$900 million'. This represented an astonishing coup, well under half the figure previously asked of Westpac.

Griswell, wary to the last, added that his legal representative had cautioned against shaking hands on this knock-down price, which would increase to $950 million if all aspects of integration went smoothly. 'So, can we hug instead?' Morgan replied, to break the ice. With that embrace, the deal was effectively complete, thus validating some inspired brinkmanship.

When the announcement was made a couple of months later, *The Sydney Morning Herald* declared: 'Good things come to those who wait.'[55] Atlas, who had seen at first hand Morgan's consuming desire to haul an agreement over the line, says: 'This one went down to the wire. David drove the transaction – it was up to him. It wouldn't have happened if he hadn't decided it would happen.'[56] Phil Chronican, by then Morgan's chief financial officer, reached the same conclusion. 'It was about David's tenacity in not letting go,' he says. 'The whole thing would have fallen apart if it had been left to the other business leaders on either side.'[57]

This piece of trans-Pacific shuttle diplomacy had lasted only a matter of hours, but it promised to buttress Westpac's position on the wealth front for years to come. Analysts at Salomon Smith Barney noted how the acquisition would tether the bank to BT's vast distribution network, while enabling relationships with a further 450,000 high-net-worth clients.[58] Even his rivals had to concede that Morgan had pulled off quite the triumph. 'It wasn't much money,' says John McFarlane, who at ANZ had overseen a far less fruitful wealth partnership with Dutch bank ING. 'On the scale of acquisitions, it certainly wasn't huge.'[59]

Later, Morgan would also negotiate the acquisition of RAMS, a successful mortgage broker, at a knockdown $140 million in 2007. On the surface, the deal seemed such a steal that some at Westpac expressed concern that the bank might face legal action for not paying enough. These successes were of a kind that prompted Andrew Cornell, of *The Australian Financial Review*, to portray Morgan as the Steven Bradbury of banking. In 2002, the year of Morgan's swoop for BT, Bradbury had become an overnight cult hero at the Winter Olympics in Salt Lake City, winning a short-track speed-skating gold medal for Australia over 1000 metres. His win, the first by any southern-hemisphere athlete in a Winter Games, was less a testament to his aggressive racing than to the fact that every one of his opponents crashed in a final-corner pile-up. Bradbury, it seemed, subscribed to the wisdom of hanging back while all about him fell by the wayside.

Morgan, according to Cornell, espoused much the same strategy as a banker, having 'understood his industry's track record of losing its feet and hitting the barriers'.[60] His eventual vindication over BT, a saga in two acts, proved as much. Morgan showed through the orchestration of this deal that he knew both the right time to walk away and the right time to pounce. As long as all that Westpac did was rooted in such discipline, he reasoned, then it would have every chance – come what may – of being the last bank standing.

CHAPTER 10

Leaders Throw Long Shadows

It was on a stroll through the gardens of Sanssouci, the stately summer palace built by Frederick the Great as his haven on the fringes of Berlin, that a decision was made to breed horses. Morgan had travelled with Kelly to Germany for the 2003 International Monetary Conference, an annual meeting of around fifty of the world's top commercial bankers, and was so smitten by the grounds' soothing country air that he craved, much like the last king of Prussia, a bucolic hinterland where he could leave his worries behind.

Uneasy lies the head that wears a crown, as Shakespeare said of Henry IV, a piece of wisdom that Morgan was inclined to believe after observing the pressures particular to those holding the highest office. During Treasury days, he had seen how Bob Hawke could switch off only by betting on the races, and how Paul Keating found precious refuge in his sprawling classical music collection. For Keating, listening to, say, Bruckner's *Symphony No. 5* also had a humbling effect, reminding him that it was in soaring musical composition, rather than the worthy work of government, where true genius lay. 'The scale of it says to you, "Sorry, you've missed out",' Keating once reflected. 'I'm a mortal, but these are immortals. We're just bit players on a very large stage.'[1]

Morgan's own way to lighten the strain of leading one of the largest banks was to seek tranquillity in nature. If it had worked for Denis Healey, the former UK chancellor of the Exchequer who found no purer contentment than on his Sussex farm, then it was good enough for him.

In his mind's eye, he envisaged a rolling rural estate, within a two-hour drive of Sydney, sheltered from the summer heat and with sufficient acreage for horses to roam. The Southern Highlands, with its blend of green pastures and dense bushland, he decided, was the place to start looking. Since the late nineteenth century, it had been the sanctuary for what Daniel Deniehy termed Australia's 'bunyip aristocracy', the landed gentry who fancied themselves as English aristocrats. Morgan harboured no such pretensions – indeed, he had identified pomposity, along with cruelty to animals, as his two abiding hates in life. But by now he possessed the capital that would enable weekend escapes from the stress of Westpac, and a verdant retreat also promised a reconnection with the creatures he had been drawn to from his days riding around Woodend in his acting youth. 'Some things you need to take up early for them to get into your soul,' he says. 'I love the spirit of horses, their independence, their loyalty. Such is the power of the noble steed.'[2]

Far quicker than they had imagined, he and Kelly found their perfect property, just outside Mittagong, with over 180 hectares and uninterrupted views across the Hawkesbury–Nepean catchment. Not only would it allow Morgan to designate Sundays as 'white space', riding out through pristine wilderness on his beloved mount, Matilda, but he could try his hand as a breeder, too, selecting quarter horses and watching them flourish. 'Breeding is indescribable carnage for one's personal finances, but the pleasure it gives me is quite irrational,' he explains. 'Equally, there is no way I could have done the Westpac job without this kind of outlet in my home life. I would have exploded.'[3]

Within this lush expanse was a small river house, which became Morgan's hideaway while a family home was built. Here, he found that he was at his most constructive, hatching sweeping plans for where he wanted to take Westpac next. A vital priority was to ensure that the bank met, to the fullest extent possible, the needs of the so-called 'fourth stakeholder', beyond shareholders, staff and customers: namely, the community.

While it might appear axiomatic that any bank has at least some regard for its standing among its community, Westpac, like its competitors, had for too long been heedless of its wider reputation. In a dramatic break from industry norms, under Morgan's leadership this fact was openly acknowledged. In 2001, Westpac's annual report had carried, on its front page, a picture of a ripe, healthy tomato. 'Juicy result...' ran the headline. So far, so positive, but one only had to turn inside to find the kicker: '...versus public resentment.' Noel Purcell, the executive who had written it, had wanted to say 'revolt' but was overruled by the board.[4] Alongside the words was an image of the same tomato, this time squashed and splattered.

Dispensing with any pacifying platitudes, the report spelt out the bank's situation in bald terms. 'Not everyone is happy,' it said. 'Anti-bank sentiment is running red-hot. Many people feel our progress has been made at their expense or, at best, without benefit to them. We stand accused of abandoning our social responsibility by pursuing the bottom line, at any cost. This view is clearly not good for business. It is an issue so fundamental to the sustainability of our long-term success that it cannot and will not be ignored.'[5] Even Morgan's letter as CEO began, bracingly: 'People don't like banks.'[6] Purcell, contemptuous of dry corporate-speak and stock photographs of board members with rictus grins, had been adamant that the language should pack a punch. 'We genuinely believed that we could change the world with this,' he says. 'David was brave to go along with it.'[7]

The irony behind this jolting awakening was that Westpac had, for the better part of its existence, conceived itself as a company that was integral to the Australian social fabric. Kim Eberhard, the keeper of Westpac's archives, has argued: 'Virtues and values, held in esteem by society at large, were inherent in the spirit of the Bank of New South Wales from its very inception.'[8] But in the rush to fathom the best response to deregulation, first by restlessly expanding and then by slashing costs, this original sense of purpose had, since the eighties, become lost. A Friedmanite view that the 'business of business is business', and that a bank's sole *raison d'être* is to make profit, went largely unchallenged.[9]

Morgan had spent many years subscribing to this logic, until he recognised that it was poisoning perceptions of the industry. If banks did not give the disenchanted public what they reasonably needed, he felt, then politicians and regulators would do it for them, and in such draconian fashion that it would threaten even worse shareholder returns. So it was that, one weekend at the river house, he drafted a statement that captured Westpac's fresh direction. 'Manage long, manage broad,' it proclaimed, 'and with a consistent set of values.'[10]

To flesh out these values, it helps to study the social charter that Morgan had brought into force in 2001. As an expression of Westpac's 'principles of doing business', the document recognised the rights of Indigenous Australians, the concerns of Westpac employees, as well as carrying a firm commitment to care for the environment. At a stroke, the bank was effectively endorsing the three focal areas of the United Nations Global Compact, introduced in 2000 to encourage businesses to adopt sustainable, socially responsible policies; Leon Davis, Westpac chairman, had written to UN secretary-general Kofi Annan to formalise support for the compact.

For Purcell, author of the principles charter, this move was not one where Westpac just offered grandiose abstractions about the necessity for banks to act more ethically. Instead, it was one where it bridged, once and for all, the gap between what it aspired to do and what it was actually doing.[11] It could hardly boast, for example, of caring profoundly about rural Australia when it continued to shut down branches in remote areas. 'The board agreed that we needed the charter,' Purcell says. 'It was very empowering, getting the agenda moving.'[12]

For all that Westpac might tacitly have espoused the values now enshrined in its charter, it was important to see them articulated. Today, many of the world's premier corporations follow this lead: to walk into the lobby of Morgan Stanley's global headquarters in Manhattan is to be greeted by an assertion of its belief in 'doing the right thing' and 'giving back' in foot-high letters on the wall. 'People need to have a centring,' James Gorman, its CEO, argues in his interview for this book. 'If you don't think that giving back to your community is important, that is entirely your call. I'm not judging you. But you're not going to convince us to do it differently, so you can go and try somewhere else.'[13]

As early as 1997, among her pushes for gender equality, Sherry had made tentative suggestions that Westpac should begin thinking along other lines of ethics, but found that the subject was far from in vogue. 'I brought it up at one of those long-winded strategy sessions, saying that our scorecard ought to include sustainability,' she recalls. 'Everyone replied, more or less: "That's very interesting, Ann, but can we just move on?"'[14] Through her years of working for the Office of the Status of Women, where she had represented the country to the UN on women's rights, Sherry had learned, first, how one tended to be rated by the public according to a basic sense of fairness and, second, how it was political kryptonite to ignore the interests of such marginalised groups as Indigenous Australians.[15] In 2001, Sherry was one of six Australians consulted by Jim Collins for his international best-seller *Good to Great: Why Some Companies Make the Leap...and Others Don't*. Out of these discussions, she emerged more convinced than ever that Westpac had to grasp the nettle in making itself truly sustainable. 'Banks were constantly looking back,' she says. 'Our reference points were in the past. But the companies that made it through were those that thought about the future all the time.'[16]

Morgan's personal attachment to a more sustainable banking model sprang, in part, from Kelly's influence, who, as environment minister for almost four years in the early nineties, had grasped the fine balance between the protection of the land and the aggressive pursuit of industrial growth. But as one who had seen for himself the grievous effects of Westpac's branch closures, fee increases and mass staff layoffs upon its prestige, Morgan understood the imperative for the bank to take action that would elevate it from the pack. At Treasury, he had done much to establish the architecture of financial deregulation in Australia. At Westpac, he had the chance to set a template for how a bank should behave in such a landscape, proving it could stand for a cause greater than itself and not be fixated purely with a licence to print money. 'I genuinely felt it was in that sweet spot of being the right thing to do and also good for business,' he says.[17]

Just as Morgan had found in Canberra, a powerful convergence of personalities was crucial in driving the boldest change. By happy coincidence, the three key executives had all been shaped by a senior public-service background: Sherry in the Office of the Status of Women, Morgan at Treasury and Purcell at the Department of the Prime Minister and Cabinet. Backing up this triumvirate was Davis, who as CEO of Rio Tinto had devised a system where all directors of mines, whether in Mongolia or Madagascar, had to specify what they were doing to respect the rights of indigenous populations – when, after all, it was their resources that the mining giants were plundering. 'From bad experiences, I was totally imbued with the idea that operating a company had a social element, one that needed to be furnished,' Davis says. 'People had to realise that it was just as important as turning a profit.'[18]

If it was Sherry who first drew the blueprint for a sustainable future, Purcell who advanced it, and Davis who championed it, then it was Morgan who, ultimately, had to own it. 'Yes, David had somebody like me pushing the boundaries, but he was the CEO – and he had to be accountable,' Purcell says. 'He didn't dodge that.'[19]

While Morgan was conditioned as an economist to analyse a policy's merits based on the business case put in front of him, this was one example where raw instinct prevailed. He saw that the time-honoured custom where big business looked after shareholder value, while government looked after the people, was outmoded. There needed to be, he resolved, a renunciation of short-termism, a decisive move away from 'delivering for just one stakeholder to delivering for all'.[20]

What exactly does sustainability mean in a corporate context? It defies easy definition, encompassing as it does strands as diverse as ecology, social justice and moral philosophy. But Gro Harlem Brundtland, former prime minister of Norway, came perhaps the closest of anyone when she expressed it in 1987 as 'meeting the needs of the present without compromising the ability of future generations to meet theirs'.[21]

There are, broadly, three pillars to any sustainable outlook: economic, social and environmental. One project where Westpac won plaudits for combining all of them was the Cape York Indigenous partnership, designed to use the bank's expertise to alleviate severe inequality in one of the poorest regions of Australia. At the tip of north Queensland, Cape York comprised several Aboriginal communities that had become both dislocated and disenfranchised. Cut adrift from an age of prosperity elsewhere in the country, people there endured living conditions that were an embarrassment to a first-world society. On an initial visit to the area in 2001, Sherry made no secret of her horror at how an affluent nation still tolerated the spectacle of people living on rubbish tips.[22]

She saw, however, that it was within the bank's gift to redress such polarities. During her time at Cape York she had listened intently as Noel Pearson, an Aboriginal leader born and raised locally, argued against welfare dependency, instead advocating a path to recovery that could be smoothed by powerful companies such as Westpac. Inspired, she returned to Sydney to look for a few internal allies, who would throw their weight behind an ambitious collaboration between the bank and Indigenous Enterprise Partnerships, the umbrella group that upheld what Pearson called 'our right to take responsibility'.[23] While she had the seniority to push it through herself for a year or two, it would require the blessing of the CEO to be a sustainable solution. Morgan needed little persuading: a million dollars spent on lifting up struggling Aboriginal businesses would, he knew, be of more lasting value than if he simply signed a cheque for the same amount.

Over a year, Sherry held scores of meetings with people in Cape York, curbing her usual zeal for quick action to form a subtler understanding of problems that had become entrenched over decades. Eventually, on her guidance, Westpac settled upon two long-term programs, assisting families or communities to develop basic budgeting skills, and dispatching staff to the area for up to three-month periods to stimulate the growth of small business.

'It was the old proverb about teaching people to fish, rather than giving them fish,' Morgan says. 'We put around one per cent of our pre-tax profits into non-commercial, charitable endeavours. We didn't just write cheques, we sent executives up there to do the work and teach useful skills to Indigenous communities. It wasn't tokenistic – it had meaning.'[24]

Those compiling the Dow Jones Sustainability Index, a cluster of indices evaluating companies on everything from labour practices to climate change mitigation, appeared to agree, heralding Westpac as the world's most sustainable bank for five years straight from 2002.[25] Such lofty recognition arose, in part, from its readiness to blaze a trail. It was already the first Australian bank even to issue a sustainability report, and the first to trade renewable energy certificates. In 2003, Westpac was among just ten founding signatories globally, and the only one from Australia, to adopt the Equator Principles, which bound financial institutions to a strict set of rules for first gauging, then managing the social and environmental fallout from their decisions. In one deeply resonant TV advertising campaign, the image of a stricken penguin, its feathers and feet coated in an oil slick, drove home the message that Westpac would not finance any projects that endangered the environment.

The same strict analysis would apply, as Davis illustrates, to its lending policy. 'We would only lend to people who had proof of record to be sustainable,' he says. 'That was something we emphasised year after year.' Under Davis's chairmanship, it was an article of faith that for any message to be fully absorbed by the workforce, it had to be repeated almost *ad nauseam*. 'My view was that whenever you said something in a staff lecture, people absorbed about 20 per cent of it, then forgot half of that as the year went on,' he reflects. 'So, "don't change what you say" – that was my diktat. Keep on saying it.'[26]

Morgan was of much the same mind, sometimes claiming that it took, as a general rule, one year to mobilise each layer of management to accept a different working culture, until it became deeply inculcated. Given that there were at least seven such tiers within Westpac, this was a task likely to span almost his entire time in charge. Still, it was one he tackled with gusto, reaching to branch-manager level to impart the bank's values to over 2500 people, twice a year, asking them to disclose any impediments or bottlenecks that hampered them from doing their jobs.[27] An intranet site was also established for employees to raise issues with the CEO confidentially. Sustainability could be a broad-based concept, of which one element was an acknowledgment of the bank's flaws.

'It included transparency of both your social and financial reporting,' Morgan says. 'This included gutsy stuff like customer complaints, and where you had screwed up.'[28] He wanted, essentially, to push Westpac beyond the idea that a sustainable bank was one wedded exclusively to charitable causes or to its environmental conscience, vital though these strands might have been. Instead, as he spelt out in an address to his executive team in 2003, the emphasis needed to be firmly on 'running a responsible, ethical and trustworthy company – day in, day out'.[29]

There were comforting signs that Westpac's rank and file would rally behind such a cause. By 2004, employee commitment was registered to have risen by 21 per cent, as Morgan made it a mantra to capture his staff's 'discretionary effort': in other words, the level of effort people could give if they wanted to, above and beyond the minimum required.[30] In one sense, Morgan was a subscriber to Jamie Dimon's wisdom that an improvement in shareholder value – and Westpac's profits had just shot up by over $350 million, then the largest annual increase of his tenure – could itself be a motivating force, as by and large people drew energy from belonging to a successful organisation. But in a speech that year to Bill Gates' congregation of global CEOs in Seattle, he put more flesh on the bone, arguing that while it was increasingly impossible to micro-manage anybody, a workforce could still be galvanised by a simple and authentic set of values. 'Shared values tell individuals within a company what is worth striving for,' he said.[31]

The three that Morgan eventually chose for Westpac – teamwork, integrity, performance – were, as he saw it, not generic ideas plucked from a management textbook, but principles long encoded in the bank's DNA. He invoked an extraordinary case from 1893 of Horace Walker, a clerk who had somehow made the journey from the gold rush Queensland town of Croydon to Georgetown, 140 kilometres away, travelling by horse he crossed flooded creeks and rivers, and sustained a fractured leg crossing one of the rivers. Nothing said 'teamwork' quite like riding to one's next assignment across sodden grasslands and through the bush while nursing a serious injury.

Brian Hartzer, Westpac's incumbent CEO, pushed for a reconnection with this heritage upon the company's two-hundredth anniversary in 2017, emphasising how inextricably its prospects had been bound up with those of the colony, then the country. The US-born Hartzer, a keen student of history from his days studying the subject at Princeton, had already learned much about Morgan's passion for this very theme. 'David embodies a love of Australia and a love of economics,' he says. 'But he also has a love for the unique role Westpac has played in the nation's economic life.'[32]

Morgan tried strenuously to exemplify the values he wished to see in his staff. 'Leaders throw long shadows,' he would often say, conscious that he was never off-duty and that many would take their cues from how the person at the top behaved. Brigitte Costa, who had assumed chief of staff duties from Trudy Vonhoff in 2002, reflects: 'We had a system of coloured folders. Sometimes, he would come into my office and start to go through them. "No, David, they won't be ready until next week," I'd say, telling him he should go home early. "I'm the CEO," he'd reply. "I can't possibly leave early."'[33]

His own intensity, he believed profoundly, could determine that of the bank's employees who were watching his example. While he made sure never to demand more of people than he gave himself, the benchmark he set was prodigiously high. 'David had the highest work rate of anyone I have ever known, to this day,' says Phil Chronican, his loyal and trusted second-in-command, appointed as CFO in 2001. 'He was unlike many I have come across in business, in that he would focus on high-level goals while insisting that every little loose end was tied up. He could translate from strategy to execution very clearly. I remember leaving our hotel in New York, where we had been for a May investor meeting, and David asking the receptionist if there had been a fax for him overnight. It turned out that a 200-page fax from Sydney had blocked the whole system. But it was printed out and handed straight to me to read on the flight home, ready for a conference as soon as we returned. That was the rate at which you had to work with him.'[34]

The relationship between Morgan and Chronican was exceptionally close, largely because their styles were complementary. At root, both were hard-boiled, numbers-driven, devotees of detail, but Chronican, a Kiwi who had earned an MBA at Insead and been part of Westpac's evolution since the early eighties, understood the bank's internal mechanisms more intimately than most. 'Whereas David would tend to know what he wanted, I knew how things actually got done,' he explains. 'I was more of a banker, in a technical sense, and he gave me the headroom and autonomy. Very rarely did he question why I was doing anything, so I felt that I had his trust.'[35]

'We were joined at the hip,' Morgan agrees. 'He knew exactly what problems to solve and what to elevate to me.'[36] Where Morgan would toil slavishly on Friday evenings, not repairing to the farm until every last 'i' was dotted and every 't' crossed, Chronican preferred to down tools at around 6 pm, enjoy a glass of wine and then tackle the next round of heavy lifting on Sundays.

As his right-hand man for several years, Chronican acquired a singular insight into what made Morgan tick, and an appreciation of the human complexities that deterred him from taking unnecessary gambles. 'For all that David had an amazing drive to succeed, he had an almost equal drive to avoid failure,' he says. 'It all goes back to the story of how his father's business failed. When things were off the rails, you could see that it really hurt him. Visibly, he hated the sense of being out of control.'[37]

One area that Morgan was fanatical about keeping in harmony was his family life. Scarred not just by the folding of the paternal hat company but by his memories of a broken home, he vowed that his role as CEO, however onerous, would not envelop all the time he could spend with Kelly and their two teenage children. Vonhoff, who as his first chief of staff would orchestrate his every working day in a way that minimised distractions, ensured a private telephone line to which only Kelly, Jessica and Ben had access. Morgan was scrupulous, too, about imparting some of his economic acumen during his daughter's and son's formative years, to protect them from the same upheavals he had suffered as a young man four decades earlier.

'Goals were set for Jess and Ben around what they wanted to achieve,' Vonhoff says. 'They would come in and do a performance assessment. David would put a lot of thought into how he could involve them in the family finances, in making portfolios, so that they were comfortable with the position they would undoubtedly inherit.'[38]

Noel Purcell was another who, on frequent road trips together, observed this trait of Morgan's at close quarters. 'After twenty hours of flying, we would arrive at JFK, jump in the car to Manhattan, and the first thing David did was ring the kids,' he says. 'It didn't matter where he was. I got the impression that he didn't want them to experience what he had gone through. I admired him in that regard.'[39]

* * *

Come 2005, the consistency of Westpac's upward curve was unmistakeable: a record net profit of $2.8 billion, a much-improved expense-to-income ratio of 47 per cent, and a thriving domestic operation that persuaded Morgan to resist any aggressive expansion into Asia. With the bank's Australasian influence surging, he declared, confidently: 'We have filled in all the gaps in our geographic footprint.'[40] Still, he was unswerving in his insistence that Westpac had to be built to roll right over whatever crises the cyclical banking industry might throw up. 'Yes, we want growth,' he told the 27,000 employees, 'but the right growth at the right time. What we don't want is growth that ultimately proves value-destroying.'[41]

Jon Nicholson, who was taken on in 2006 as chief strategy officer, was deeply struck by Morgan's hard-nosed stance on risk. The pair shared some Canberra background, from Nicholson's time as senior private secretary to Bob Hawke, and he noticed echoes of Morgan's Treasury training in the way Westpac was now being run.

'David had a very strong sense of public policy and of the social licence to operate,' he says. 'Plus, he understood, from Westpac's nightmare in the early nineties, what it meant to put a major institution at risk.'[42] Morgan could not be swayed from his conviction that there was far more downside than upside attached to decisions in banking, a view that his lieutenants would seldom second-guess. 'It's the saying no that saves you,' Nicholson argues. 'It's the most important skill. People tend to move with the herd, because saying yes makes your short-term profits look better. The crash, however, always comes.'[43]

Focus, Morgan found, was the most underrated concept in the management lexicon. All too often, a chronically unfocused approach seemed to lie at the root of corporate mediocrity, whether in Westpac's restless thrust into exotic geographies and financial services during the eighties, or in NAB's myopic preoccupation with mergers and acquisitions throughout the nineties.

Morgan had little time, though, for any such glamour fever or grass-is-greener syndrome. Having swooped to capture BT at a knockdown price in 2002, he was content for Westpac to concentrate on enriching its core business, lending prudently and sustainably, while ensuring that hard-won customer satisfaction did not slide back into disillusion. In particular, he set stall by the bank's 'Ask Once' commitments, which pushed it to answer all customer queries the first time. 'It was very well regarded within the market,' says Hartzer, then a competitor running ANZ's retail division. 'We thought it was very clever.'[44]

Nicholson, likewise, discovered that the Westpac he joined had weathered the blowtorch of wider public criticism, by signalling that it would place the concerns of the community ahead of its own short-term economic interests. 'In championing corporate social responsibility, David was a pioneer,' he says. 'In Australia, there is an "all banks are bastards" school of thought, so the public was taken aback at the notion that a big, greedy bank would do what was right. It seemed incomprehensible.'[45]

These deeper forces are vital, according to Andrew Cornell, long-time observer of the banks at *The Australian Financial Review*, to any overarching perspective on Morgan's body of work. 'As there weren't too many acquisitions in his time, people might assume that he was just a steady-as-she-goes CEO, but this would be a misreading of what went on beneath the surface,' he explains. 'David was very clinical on banks being safe, resilient, capable of absorbing shocks. He was the stand-out banker of his generation.' It is a sentiment endorsed even by John McFarlane, Morgan's counterpart at ANZ from his accession to the role in 1999, who reflects: 'Of the banks, I thought that he had the most successful tenure.'[46]

In early August 2007, Australia's banks had a preview of the global picture changing for the worse. Short-term credit markets in the US had shut down, as France's BNP Paribas opted to freeze three of its funds, indicating that it had no means of valuing the bundles of complex assets within them, known as collateralised debt obligations (CDOs). As such, it became the first major bank to acknowledge openly the risk of exposure to the murky world of subprime mortgages.

Within Westpac, this first blip on the seismograph did not go unnoticed. 'I remember Curt Zuber, then as now the bank's treasurer, coming into my office unannounced to tell me, "David, something really funny is happening with the markets,"' Morgan says. '"They're saying it's just because the traders are on holiday, but we think there's something else going on." I could see the look in his eyes – it's one of those moments that stay with you. It turned out to be the first breaching of the dam wall.'[47]

The two of them sat together for an hour, thrashing out how best to proceed. Morgan, mindful of the benefits that NAB had derived in the early nineties recession from being the nation's lowest-risk, most resilient bank, had made it the abiding quest of his tenure to ensure Westpac was the best conditioned to withstand the next worldwide shock. On this front, the portents were promising: even at the early signs of crisis, Westpac was the least likely to follow the lemmings jumping off a cliff.

Nicholson recalls the example of one junior credit officer at the institutional bank, who penned a memo that advised against succumbing to the fashion for CDOs: 'The guy said, "I've had a good look at some of the derivatives and home loans that they're selling in the US. I can't for the life of me understand them. Therefore, we shouldn't buy them." It was about doing the sums, being hard-nosed.'[48]

All around, the threads that bound the entire financial system together continued to fray. Come September 2007, Northern Rock, a British building society that had taken too many risks and found itself with no alternative sources of funding once the markets dried up, ran out of money. This prompted the first run on a UK high street bank for 150 years. In the US, four months later, analysts announced the largest single-year drop in home sales in a quarter of a century.

The anomaly was Australia, which skated over the escalating crisis. The reasons behind such durable performance ran deep, with household credit growth in the country underpinned by rising incomes and employment, as opposed to declining credit standards. The strength of the Australian relationship with China sheltered national resources from precipitous falls in demand elsewhere, while a catalogue of recent failures, not least Westpac's own brush with insolvency in 1992, had brought more robust regulation.

Ian Macfarlane, from his vantage point as Reserve Bank governor until 2006, posits a different theory: namely, that the greatest protection for Australia lay in its strict curbs on corporate control of the banking sector. 'Now people say that we did well because we had effective supervision, but I don't think that's the explanation,' he says. 'In other countries, banks were competing not just for customers, but to save their own lives. Due to our "Four Pillars" policy in Australia, there wasn't the same intensity of competition, or the same temptation to chase short-term profits. It is no coincidence that the only two countries with prohibitions on the major banks taking each other over, Australia and Canada, were the same two that came through events unscathed.'[49]

There were, however, some stark disparities between the Big Four in terms of how convincingly they prevailed. NAB had its fingers badly burnt when, at the solicitation of US investment banks, it bought $1.2 billion of CDOs in 2006, only to write down 90 per cent of the investment later on. Westpac, by contrast, refused to take the bait, wary of repeating the same careless dabbling that had dragged it to the edge of extinction. Under Morgan's direction, resolve had hardened to avert the volatility of what had gone before.

Even before the global economy started to creak alarmingly, Morgan had asserted an aim, at all his public meetings, to make Westpac 'second to none' in its ability to ride out a storm. Today, the judgment by one of Australia's most respected banking analysts is that he succeeded. 'When Westpac entered the global financial crisis, it was in a much stronger position than its peers by virtue of what David had done,' reflects Brian Johnson, then of J.P. Morgan. 'For me to be complimentary about bank CEOs is not a normal state of affairs. While ANZ and NAB had a torrid time, Westpac and Commonwealth Bank more or less breezed through. "De-risking" the bank might hurt your earnings there and then, but it makes them more resilient for the future. Commonwealth's power was essentially a legacy of history: a very large, stable deposit base, not much institutional lending. But Westpac genuinely went into the GFC lean and strong.'[50]

To this day, Morgan's record of buttressing the bank against cataclysmic change is one recognised by its leaders. 'You're there to increase shareholder value,' says Hartzer, the chief executive since 2015. 'To do that, you need to manage your return on equity, simplify your business, cut costs, focus on your knitting. Those are important parts of why we sailed through the GFC so well.'[51]

That legacy is firmly entrenched. Indeed, in a book to herald Westpac's bicentennial in 2017, the double-page spread on Morgan's CEO-ship was headlined: 'Recovery, Responsibility, Resilience'.[52] Not that he could have predicted such eulogies a decade earlier, when the full repercussions of the GFC had still to play out.

In late 2007, the sweep of economic horror unfolding beyond Australia's shores was as yet unleashed: the failure of Bear Stearns, the collapse of Lehman Brothers, the unprecedented stock market meltdown. Morgan, though, already knew that he was leaving the company to which he had rendered eighteen years' service.

There are no hard-and-fast benchmarks for CEO longevity – Jamie Dimon, who has presided over the J.P. Morgan Chase empire since 2005, argues: 'What difference does it make? An average of ten years? You can't have set rules for every person.'[53]

But Morgan's thoughts had turned, beyond his fifth year, to the issue of succession planning. 'I used to say that if you haven't given your best as a CEO to a company in nine years, then you haven't been doing your job properly,' he says.

Still, this cold logic did not make the task of stepping away any easier. Emma Beames, his chief of staff at the time, describes the conflict of emotions with which he struggled deeply. 'David knew it was time to go, but he agonised,' she says. 'He was tangled up about it, having increasingly frequent conversations with executive coaches about when to announce a successor. He wanted to minimise the lame-duck period.'[54] Or as Brigitte Costa, Beames' predecessor, puts it: 'Westpac was his baby. The question was, "The baby has grown up. What do I do next?"'[55]

It was during Morgan's sixtieth birthday party at the family farm, an affair grand enough for guests to be asked on official invitations whether they would bring their own horses, that the name of Gail Kelly first surfaced as a prospective next in line. Born in South Africa and a former Latin teacher, Kelly had worked her way up from teller level to lead St George,

Australia's fifth largest bank. As the country's first female banking CEO, Kelly had carved a formidable reputation for her powers of persuasion and empathy, going so far as to answer some customer complaint emails herself.

Ted Evans, who, in a neat symmetry, had gone from being one of Morgan's closest Canberra friends in the eighties to his chairman for his final years at Westpac, was among Kelly's most fulsome admirers. 'At David's party, Ted spoke to me about the possibility of being "in the mix", about whether I was willing to be considered,' Kelly says. 'Soon after, we went into the process.'[56] Evans, for his part, is not shy of illustrating why she leapt straight to the top of his candidate list. 'Gail was an extraordinary individual,' he says. 'In particular, she was a wonderful public speaker. She could speak for forty minutes, never using notes, never putting a word wrong.'[57]

Kelly came with the recommendation of both Morgan and Ros Kelly, with whom she shared a commitment to advancing the cause of women in business. From Morgan's perspective, the one regret was that Chronican, his steadfast deputy, would miss out on a job for which he was eminently qualified. 'In my heart, I wanted to give it to Phil,' he concedes. 'I felt absolutely wretched about it, actually.'[58] It was an awkwardness of which Gail Kelly herself was aware. 'I knew it would be difficult for David,' she says. 'He and Phil had a very close and long-standing relationship.'[59]

An elegant transition had come to be regarded as a distinguishing feature of any well-run bank. Indeed, the board of NAB had made it clear to chief executive John Stewart that it would form a central part of his performance review. There were few unsightly joins when, on 17 August 2007, Westpac confirmed that the flame would be passed from Morgan to Kelly. It seemed, wrote Macquarie Research experts struck by Kelly's relentless emphasis on customer satisfaction, a 'sensible fit'.[60]

On reflection Kelly is candid, too, about the robustness of the position bequeathed to her. 'There was real credit quality,' she says. 'David had been there during the whole 1991–92 scenario, and it had embedded itself deep in the psyche of Westpac-ers. He systematically strengthened the risk management framework of the bank. Where our counterparts had been seduced by US-structured credit, he had made a conscious decision not to get involved.'[61]

Fastidiously resistant to risk though he might have been, Morgan took his impending departure as a cue to speak more freely. Having learned from bitter experience to be guarded in public statements, he marked his twilight at Westpac by firing off a few Exocets. At one trans-Tasman business circle lunch in Sydney, he lambasted the Four Pillars banking structure as anachronistic and inimical to growth, deriding it as a 'woolly mammoth dug from the Siberian tundra and shipped still frozen to Australia'.[62]

Across his nine years at the helm, the tale of the tape for Morgan, a numbers man to his core, stood up to any scrutiny: an unbroken run of record increases in cash earnings, total shareholder returns of almost 15 per cent every year, and a share price rising, on average, more than 11 per cent per annum, from $9.50 when he took over to a peak of nearly $32.

Equally, it was a source of much pride that the proportion of women employees had swelled from 25 per cent in 1998 to

42 per cent by 2007. 'What mattered was the way in which it was done,' Morgan says. 'It's wasn't by setting rigid quotas, but by allowing paid maternity leave or working from home, avoiding unsocial hours for meetings. We got rid of the unconscious discrimination, and the barriers to a true meritocracy.'[63]

The path did not always run smooth: during a talk in 2006 at the University of New South Wales Business School, attended by his daughter, Jess, Morgan was told by one female member of the audience, an employee at the state Treasury, that it was a 'turn-off' for women to hear him extolling the virtues of working six days and five nights a week.[64] There was broad support for his approach, though, from the women on his senior team.

Ilana Atlas, who served as group secretary and general counsel from 2000, attests to his contribution in moving beyond the old boys' club of the past. 'In a way, David was agnostic on matters of gender, which for the time was highly unusual,' she says. 'I didn't feel, when he hired me, that my gender was ever an issue. While Bob Joss had started the organisation on this journey, David was a very significant part of women having opportunities there.'[65]

But as Morgan faced up to his exit, even a stocktake of all that had been achieved did not palliate the pain of leaving. A position to which his entire career had built, at a company with whose history and philosophy he felt inextricably wedded, could hardly be vacated without some pangs of emotion. Walking out of his office for the final time would, he accepted beforehand, be a 'hard thing'.[66]

Throughout his working life, Morgan's wisdom had often intersected with that of Bill Clinton. 'It's the economy, stupid,' a slogan adopted for Clinton's victorious 1992 presidential campaign against George Bush, was a truism of which he was fond. In times of peace, it had tended to be concerns about jobs, trade and economic growth that preoccupied the typical voter above all else, and it was these that had most animated Morgan since his earliest days at university. It seemed fitting, then, that he ended his valedictory speech at Westpac by adapting another example of Clinton's folksy charm.

Invoking the pay-off line of the former president's autobiography – 'I think it's a good story, and I've had a good time telling it' – Morgan told the gathering at the Sydney Institute: 'For nearly two centuries, Westpac's story has weaved in and out of Australia's story. The two are inseparable. It was true of the bank's first thirty years, and profoundly true of the last thirty. To have been a part of that, to have participated in the drama of it, I count as one of the great privileges of my privileged life. This is my story, and I've had a wonderful time in the thick of it.'[67]

Four months after Morgan delivered those words, the bank agreed to a dramatic, uncontested $18.6 billion takeover of St George. At a stage when much of the developed world was engulfed by the economic conflagration of 2008, Westpac was completing one of the largest deals in Australian corporate history. The merger, running counter to the currents of the global credit crunch, created a financial institution of far-reaching power, as Gail Kelly swooped quickly to buy a bank that she had led for six years.

While it represented an undoubted coup for Kelly, mere weeks into her reign, the idea had long since been mooted.

As far back as 2002, Morgan had held talks with Kelly, in her capacity as St George CEO, about the prospect of a merged entity. While she expressed a preference for St George to remain independent, Morgan would later endorse her elevation to the Westpac job partly in a belief that it was the best hope of consummating a deal. Jon Nicholson, retained by Kelly as head of strategy, also identifies Morgan's success in making Westpac the safest of the Big Four as a critical factor behind the eventual move.

'If things had got worse, Westpac would have been the last player standing – no question,' he argues. 'The prize for that was St George. It would have been impossible unless we were in good shape and our competitors were not.'[68] It was a feat that could scarcely be overstated. 'When David took charge, Westpac was not a well-run bank,' Nicholson says. 'But he made it a very strong and safe one. You can't really do anything better. People will never understand the value of that to every single person in Australia. He created a bank strong enough to survive, with hardly a glancing blow, the biggest economic event since the Great Depression.'[69]

In the eyes of James Gorman, the seamlessness of the handover from Morgan to Kelly counts among the most telling tributes to his near decade at the top. 'He brought a highly disciplined management philosophy to an Australian institution,' says Gorman, still one of Wall Street's most influential bankers. 'He handed it off to his successor, and he gave her room to grow. There are very few testaments more powerful than that.'[70]

CHAPTER 11

Life's Third Act

Jane Fonda, the Hollywood actress who epitomises the elegant defiance of ageing, has long fought the idea that one's later decades should signal a slide into decrepitude. At seventy-two, she gave a talk about American society's struggle to come to terms with the fact that people were living, on average, thirty-four years longer than during their great-grandparents' generation. Fonda described how, in the lead-up to her sixtieth birthday, she wrestled with the question of what she was supposed to accomplish in the time that remained. 'Life's third act,' she called it.[1]

Morgan, who had turned sixty just ten months before stepping aside at Westpac, felt, if not quite the same existential angst, then an anxiety about how best to map out his own Act III. The suddenness with which a chief executive could be thrust from business stardom to relative anonymity brought, at first, an acute sense of disorientation.

'It's a very personal thing, but it was strange to walk around Sydney as a CEO one week, then as a mere mortal the next,' Morgan recalls. 'Ralph Norris, CEO of the Commonwealth

Bank, later talked to me about this. After he stepped down as head of Commonwealth Bank, he went from getting 560 Christmas cards a year to just seven. You are vaguely aware, even when you are in the job, that half the people fawning over you are just in it for a transactional relationship.'[2]

But while it was one matter to have the intellectual realisation about the change that would come, it was quite another when it finally happened.

As Morgan saw it, there were three distinct forks in the road he could take. The first was beguiling enough, comprising as it did a spell of unadulterated leisure. Together, he and Kelly could savour holidays they had long promised themselves. This footloose existence did not hold its lustre for long, though. Morgan realised, on his umpteenth visit to the farm stables to check on his horses, that a listlessness was already setting in.

'I can remember thinking, I've still got too much drive and energy just to be kicking around like this,' he says. 'I didn't want another minute of CEO life, but I felt that I risked becoming rather a bludger on society, that I wasn't pulling my weight. I didn't expect that what should have been a happy phase of my life would turn out to be among the least enjoyable.'[3]

Sir Alex Ferguson, held in such esteem for his eleven Premier League titles as manager of Manchester United that he has since run a course at Harvard Business School, has often spoken of hard work as a life-sustaining force. Citing the example of his father, Alexander, diagnosed with lung cancer within a week of retiring from his job at a Glasgow shipyard, he once said: 'There are too many examples of people who retire and are in their box soon after – because you're taking away the very thing that makes you alive.'[4]

After a while, Morgan came to a Fergusonesque view of retired life, in its most indolent form, as a shapeless, unappetising prospect. It was a comfort, then, that one day after departing Westpac in January 2008, he could choose a second path by stepping straight into a board seat at BHP, 'The Big Australian'.

Back in 2005, Don Argus, BHP's redoubtable chairman, known to many by his moniker of 'Don't Argue', called Morgan with the words: 'I want to have a chat about the Big Fella.'[5] In principle, the attraction of a place at the table with BHP, which had evolved from ramshackle outback origins into the largest mining company on the planet, hardly needed spelling out. But in practice, the relationship proved nothing like as fruitful as Morgan had hoped.

A belief hardened in him that, as a non-executive director, without any significant equity stake, he was incapable of exerting the influence he craved. For all that he had allies in the boardroom – including former chief executive Paul Anderson, a customer of his at Westpac – he felt painfully marginalised. Warren Buffett, no less, had cautioned him during a conversation in Seattle: 'David, the best business model is a dominant shareholder with separate management. You won't like public company boards, but you would like Berkshire Hathaway.'[6] Morgan could never be sure if, in that moment, Buffett had been dangling an invitation for him to join Berkshire's board, but the BHP experience taught him that the personal message had been a prescient warning. At a tempestuous time, with BHP preparing a doomed hostile takeover bid for Rio Tinto, he felt oddly peripheral.

'I just like being useful and making a difference,' he says. 'But it is a rude shock how little power and influence one has, relative to having sat in the boardroom for almost a decade as CEO.'[7] John McFarlane, the same age as Morgan and for so long his direct rival while running ANZ, does not hesitate to describe Morgan's move to BHP as mistaken. 'They weren't leveraging the edge that he had,' he says. 'They were in an entirely different sector, with very long-term investment focus and volatile resource prices. He would have been much better off chairing a bank, but he would have needed to leave Australia to do it, because you wouldn't chair a competitor.'[8]

One way for Morgan to reassert his presence – and his third post-Westpac option – was through a return to the public policy-making that had been his lifeblood in the eighties. That chance unexpectedly arose when, early in 2008, Kevin Rudd, the newly elected Labor prime minister, made a splash by ordering a sprawling conference at which 1000 prominent Australians would lay out their visions of the nation's future. Everyone from economists to Indigenous leaders, scientists to artists would converge at the Great Hall of Parliament House for a mammoth two-day brainstorm, as if to illustrate Rudd's argument that 'government, irrespective of political persuasion, does not have a monopoly on public wisdom'.[9] Thus did Morgan, after sitting down for dinner at the Lodge with Rudd, major ministers and state premiers to launch 'Australia 2020', as the summit was billed, find himself chairing the working group on future directions of the Australian economy.

'Rudd appeared gloriously relaxed about it,' says Morgan. 'He said, "I just want to get the best ideas out there."'[10]

With that instruction in mind, Morgan and his team set to work on a prescription for how Australia could become the best place in the world to live and do business. While that objective sounded dauntingly grand, the commitment of those present could not be gainsaid, with discussions far more rigorous than at the usual talking shops. 'It had seemed to me a corny idea at the time, but it turned out to be quite an extraordinary thing,' says Ken Henry, then secretary to the Treasury. 'David's group came up with the idea that we needed to pursue generational tax reform.'[11]

Such an undertaking promised to be a logical extension of Morgan's expertise: after all, he had taken a central role during the Hawke–Keating years in transforming the tax system on an unprecedented scale, so why not again now?

For all that Australia's tax model had made vast advances over the twenty-three years since, it retained its share of imperfections. There were still wasteful taxes that created perverse incentives, not least a fringe benefits tax threshold that merely encouraged people to increase their driving mileage. In response, the summit's experts called for a comprehensive review that would reduce the number of taxes, eliminate stamp duties, and ensure that Australia was not permanently disadvantaged vis-à-vis the simpler, flatter taxation at work in Asia.[12] While the review was taken up, the 138 separate recommendations proved harder to sell, with the Rudd government ultimately approving just three of them. As Nicholas Stuart, author of an unauthorised biography on Rudd, later wrote: 'The 2020 summit provided a paradigm for much of the activity in Rudd's term of office. His rhetoric inspired and enthused voters. And yet…nothing happened.'[13]

While disappointed by such inertia, Morgan was not altogether surprised, given how the distance between 2008 and his own period in public service was measured in more than years. Contrary to life in the Keating Treasury, there was, to his mind, no longer the same mountain of necessary reform to implement or, indeed, the same quality of politician or bureaucrat to champion audacious change. 'Look back at the talent of the ministers in the Expenditure Review Committee in 1985, compared to those with whom we were dealing in '08,' he says. 'I just couldn't talk of them in the same breath.'[14] It is a perspective that journalist Laura Tingle, whose career spans the service of nine prime ministers, extends to the federal bureaucracy. In her 2015 *Quarterly Essay*, she says: 'In the narrower but crucial world of policy advice, there has never been a greater need for intellectual firepower, or for a deep memory.'[15]

Although the vaulting ambition of 'Australia 2020' was thwarted, in part, by the failure of the political class to match rhetoric with action, it was also suppressed by the capricious hand of fate. Six months after delegates dispersed, Lehman Brothers collapsed, and with it went Australia's optimism about buoyant budgetary conditions for years to come. 'The position had been so good beforehand that the previous government, under John Howard, had provided three personal income tax cuts in its last two years in office,' Henry says. 'There was so much money flowing into the budget, the government was determined to redistribute it to taxpayers. But then the GFC hit, and the budget just disappeared.'[16]

* * *

The minimal enactment of the summit's blueprint taught Morgan that it would be near impossible to have a truly influential voice on public policy in the autumn of his career, unless he returned at the level of secretary to the Treasury or governor of the Reserve Bank. As such, he resolved to find a fresh direction, one that would bring both enjoyment and a chance to apply his particular aptitude.

Early in 2008, he received his first offer to switch to the world of private equity, as Mervyn Davies, chairman of Standard Chartered Bank – with whom Westpac had forged a strategic alliance in 1998 – approached him about joining Corsair Capital. Given that Corsair had been spun out of J.P. Morgan after the financial giant's purchase of Bank One, Morgan thought it prudent to contact his friend Jamie Dimon about the merits of such a leap.

'David, that's a great offer,' said Dimon, then in the throes of negotiations to pluck Bear Stearns from the crucible of a historic Wall Street crisis. 'But before accepting, you should probably jump on a plane and meet a couple of other people.'[17] Within days, thanks to Dimon's overtures, two further openings had appeared: one with KKR, run by Henry Kravis, an investor of such renown that his firm's record buy-out of RJR Nabisco inspired the film *Barbarians at the Gate*, and another with J. Christopher Flowers, once one of Goldman Sachs' youngest ever partners and now a global dealmaker extraordinaire.

In Dimon's judgment, it was Flowers' company that promised Morgan the deepest satisfaction. 'One really important thing I told David was, "Don't take on a lot of little things right now,'" he says. "'I know you may be restless, but if you accept this board and that committee, then before you know it you will have made a decision about your next career. That may be fine, but you should make that decision actively and thoughtfully. Step back, and think about every single detail of how you want the next stage of your life to look.'"[18]

So it came to be that on 1 April 2008, Morgan met Flowers in his top-floor Manhattan office at 767 Fifth Avenue, with a view to being made an operating partner of J.C. Flowers & Co., which in just seven years had established itself as a major player in financial services across multiple jurisdictions.

Flowers himself carried a formidable reputation, having emerged in the late eighties as the outstanding mergers-and-acquisitions specialist of his era, whom all the world's leading financial houses wanted on their side. He had a lightning-fast head for figures, born of graduating *magna cum laude* from Harvard in applied mathematics, and could work through complex numerical models without so much jotting down a calculation. 'The Zelig of finance', *Fortune* magazine titled him, in a nod to the Woody Allen character able to ingratiate himself with every sector of society.[19] Even the family Monopoly games that he had played as a young boy would tend to end with his sister, Katie, hopelessly in debt.

Flowers had crossed Morgan's radar before, after poaching David Fite, a highly regarded member of Westpac's executive team, from him in 2000. In person, Morgan found that the intellect and sometimes brooding persona ascribed to Flowers in business profiles was leavened by a healthy dose of self-deprecation, and a perhaps surprising degree of humility. 'Doubt is a virtue of intelligence,' ran a favourite saying.[20]

While Morgan analysed the pluses and minuses of each offer with trademark fastidiousness, his instinct, from the face-to-face meeting, told him that Flowers offered the best fit. That inkling was confirmed during a May dinner in Positano, on Italy's Amalfi Coast, where he and Kelly, together with Dimon and his wife, Judy, had gone to celebrate their twenty-fifth wedding anniversaries. Over a couple of gin and tonics at Le Sirenuse Hotel, Dimon left no doubt as to which course Morgan should pursue.

'It's very personal, who you relate to, but Flowers was a natural for David,' Dimon reflects. 'When you are a banker, you're involved in valuations as well as people decisions, and these private equity companies also need an operating director, someone who can evaluate a management team. It was the best of all worlds for him.'[21] Won over by such logic, Morgan, feeling a renewed vigour, embarked upon his next chapter as part of the Flowers project only five weeks later.

The role was Sydney-based, which presented its own challenges, given that Morgan had to join the weekly conference call at 1 am local time. Making a fist of an essentially one-man show, far removed from the main J.C. Flowers offices in New York and London, seemed a fiendish exercise logistically, and yet somehow, against the odds and with the founder's active support, it worked.

As the de facto Australian chairman, Morgan used his network to explore a plethora of potential buy-outs, including an aborted $5 billion bid for Suncorp Metway, the Brisbane bancassurer that fell into difficulty as markets plunged during the worst of the GFC. Indeed, the more the crisis bit, the more a figure such as Flowers could call on his eagle eye for a deal. Running the sums on every listing ship from Bear Stearns to Northern Rock, Flowers famously declared: 'This is the Super Bowl of investment. It's no time to be sitting in the bleachers.'[22] He expressed it even more bluntly at a New York conference called 'The Big Fix', predicting that 'lowlife grave dancers like me' would make a 'tremendous fortune' from the detritus of a worldwide collapse.[23]

Sure enough, when Lehman Brothers fell over on that fateful day in September 2008, Flowers turned up right in the thick of it. In the space of a weekend, he pored over Lehman's books for fourteen hours in a quest to save the moribund firm, studied ways to stem the spiralling debts of insurance colossus AIG, before finally advising on Bank of America's acquisition of Merrill Lynch. The experience of shuttling from one near-calamity to the next was, he claimed, 'like being at D-Day'.[24] Not for nothing was his contribution in those darkest days a key element of Andrew Ross Sorkin's book *Too Big to Fail*, which in 2011 became an Emmy Award–winning film.

The jewel in the crown of Flowers' portfolio, by the time Morgan came on board, was Shinsei Bank, formerly the troubled Long-Term Credit Bank of Japan. In 2000, Flowers and Tim Collins, chief executive of Ripplewood Holdings, had combined forces to pull off what billionaire investor David Rubenstein described as 'one of the greatest buyouts ever done…the defining transaction in Chris's life'.[25] The deal was structured cleverly, with the government providing downside protection on the bank's entire loan portfolio. Plus, the name change to Shinsei, Japanese for 'reborn', was far more than cosmetic, as jobs were cut, excesses curbed, bad debts cleared and divisions recast. When the bank was partially floated on the Tokyo Stock Exchange in 2004, buyers made up to seven times their money, while Flowers himself, with a 33 per cent stake, reaped an estimated $1.3 billion windfall.

Barely had Morgan completed his first year at the company when a gold-plated package was presented for him to take the reins as Shinsei's chief executive. The bank had been hit hard by the GFC, with four-fifths wiped off the share price and Thierry Porté, the American CEO, removed under government pressure. In response, Flowers had aired a proposal with Warren Buffett to take the bank private. The peerless investor considered it carefully, before calling Flowers to decline. Five minutes later, Flowers rang back, asking: 'What about if David Morgan is CEO?' 'If David is CEO,' Buffett replied, 'and puts some of his own money in, I'm in.'[26]

While an uprooting from Sydney to Tokyo threatened to be a substantial dislocation for Morgan's family, the sweeteners were eye-watering: a place on the L'Oréal board in Japan for Kelly, as well as a university posting and a private jet on permanent standby. This was without even taking into account the US$150 million (A$210 million) that Morgan and Flowers stood to make individually. 'We had some talks with Buffett about him buying a significant stake,' Flowers confirms. 'He was quite interested actually. But what Buffett wanted, if he did do that, was for David to be CEO. He knew David, and that plan sounded good to me, too. I'm not sure that Ros liked the idea, though.'[27]

His suspicion was correct, with Kelly unenthusiastic about being based in Japan. She was not opposed, however, to a move that would require less dramatic cultural displacement. So when, one fine September morning at the MCG ahead of the 2009 AFL Grand Final, Morgan took a call from Flowers asking if he would consider an immediate switch to head up the London office, Kelly insisted that he ring back immediately with their acceptance. The timing felt propitious, with both their children by now in their mid-twenties, Jess having headed to California to pursue an MBA at Stanford, and Ben having emulated his father by qualifying for a masters course at the London School of Economics (LSE). While Morgan had relished his adventures at LSE and the IMF throughout the seventies, Kelly had never lived overseas and was hell-bent on grasping the opportunity.

It was an opening that came about in fraught circumstances, after Ravi Sinha, the head of Flowers' operations in the UK and the man who had led the attempts to buy Northern Rock prior to its nationalisation, was found to have charged £1.3 million ($2.3 million) in fictitious invoices. From May to July 2008, the Indian-born financier, once a star at Goldman Sachs, had borrowed $17.5 million to support his personal interests, some of which even lay in companies where J.C. Flowers funds were invested.[28] Eventually, with the full scale of Sinha's wrongdoing unmasked, he was fined almost $6 million, then a record for the UK's Financial Services Authority, and banned from working in any such sphere of business for life. But when the scandal first broke, Flowers' primary concern was to restore leadership to the London office, a vacuum that he believed Morgan was best-equipped to fill.

It took Morgan only a few hours to arrange to board the next flight out. He resigned from the BHP board the following day. For all the suddenness of the change, there was an exhilaration in sensing that he had, even after Westpac, found a métier that would suit his strengths. 'Something I am reasonably good at is fixing a busted bank,' he says. 'That was how I had spent a good deal of the past twenty years, and there was no substitute for having seen it through to a successful conclusion. With the GFC, there was a situation where I could genuinely make a difference in rehabilitating broken banks.'[29]

No sooner had he settled in London, the city that he recalled in a more down-at-heel seventies guise from his days as an LSE postgraduate, than he was called upon to make this reputation count.

Come July 2010, J.C. Flowers had announced its intention to buy a large minority stake in Kent Reliance, a UK building society that closely fitted the definition of 'busted', having almost tipped into bankruptcy before a dramatic £50 million investment was proposed. In many ways, it seemed an odd marriage, this coupling of dyed-in-the-wool British regional management with the ruthless opportunism of New York private equity. But it fell to Morgan to ensure that it worked.

He grasped the task with gusto and set about sidelining all those who had run the company into the ground, appointing a dynamic young chief executive, Andy Golding, converting Kent Reliance from a building society to a bank, and even giving it a different name. OneSavings Bank, as it is now called, remains a prime example of an institution that Morgan helped repair from the ground up. Having attained a market value of over £875 million ($1.5 billion), it has become firmly established in the FTSE 250 index, and returned the money originally injected by J.C. Flowers six times over.

Morgan's natural tendency towards bravado did not go unnoticed in a country where top-rank bankers traditionally shrank into the background. A 2010 interview in *The Mail on Sunday*, which depicted him as an 'archetypal Australian, brash and brimming with confidence', put it thus: 'Private equity bosses are widely reviled for their lack of finesse and slash-and-burn approach. But if there is one big-hitter in the sector who defies stereotypes, it is David Morgan.'[30]

For all the glaring divergence in personalities, with Morgan's extravagant bonhomie standing at odds with Flowers' understated, intensely cerebral nature, the two quickly formed an effective business bond. Where Flowers' brilliance at spotting a deal was undisputed, Morgan, as managing director in charge of Europe and Asia-Pacific, added a precious and fine-grained understanding of how to operate financial services companies.

'David's a much better manager than me, more disciplined, and a lot more gregarious,' Flowers acknowledges. 'But my strength is a facility with numbers. I have an intuitive feel for them, and for going behind them in great detail. Most people aren't as good as I am at that, to tell you the truth.'[31]

On one occasion, Dimon, who had brought the pair together in the first place, told Morgan that he thought his contribution made J.C. Flowers less of a one-man band.[32] 'It's the thing that's true about David: management,' Dimon says. 'You can't separate management and leadership. The two are closely intertwined.'[33]

An essential element of the job's appeal, in Morgan's eyes, was the invigorating cross-cultural dimension. His remit at J.C. Flowers offered such variety that before long, he held board positions simultaneously in five different countries. One week he could find himself in Tokyo, trying to persuade Shinsei executives of the virtues of meritocracy – not always an easy sell in Japanese banking, where an assumption of jobs for life lingered – and the next he could be trouble-shooting in The Hague for NIBC, a major Dutch bank acquired in 2005. Similarly, a brisk trip to Luxembourg, to monitor progress at NPG Wealth Management, could be bracketed with a board session in Hamburg at HSH Nordbank, an experience that taught Morgan all about the problems of building an outstanding bank within the highly restrictive German system. Although Germany looks on the surface like a model economy, with robust growth and a low public debt ratio, the profitability of its banks is strikingly weak. As of 2018, only one of its banks, Deutsche Bank, features in the world's top 100 by market capitalisation, and even then in the bottom half. In Morgan's judgment, reached in discussions with IMF experts in Washington, an antiquated banking structure, characterised by heavy-handed government intervention and excess capacity, has long kept profits far lower than is logical or necessary.

Through his travels, he saw how directly certain national characteristics would bleed into corporate strategy. For instance, while he had sought at Westpac to embolden employees to challenge authority – to tell the emperor he had no clothes, as he expressed it – he realised that such a system would be impossible to replicate in Japan, where deference towards a person's rank in society was a deeply ingrained trait. Certain awakenings proved a shock: while he had left Australia imagining that his compatriots' talent for bluntness was unsurpassed, he was disabused by his first taste of the typical negotiating style in Holland, which he could only describe as 'utterly charmless'.[34]

At his first NIBC board meeting in 2010, as executives proposed paying themselves a hefty bonus in spite of a dismal financial result for the previous year, Morgan told them, in no uncertain terms, that he considered their ruse entirely inappropriate. The message, perhaps unsurprisingly, was not at all appreciated, as the Australian and Dutch forms of plain speaking collided head-on. As Ben Coates, author of *Why the Dutch are Different*, said: 'There is a sense that people have the right to say whatever they want and be as direct as they want. And if people don't like that, it's their fault for getting offended.'[35] *Eigenwijs*, a Dutch word with no direct translation but implying an implacable faith in one's own knowledge, defined the temperament best.

It was, in Morgan's words, a 'challenging cultural interaction', but a valuable one. After all, national culture could be a crucial determinant of business success or failure, a theme that would later be expanded by Kai Hammerich and Richard Lewis in their book *Fish Can't See Water*. 'As human beings,' the authors write, 'we are culturally programmed to view the world from our own national perspective.'[36] While most of the literature prescribed at American business schools was, as Morgan knew from his own time at Harvard, myopically US-centric, the vivid contrasts of his work with Flowers showed him how radically one needed to adapt on the international stage.

Nowhere did this rule hold truer than in Japan. For over 200 years, under the *sakoku* (closed country) policy of the

Tokugawa Shogunate, the country was essentially off-limits to the outside world, until the arrival of US Commodore Matthew Perry's warships in 1853 compelled it to open to Western trade. Remnants of such isolationism endure, whether in the restrictions on immigration, still the most draconian in the developed world, or the strength of anti-*gaijin* (anti-foreigner) sentiment, as manifested in the lack of inward foreign investment and the startlingly low level of foreign participation in banking. 'When I travel to New York, I am always struck by the percentage of white Caucasians in the banks there,' one corporate banker told *The Guardian*, anonymously, in 2012. 'Here in Tokyo, it's overwhelmingly Japanese.'[37]

For all that resistance to foreign workers has softened slightly under the premiership of Shinzo Abe, the corporate emphasis upon social harmony is as strong as ever, while the involvement of J.C. Flowers at Shinsei continues to be the most conspicuous example of external influence over a Japanese bank. 'On the human and psychological side, banking in Japan has a very different feel to it,' Flowers says. 'I've been going there for almost twenty years, and it's the strangest place, of everywhere we operate, to do business.'[38]

As Morgan would soon recognise, the Japanese customs of strong work ethic, loyalty to the firm and unfailing politeness in the workplace, all laudable in principle, could be double-edged. Putting in long hours, he discovered, sometimes amounted to nothing more than hanging around the office until the boss left. Likewise, the flipside of impeccable manners was that executives would agree on a course of action to his face, but then show no willingness to follow through with

Morgan's mission

Why Westpac is on a roll

DAVID MORGAN
CEO, WESTPAC

ISSN 07277458
9 770727 745003

PLUS NEWCREST RIPE FOR TAKEOVER

In 2004, five years into his tenure as Westpac chief executive, Morgan spelt out the areas where he expected the bank to outperform in the long term: sustainability, wealth management, avoiding major overseas investments, and resilience. 'Whatever unforeseeable shock comes to us,' he said in an interview at this time, 'we will be in a more resilient shape than our peers.' It was a prophecy that would soon be borne out by global events.

Morgan and Bill Gates hit it off when they met, despite being polar opposites as personalities. Gates strictly controlled the list of ninety-nine invitees to his annual Microsoft CEO Summit in Seattle. The norm was to be invited only once. Morgan attended for six years running.

Morgan first encountered Jamie Dimon, then chief executive of Bank One and later head of J.P. Morgan Chase, at the CEO Summit in 2001. They struck up an instant rapport on a boat trip across Lake Washington. 'At the end of the boat ride, David told me, "Hey, we've got to stick together,"' Dimon says. 'And we have.'

Morgan with Jeff Bezos, founder of Amazon and, in 2018, Gates' usurper as the world's richest man. Morgan admired Bezos' philosophy on corporate culture.

Morgan grew friendly with legendary investor Warren Buffett after a paper he delivered in Seattle in 2004. Five years later, in a proposed 50-50 deal to take Japan's Shinsei Bank private with J.C. Flowers, Buffett initially declined. But within minutes, he said to Flowers: 'If David is CEO, and puts some of his own money in, I'm in.'

Morgan with John Howard, treasurer from 1977 to 1983. He told Howard of his relationship with Kelly as soon as it began, conscious of the perceived political complications of a senior Treasury bureaucrat dating a Labor member of the House of Representatives. 'Thank you, David,' Howard replied, calmly. 'That's your business.'

Morgan with Jack Welch, chairman and CEO of General Electric. He asked Welch for his views on how long a CEO should typically stay in post. 'It all depends,' Welch replied in a personally handwritten note, 'on your capacity to reinvent yourself.'

Morgan and son, Ben, at the tennis court, just as he assumed his duties as Westpac CEO in early 1999. They began playing the game when Ben was just three, on a gravel court in their back garden in Canberra, and enjoy a vigorous weekly singles match to this day.

Morgan being dressed as Santa Claus by daughter, Jessica, at their family home, ahead of the annual Christmas party that he would arrange for around 100 Westpac staff and their families.

In July 2006, *The Australian Financial Review Magazine* described Morgan as 'the closest thing Australia has to technocrat aristocracy'. Headlined 'The Power of Two', it traced Morgan's transition, with Kelly's significant assistance, 'from policy wonk to talented all-rounder'.

Cartoon by Eric Löbbecke of *The Australian*, 2007, reflecting the remarkably cheap price Morgan paid to acquire mortgage broker RAMS, just as the global financial crisis was about to strike. (Newspix)

In Jamie Dimon's judgment, it was Chris Flowers' private equity company, which had established itself as a major player in multiple jurisdictions, that promised Morgan the deepest satisfaction post-Westpac. So it came to be that on 1 July 2008, Morgan became a partner in J.C. Flowers & Co. (Louie Douvis, *AFR*)

Morgan in his London office, decorated with photographs of his horses in the Southern Highlands. He moved to the UK in early 2010 to become J.C. Flowers' managing director in charge of Europe and Asia-Pacific. (Julian Andrews)

Morgan and Kelly with their two dogs, Ollie and Charlotte, outside their London home, 2016. (Andrew Parsons)

The Morgans together in Central Park, Manhattan, 2018. Jessica, who has completed a Masters of Business Administration at Stanford, lives with her husband and their two daughters in New York. Ben followed his father by undertaking graduate work at LSE, before pursuing a career in banking. He lives in London with his wife and son.

it. As for the concept of loyalty, this could easily become warped when the cult of the *sarariman* (salaried man) was alive and well, with some white-collar workers automatically expecting job security and gradual pay increases for the rest of their lives.

Turning around a Japanese bank on Shinsei's scale would, it became clear, be a painstaking labour. Since 2010, Morgan and Flowers have travelled to the bank's Tokyo headquarters six or seven times a year, for a week at a time, but progress has been hard-won. Guided by his successes at Westpac, Morgan concentrated his efforts on encouraging candid performance appraisals, performance-orientated reward and measurement systems, productivity enhancement programs, clearing out staff who were falling short, and moving to a more fast-acting, top-down leadership style, as opposed to the ponderous, bottom-up, consensual decision-making that appeared to be the norm. Most ambitiously, he tried to find a way where bad news could be transmitted straight to the chief executive. This idea flew in the face of Japanese custom, risking the grave sin of *mentsu wo ushinau* (causing somebody embarrassment in public). The country's corporate history was littered with cases of problems being swept under the carpet to protect leaders from losing face.

Perhaps most memorably, Olympus, the Tokyo-based optical equipment manufacturer, was shaken to its foundations in 2011, when British-born CEO Michael Woodford was ousted after exposing one of the largest and longest-running loss-hiding arrangements ever recorded in Japan. Over $1.4 billion in losses, dubious fees, and even suspected covert payments to criminal enterprises were traced back in Olympus's books to the eighties. The scandal, which wiped 80 per cent off the company's market valuation and led to Woodford receiving $15 million in damages for defamation and wrongful dismissal, had been born of a familiar impulse to swerve uncomfortable truths. It was still possible to believe, wrote John Gapper in *The Financial Times*, that the accused directors 'thought they were behaving honourably', so as 'not to make their predecessors lose face'.[39]

Changing habits with such deep and tangled cultural roots would not be accomplished overnight. Indeed, any pride that Morgan feels in moving Shinsei forward, whether in cost efficiency or shareholder value, is set against the knowledge that, ideally, it should not have been nearly so hard to achieve. 'There is massive time and effort required to get even these basic outcomes,' he says. 'It wears one down a little.'[40]

The more widely Morgan roamed, the more convinced he became of the superiority of the private equity model over its public company equivalent. Despite having devoted eighteen years of his life to a public company, at Westpac, the transition to J.C. Flowers reminded him that the period had not been without its drawbacks.

As Dimon has observed in his most recent annual letter to J.P. Morgan Chase shareholders – a document that has become almost a canonical text for the banking industry – public-company life can be beset by such irritations as 'frivolous shareholder litigation, burdensome disclosures that don't get to the core of investor concerns, and an unhealthy focus on short-term results'.[41] It is for such reasons that there has been a precipitous decline in the number of US publicly listed companies, from a peak of 8090 in 1996 to just 4381 by 2015, a seismic shift in the corporate architecture.[42]

A relentless short-term fixation is, Dimon suggests, unwise, in that it tends to force companies to hold back on technology and other investments in the future just to meet a forecast affected by factors outside their control, such as fluctuating commodity prices or a volatile stock market. These arguments chime with Morgan's personal experience. After bucking the trend where former CEOs in his position would simply take a public-company chairmanship elsewhere, he believed he had found a far more rewarding, energising alternative. Through serving on eleven boards over the past decade, seven public and four private, he has been afforded a prime vantage point to study the disparities. 'Private equity is more exciting, more dynamic, and it gets away from the tyranny of those quarterly earnings,' he explains. 'You can take a longer-term view, and you're much more involved in the running of the company, because you're a significant investor. You're not just there as a prestigious patsy, waiting for your board director's fee.'[43]

For Morgan, another great pleasure of life's third act was that he could channel his expertise into an informal mentoring role for incumbent chief executives. While he had no desire to spend another minute in the CEO's chair himself, he retained an appetite to advise others on how best to make a success of it. In part, this sprang from an eagerness, even well into his seventh decade, to resist slowing down too much. Dimon, with whom he has enjoyed regular tête-à-têtes in New York, says: 'David likes to stay involved and connected – and relevant. That's a good thing. He's a rather young man relative to his energy and capability, and he wants to keep exercising his skills. When you have been through all the ups and downs, all the board issues, all the public issues, it is helpful to have someone who is independent and who has had real experience. If you watch boards, they are like jurors – they can go this way or that way. So, it is very helpful to a CEO to have someone impartial, someone to whom you ask the tough questions, and know that with the answers you'll be getting closer to a solution.'[44]

But a separate motivation for mentoring was the simple fact that CEO life, in all its relentlessness, was seldom openly discussed. As Louis Gerstner, head of IBM in the nineties and widely credited with turning around the technology giant's fortunes, asked in the foreword to his memoir, *Who Says Elephants Can't Dance?*: 'After a twelve-hour day at the office, who would want to go home and read about someone else's career at the office?'[45]

Still, Morgan was aware, from his nine years running Westpac, that CEOs almost invariably carried some concerns that they could not share with their boards, their peers, or even their spouses. What if you faced a problem with the chairman, or an errant board member? What if, as you attended to the morale of everyone else in the company, you needed someone to look after yours? Morgan had held such conversations, during the Westpac years, with an industrial psychologist at the University of Sydney, but understood that few were so fortunate to have the same sounding board.

'Most people don't talk about it honestly,' Morgan says. 'Yes, CEO life is very glamorous. You're recognised, you're given the best seats in restaurants, and you're ridiculously overpaid. But you need stamina. As the leader, you rarely play the grand final, but more an endless succession of semi-finals. You can hardly ever relax, and that creates intense strain. Behind closed doors, some CEOs literally weep.'[46]

These tensions would erupt into the open in London, with a man Morgan knew well. Late in 2011, António Horta-Osório, the Portuguese chief of Lloyds Banking Group, was signed off for six weeks with exhaustion. It was, the *Evening Standard* later noted, the most high-profile case of sick leave that anybody could recall in the Square Mile.[47]

James Gorman, who as CEO of Morgan Stanley had to prove his mettle to the singularly unforgiving audience of New York investment bankers – once candidly admitting he was 'not of their world' – makes the broader argument that executive stress, specifically the nervousness that every misstep can be magnified, is an occupational hazard at this rarefied level. 'It's kind of the job,' he says. 'It's like saying you play Australian Rules football but you don't want to get bumped. It all depends on whether you come into this job feeling as if it owes you something. My philosophy is that it owes me nothing. I'm lucky to have it. A lot of other people want it. But while I've got it, I'm going to do it my way.'[48]

To Morgan, who had witnessed episodes of CEO burnout before, Horta-Osório's problems were a salutary reminder of the stresses unique to the corner office. In a commentary for *The Times*, he put forward a ten-point plan for how newly ensconced CEOs might better adjust, explaining how they could only hope to change their businesses incrementally, not with one big bang, and warning that their personal lives would be scrutinised mercilessly. 'One transgression,' Morgan wrote, 'can have fundamental repercussions.'[49]

It turned out to be prescient advice for the figure who had inspired the article in the first place. Five years later, Horta-Osório had to issue an abject apology to his staff after reported misconduct while travelling abroad.

A subject that preoccupied Morgan deeply was the necessity for all leaders to show humility. It was a quality he had twice been directly accused of lacking, first by his late friend Chris Higgins and then by his first Westpac chairman, John Uhrig, but he had sought, as befitting his borderline obsession with self-improvement, to iron out these ruffled edges as a CEO. The most glaring pitfall for any occupant of such a position, he thought, was to succumb to hubris. To guard against it, he made it an article of faith to be respectful and accessible to staff at every level of the organisation. His Westpac chiefs of staff attest to how diligently he worked at these interpersonal skills. 'At various Christmas gatherings, you would each get your three minutes in the sun – 100 per cent, full-throttle focus, exactly on you,' Emma Beames reflects. 'His eyes wouldn't waver.'[50] Her predecessor, Brigitte Costa, says: 'When he used to do that to anyone who was in the lift with him, he would make you the centre of the universe for those minutes. He took the time.'[51]

This attention on being seen by employees, on listening to their concerns, is an area where Dimon has drawn great renown at J.P. Morgan Chase. In summer, he forsakes the company jet in favour of an election-style battle-bus, trundling across the American heartland for a series of open roadshows from Denver to Detroit. 'I believe that everyone should be treated equally in the company, including the janitor, the receptionist and the people who clean the kitchen,' Dimon says. 'David thinks about things the same way. You don't go out to show the flag, you go out to learn and show respect for the people on the front lines. When you leave the headquarters, you're learning from your tellers, your operating specialists and your financial advisors. I've done town halls at JPMC all around the world for every year for fifteen years now, and I answer each and every question. And the ones I can't answer off the top of my head, I write down, and I send an email two weeks later with the detailed response. And when we make mistakes, we change things. That's how we show respect to all employees.'[52]

From Sydney to London to New York, Morgan has cemented himself as a confidant to many of the world's pre-eminent bankers, a discreet source of counsel on matters that CEOs would be loath to raise in a public forum. Gorman, presently the most influential Australian financier on the world stage, and one who has had several talks with Morgan about what it means to be a leader, offers clear reasons as to why. In his office high above Times Square, he says: 'David was among the strongest banking CEOs of the last couple of generations in Australia. I thought the discipline and professional management that he brought to it was more akin to a global market than to a closed and frankly comfortable domestic market. At Westpac, he suppressed the urge to do the type of transactions that distracted ANZ and NAB. I have known all the CEOs of Australian banks over the past twenty years, and he was definitely one of the best. The banks are big down there, it's non-trivial. And David's natural style is to be out there, involved in leadership issues. CEOs don't have many people they can talk to about that, people who have done it. But with David, you have someone who is an incredible source.'[53]

It helps that the two are aligned in regarding much of the literature about leadership, with its fixation on specific characteristics needed to reach the top, as essentially redundant. 'Look at all those eighties slogans, like "true grit", "only sharks can swim", or "nice guys finish last",' Morgan says. 'They do not exactly celebrate the diversity of the human condition.'[54]

If Morgan has learned anything about the nature of leadership, it is that it could be messy, heterogeneous, requiring the subtlest balance of qualities. He has lived long enough to realise that narcissists and misanthropes make lousy CEOs, but the task of saying, definitively, what would make an effective one is much trickier. One does not need, necessarily, to be the most determined person, the most empathetic, or the most nimble in analysing complexity, or the best at execution, but to possess all such virtues in healthy proportion.

'There's not one thing,' Gorman agrees. 'Leading a bank in Australia is different from leading a soft-drinks company in Atlanta called Coca-Cola. It can't be simplified down to a single statement. What matters is how you complement your own skills with those around you, how you handle the relationship with your board, how you master all the tools that make you a better leader. We all bring a different body. Therefore, any leadership manual that tries to treat us as if we are all the same, or to offer an identical prescription for success, is absurd. It's situational to who you are.'[55]

It is a theme of discussion that Gorman has often touched upon with Morgan. 'David is very focused on the nature of leadership – the role and values of the leader, the way the leader interacts with the board – and that makes him something of an expert versus most CEOs, who haven't spent much time thinking about it. It's his obsession. I'm comfortable talking to him about board relationships, how to manage succession, how to stay in the job. I ask him, because he's done it, and he wants to share. He's very selfless like that. He wants to be engaged, to help you think through problems and be successful.'[56]

Morgan was scrupulous about applying this expertise to whatever lessons he gave his children. While he had no great wish to swap any particular chapter of his life to date, he did not seek to impose his own rules for living upon them. If there was any hard-and-fast rule, it could be found on the small poster that he bought one morning at Columbia Road markets in East London, and that hangs to this day at his office in The City. 'Work hard,' it reads, 'and be nice to people.'

* * *

More than a decade on from Morgan's exit at Westpac, these are, by any stretch, complicated times to be a banker in Australia. The Royal Commission into Misconduct in the Banking, Superannuation and Financial Services Industry, better known as the Banking Royal Commission, long advocated by consumer groups, whistleblowers and many MPs, has, since its first hearings in March 2018, unmasked major malpractice. While former prime minister Malcolm Turnbull infamously rejected the need for an inquiry at first, Morgan supported it, believing that it could be a 'circuit-breaker' for banks eager to rebuild their battered public image.[57]

Peter Costello, Australia's longest-serving treasurer, has dated bankers' most egregious lapses to the period immediately after the GFC, arguing that their relief at the system emerging unscathed bred both a complacency and a detachment in their attitudes.[58] The GFC undoubtedly caused a major diversion of focus among the banks, from non-financial towards financial risks. A second crucial factor was the introduction of the federal parliament's Future of Financial Advice (FOFA) legislation in 2013, designed to impose strict obligations on any companies providing financial advice. In reality, the banks, Westpac included, did not embed strong enough controls to ensure that customers received the ongoing advice for which they had signed up, or to stop fees being paid once the advice relationship ceased.

Morgan has no desire to pre-empt the final report of the royal commission, not available at the time of this book going to press. While he has not found his years as a chief executive singled out for criticism, he does have some initial views on what now needs to be done to repair the damage. 'I would advise Hayne to focus on two main things: first, for banks to act in an ethical and responsible manner. Second, to ensure product sales are resolutely and completely aligned with customer needs.'[59] These are consistent with the six normative principles set out by Hayne in his interim report in September 2018: namely, that banks must obey the law, not deceive or mislead, be fair, provide services fit for purpose, deliver them with care, and honour the best interests of those for whom they act.

From his own experience as a regulator and practitioner in financial services, Morgan is equally sure that the answer to raw and justified public anger is not stringent re-regulation, but a simplifying of the existing rules, in line with what the royal commission proposes, so that they cannot be legally or ethically gamed. 'Those who forget history are doomed to repeat it,' he says. 'Back in 1981, I was in charge of turning the Campbell Committee Report into government policy. The lesson was that if you had regulation focused on specific institutions in the financial sector, you were doomed to failure. New institutions would just be set up outside the circle. Cutting the supply of something does not mean that the demand goes away.'[60]

It ill behoves banks to be too defensive about the backlash that has engulfed them. But Morgan harbours an anxiety that the feeding frenzy could yet fuel too much of a sledgehammer response. Already, Hayne has signalled an intention to pursue miscreant banks through the criminal courts, so as to inflict prominent casualties that serve as potent deterrents to any would-be transgressors in future. The approach has stirred some opposition, with Richard Gluyas warning in *The Australian* that it risks creating a 'crapshoot', where 'facts get twisted into fake news, and honest but nervous witnesses appear dodgy'.[61] Morgan, similarly, is unshakeable in his belief that the country should not, even in its outrage at some bankers' unforgivable behaviour, be excessively adversarial in the search for remedies. 'It serves the legal practitioners well, but few others,' he says. 'It is essentially the American model, and one of the worst I have seen in the world. It should not be the Australian one. The US is a "me" society. Australia is much more of a "we" society. We have gone down the adversarial route in our political system for the past half-decade. Few would argue that it has served us well.'[62]

Morgan endorses firm action, too, to enhance the effectiveness of the regulators. Observing how, over the last twenty-five years, regulators have dramatically lost out to the private sector in the war for talent, he has tried to help redress the imbalance through his involvement in the review of the Australian Public Service set up by Turnbull. He expresses the same support for certain radical steps on remuneration, not least for mortgage brokers, urging a move from product commissions to a transparent regime of the customer paying. Already he has witnessed the benefits of such an approach in the Netherlands, where he has served as deputy chairman of NIBC for eight years. He is uneasy, though, about any draconian curtailing of variable remuneration, despite Hayne's concerns over how incentives can invite wrongdoing. They remain, to Morgan's mind, indispensable to any company that values performance, improving results in everything from compliance to sustainability. 'Let's not,' he advises, 'throw the baby out with the bathwater.'

Morgan appeals for a recognition that boards and regulators are only ever distant second lines of defence against malpractice. Behind any corrosion of banking behaviour, he suggests, lies a breakdown of culture, manifested not simply in the CEO's conduct but in that of the company's top 2000 employees. 'It takes a long time to change cultures in such organisations,' he says. 'That might be an inconvenient truth, but it is a fundamental one.' At Westpac, he made it the *sine qua non* of his leadership to ensure that failures were accounted for, mistakes openly acknowledged, publishing a Social Impact Report each year from 2002 to help repair the relationship between the bank and its customers. He expresses this in the biblical truism that 'the truth sets you free'.[63] If Westpac could be candid enough then to depict its shortcomings in the graphic form of a squashed tomato, why not now? Morgan's preference would be to mandate banks to release the results of their own culture surveys each year, just as NAB was compelled to do on the final day of the royal commission's hearings in December 2018.

In a sense, the toxic fall-out from the royal commission signals the fulfilment of his prophecy, delivered early in his Westpac reign, that the banks would face dramatic regulatory blowback if they did not take community concerns seriously. In the quest for fuller accountability, Morgan intends to press hard for an amendment to the *Corporations Act* that reflects banks' obligations to the wider community. While it might still be unfashionable for bankers to accept a social conscience, Morgan has spent the last ten years dealing with a broadly analogous system in Western Europe. If it can work there, he concludes, then there is no reason why it should not translate successfully to Australia.

Indeed, Morgan's record of working in the financial sectors of six separate advanced economies since 2008 reinforces his conviction that Australia retains, even in tumultuous times, a globally competitive banking system. 'We have four of the top thirty banks in the world by market capitalisation,' he says. 'We have very few industries in Australia that can make that claim. The system was also one of the top two in the world, alongside Canada, to come through the GFC strongly. Whatever is implemented as a consequence of the royal commission should seek to ensure that this vital Australian industry becomes more internationally competitive, not less.'

As Costello puts it: 'I'll tell you what's worse than a very profitable bank – a loss-making bank. That is a real problem.'[64]

***

There comes a moment in any person's life when one searches the past for possible regrets. But it is not one over which Morgan has been known to agonise, openly at least. 'I had lunch with David in Melbourne some years ago, and he simply said that he was sublimely happy,' says Don Watson, his old confrère from La Trobe, who treats the very idea of *Non, je ne regrette rien* with some scepticism. 'Getting old is getting regrets. We like that Édith Piaf song because it's wrong.'[65]

To ask Morgan directly if he harbours any lingering regret is to receive an illuminating answer. He rewinds not to any frustrations at Westpac, or at Treasury, or at any juncture of his academic career, but to the scalding memory of his father Ray's bankruptcy. Even after so many conspicuous accomplishments, from shaping lasting economic reform to commanding a global top-20 bank, the shock at that 'For Sale' sign is one that has never left him. Memories of the paternal pain that ensued, and of how he dealt with it as a child, have also been a source of lasting unease. 'I perhaps judged Dad too harshly,' Morgan reflects, with no little emotion. 'In a way, I sold him a bit short.'[66] And yet the spectacle of Ray's struggle forged in his son a resolve never to risk the same financial peril himself. 'The defeat of the father,' Watson says, 'is in David forever.'[67]

Ray Morgan died in 1983, aged eighty, after a battle with Parkinson's Disease. Verna, David's mother, passed away two years later from Alzheimer's, her later life centred on the gift shop she ran at the 'Paris End' of Collins Street, and her precise age as fiercely guarded a secret as it had been during her children's youth. Cherry, his sister and the figure who did much to shield him from the traumas of a broken home, continues to live happily in Hawthorn East, her family successes reflected in the election in May 2018 of her daughter, Sally Capp, as the Lord Mayor of Melbourne.

A message that Morgan often imparts to strung-out CEOs is the need to find an island of stability, far removed from the pressures of the business life. He has learned as much from the love, closeness and happiness experienced with Kelly and their two children, Jess and Ben, recognising beyond doubt that he could not have forged the same career without such support. Beyond this, he derives, even today, no deeper solace than from riding his horses. In more soothing moments, he will take his favourite mount, Matilda, off on a foray into the virgin bushland that lies beneath the family farm in the Southern Highlands. While not an overtly religious person, Morgan has long ascribed a spiritual dimension to the bush, the place where Australia's most ancient myths dwell and where, under the vastness of the southern sky, it is possible even for agnostics to experience an elevated state of being. 'To spend time alone in the Australian bush is to experience our union with nature,' the actor Jack Thompson once said. 'It is powerfully reassuring.' On horseback, it remains Morgan's treasured, private sanctuary, the one hideaway where he cannot be disturbed. It is the setting where his thoughts assume the greatest clarity and where, however fleetingly, he has the luxury of reflecting upon a life richly lived.

ACKNOWLEDGEMENTS

A book of this nature ideally requires the utmost commitment and candour from its subject, and I could not have asked for a more dedicated interviewee than David Morgan. Across 100 hours of conversations, no question was off-limits and no answer ever less than expansive. As a highly disciplined former CEO, he would sometimes be taken aback by my fondness for working without copious notes – as a journalist, I like to leave room for interviews to take unexpected directions – but the combination of styles has, I hope, helped produce material that is revelatory. I would like to place on record my gratitude to Morgan's family, in particular to his wife, Ros Kelly, for being so supportive throughout the book's development.

I am greatly indebted to Garrie Hutchinson, an author and editor of over thirty-five books and blessed with a knowledge of Australian Rules football that an Englishman could never hope to rival, for his assiduous research at every stage. Truly, Garrie has been an invaluable asset. So, too, has Sarah Robinson, Morgan's assistant at J.C. Flowers & Co., who has coordinated everything from travel to transcription with impeccable skill and patience. Every major organisation should aspire to have somebody of Sarah's multi-tasking talents.

I am hugely thankful to Sandy Grant and Pam Brewster at Hardie Grant for their backing of this project, to Emily Hart for guiding it so expertly to completion, and to Bernadette Foley for her exceptional editing.

If I may be permitted the indulgence of two personal mentions, I would also like to thank my parents, who are my inspiration to write for a living, and my partner, Jacquelin Magnay, for all her love, encouragement and insistence that she will make an honorary Australian out of me yet.

INTERVIEWS
(conducted 2016–18)

Ilana Atlas

Emma Beames

Christine Bindert

Peter Boxall

Cherry Capp

Edna Carew

Phil Chronican

Andrew Cornell

Brigitte Costa

Leon Davis

Jamie Dimon

Ted Evans

Chris Flowers

Bernie Fraser

James Gorman

Gary Gray

Brian Hartzer

Ken Henry

Brian Johnson

Bob Joss

Mike Keating

Paul Keating

Gail Kelly

Margaret Kelly

Ros Kelly

Bill Kelty

Helen Lynch

Ian Macfarlane

John McFarlane

Rob McLean

Karen Miller

David Morgan

Jon Nicholson

Martin Parkinson

Noel Purcell

Tony Sheehan

Ann Sherry

John Uhrig

Trudy Vonhoff

Don Watson

Garry Weaven

Elizabeth Welsh

NOTES

Chapter 1. Stage Fright

1   Interview, David Morgan, Sydney, 20 January 2016
2   Interview, David Morgan, Sydney, 24 January 2016
3   Interview, David Morgan, London, 25 February 2016
4   Interview, Cherry Capp, Melbourne, 29 January 2016
5   ibid
6   ibid
7   Interview, David Morgan, London, 25 February 2016
8   Alan Gregory, 'Melbourne High Principal was a 24-Carat Teacher in a Golden Age', *The Age*, 1 February 2016
9   ibid
10   Interview, David Morgan, Sydney, 20 January 2016
11   Michael Smith, 'My Epic Year with Lawrence of Arabia', *The Age*, 11 January 2014
12   Interview, Gary Gray, Melbourne, 29 January 2016
13   ibid
14   ibid
15   Interview, David Morgan, London, 25 February 2016
16   Question-and-answer session with David Morgan, University of New South Wales Business School, 11 July 2006
17   Interview, Gary Gray, Melbourne, 29 January 2016
18   ibid
19   Interview, David Morgan, Sydney, 20 January 2016
20   Interview, Gary Gray, Melbourne, 29 January 2016
21   'Isa Lei', a traditional Fijian song of farewell, understood to have originated in 1916
22   Interview, David Morgan, Sydney, 24 January 2016
23   Interview, Gary Gray, Melbourne, 29 January 2016
24   Interview, David Morgan, Sydney, 24 January 2016
25   Gary Carey, *Marlon Brando: The Only Contender*, St Martin's Press, 1985, p. 228

Chapter 2. Escaped Hamsters

1   Interview, Don Watson, Melbourne, 29 January 2016
2   *The Australian*, 8 March 1967
3   William J Breen (ed.), *Building La Trobe University: Reflections on the First 25 Years*, in La Trobe University Press, 1989, p. 146
4   Interview, Bill Kelty, Melbourne, 28 January 2016
5   ibid
6   Interview, Don Watson, Melbourne, 29 January 2016
7   ibid
8   Interview, David Morgan, London, 25 February 2016
9   Interview, Don Watson, Melbourne, 29 January 2016
10   Interview, David Morgan, London, 25 February 2016
11   Interview, Bill Kelty, Melbourne, 28 January 2016
12   Breen, *Building La Trobe University*, p. 153
13   Bruce Dawe, 'Life Cycle', *Sometimes Gladness: Collected Poems, 1954–1978*, Longman, 1978, p. 56
14   Interview, Don Watson, Melbourne, 29 January 2016
15   Interview, Tony Sheehan, Melbourne, 29 January 2016
16   ibid
17   Interview, Don Watson, Melbourne, 29 January 2016
18   Interview, David Morgan, London, 4 May 2016
19   Speech by David Morgan, La Trobe University, Melbourne, 21 March 2007
20   Interview, Tony Sheehan, Melbourne, 29 January 2016
21   Interview, Don Watson, Melbourne, 29 January 2016
22   Interview, David Morgan, London, 25 February 2016
23   Interview, Garry Weaven, Melbourne, 28 January 2016
24   ibid
25   Interview, Bill Kelty, Melbourne, 28 January 2016
26   ibid
27   Telephone interview, Elizabeth Welsh, 28 January 2016
28   Interview, Don Watson, Melbourne, 29 January 2016
29   Interview, David Morgan, London, 26 April 2016
30   Interview, David Morgan, Sydney, 20 January 2016
31   Interview, David Morgan, London, 25 February 2016
32   From the file, David Morgan, *Goal Goliath*
33   Interview, David Morgan, Sydney, 20 January 2016
34   Interview, Bill Kelty, Melbourne, 28 January 2016
35   Jack Welch, *Straight from the Gut*, Warner Business Books, 2003, p. 38
36   Interview, David Morgan, London, 4 May 2016

Chapter 3. Journey Without Maps

1   David Remnick, 'Vladimir Putin's New Anti-Americanism', *The New Yorker*, 18 August 2014
2   Interview, David Morgan, Sydney, 20 January 2016
3   Interview, David Morgan, London, 25 February 2016
4   Interview, David Morgan, Sydney, 24 January 2016
5   UK Complete University Guide, 2019
6   Interview, David Morgan, London, 25 February 2016
7   ibid
8   UK television address by Edward Heath to the nation, 13 December 1973
9   Kenneth O. Morgan, *Britain Since 1945: The People's Peace*, Oxford University Press, 2001, p. 227
10   Email correspondence from Bronwyn Curtis, 13 October 2016

11   Podcast by Jeffrey Golden, 'Tales from Houghton Street', London School of Economics, 11 July 2015

12   Interview, David Morgan, London, 25 February 2016

13   ibid

14   Interview, David Morgan, Sydney, 20 January 2016

15   Remark by John Dean, Watergate Prosecutor Transcripts, 21 March 1973

16   Interview, David Morgan, Sydney, 20 January 2016

17   Speech by David Morgan, 'Taking a Positive Look at Failure', Stanford Business School, 20 April 2009

18   Interview, David Morgan, Sydney, 20 January 2016

19   Telephone interview with Peter Boxall, 4 November 2016

20   Interview, David Morgan, London, 25 February 2016

21   ibid

22   Interview, David Morgan, Sydney, 24 January 2016

23   Final report by the Mathews Committee of Inquiry into Inflation and Taxation, 22 May 1975

24   Statement by Phillip Lynch, Deputy Leader of the Opposition, 22 May 1975

25   Interview, David Morgan, Sydney, 20 January 2016

26   Interview, David Morgan, London, 25 February 2016

27   David Morgan, *Over-Taxation by Inflation*, Institute of Economic Affairs, March 1977, pp. 45–6

28   Commentary by Economics Correspondent, *The Times*, March 1977; Editorial by *The Daily Telegraph*, March 1977

29   John Pardoe, Liberal MP for North Cornwall, *Hansard*, 3 March 1977

30   Telephone interview with Margaret Kelly, 29 November 2016

31   Interview, David Morgan, London, 25 February 2016

32   John L. Hirsch, *Sierra Leone: Diamonds and the Struggle for Democracy*, Lynne Rienner Publishers, 2001, p. 29

33   Victor A. B. Davies, 'Sierra Leone, Ironic Tragedy', *Journal of African Economies*, 9.3, 2000, p. 353

34   Interview, David Morgan, London, 25 February 2016

35   ibid

36   ibid

37   ibid

38   Letter from David Morgan to Chris Higgins, Washington, 21 December 1978

39   Telephone interview with Peter Boxall, 4 November 2016

40   Telephone interview with Christine Bindert, 10 December 2016

41   ibid

42   ibid

43   Interview, David Morgan, London, 25 February 2016

44   ibid

45   ibid

46   Interview, David Morgan, Melbourne, 27 January 2017

47   Interview, David Morgan, London, 25 February 2016

48   Daron Acemoglu & James A. Robinson, *Why Nations Fail*, Crown, 2012, pp. 1–5

49   Letter (aerogram) by David Morgan to Chris Higgins, 11 March 1978

50   Telephone interview with Christine Bindert, 10 December 2016

51   Interview, David Morgan, London, 3 March 2016

Chapter 4. The Stone Age

1   Interview, Ken Henry, London, 27 June 2016

2   *The Centenary of Treasury, 1901–2001: 100 Years of Public Service*, Department of Treasury, 2001, p. 89

3   ibid

4   *Between the Lines*, ABC Radio National, originally broadcast
     27 August 2015

5   From interviews with John Stone by Bernadette Schedvin, 1991–1994,
     Parliament Oral History Project, Australian Parliamentary Library

6   Letter by Warren Buffett to the shareholders of Berkshire Hathaway Inc.,
     1 March 1993

7   Interview, David Morgan, London, 30 March 2017

8   Speech by Lee Kuan Yew, former prime minister of Singapore, 1980

9   Interview, Ian Macfarlane, Sydney, 29 August 2016

10   Dick Bryan, 'Getting Blood out of a Stone: What John Stone Reveals about
     Treasury', *Australian Left Review*, 91, Autumn 1985, pp. 26–9

11   Interview, Ken Henry, London, 27 June 2016

12   Interview, Mike Keating, Canberra, 31 August 2016

13   Mike Keating, 'Christopher Ian Higgins', *Australian Dictionary of Biography*,
     vol. 17, 2007

14   Interview, Mike Keating, Canberra, 31 August 2016

15   Letter (aerogram) by Chris Higgins to David Morgan, 18 April 1979

16   Letter (aerogram) by David Morgan to Chris Higgins, 23 April 1979

17   Interview, David Morgan, London, 30 March 2017

18   Interview, David Morgan, London, 25 February 2016

19   Letter by David Morgan to Chris Higgins, 7 January 1979

20   Interview, David Morgan, London, 25 February, 2016

21   Interview, Bernie Fraser, Canberra, 31 August 2016

22   Ros Kelly, *Ros Kelly: A Passionate Life*, Hardie Grant Books, 2017, p. 44

23   ibid, p. 27

24   Letter by David Morgan to Chris Higgins, 4 May 1980

25   Speech by David Morgan, London, 17 March 2017

26   Kelly, *Ros Kelly*, p. 40

27   Interview, David Morgan, London, 19 May 2016

28   Letter by David Morgan to Chris Higgins, 2 February 1981

29   Interview, David Morgan, London, 30 November 2016

30   ibid

31   Interview, Ted Evans, Queanbeyan, 31 August 2016

32   Interview, Ken Henry, London, 27 June 2016

33   David Wroe, 'Treasury was Disloyal, Says Ex-Bureaucrat', *The Age*,
     1 January 2005

34   Patrick Weller, *Malcolm Fraser PM: A Study in Prime Ministerial Power in
     Australia*, Penguin, 1989, p. 262

35   Malcolm Fraser and Margaret Simons, *Malcolm Fraser: The Political Memoirs*,
     The Miegunyah Press, 2010, p. 371

36   Interview, Ken Henry, London, 27 June 2016

37   Interview, Don Watson, Melbourne, 29 January 2016

38   Interview, David Morgan, London, 3 March 2016

39   Paul Kelly, *The End of Certainty*, Allen & Unwin, 1994, p. 27

40   *Labor in Power*, ep. 1, Australian Broadcasting Corporation, originally
     broadcast 10 June 1993

41   Interview, David Morgan, London, 25 February 2016

42   Interview, Don Watson, Melbourne, 29 January 2016

43   Interview, David Morgan, London, 30 November 2016

44   Press conference by Bob Hawke, Canberra, 8 March 1983

45   Paul Kelly, *The Hawke Ascendancy*, Allen & Unwin, 2008, p. 325

46   John Edwards, *Keating: The Inside Story*, Penguin, 1996, p. 200

47 Sue Johnson, 'The Well-Mannered Summit', *The National Times*, 15–21 April 1983
48 Interview, David Morgan, London, 4 July 2016
49 Paul Keating, Speech to the National Economic Summit, Canberra, 11 April 1983, p. 46
50 ibid, p. 134
51 *Labor in Power*, ep. 1, 10 June 1993
52 Interview, David Morgan, London, 19 May 2016
53 Cartoon by Geoff Pryor, *The Canberra Times*, 28 August 1983
54 Kelly, *Ros Kelly*, p. 64
55 Interview, Mike Keating, Canberra, 31 August 2016
56 *Labor in Power*, ep. 1, 10 June 1993
57 ibid
58 Interview, David Morgan, London, 26 April 2016
59 Press conference by Paul Keating, Canberra, 12 December 1983
60 Interview, David Morgan, London, 3 March 2016
61 Kelly, *The End of Certainty*, p. 134
62 Interview, David Morgan, London, 16 May 2017
63 Evan Whitton, *The Hillbilly Dictator: Australia's Police State*, ABC Enterprises, 1989
64 Interview, David Morgan, London, 16 May 2017
65 Interview, Ian Macfarlane, Sydney, 29 August 2016
66 Interview, Don Watson, Melbourne, 29 January 2016

Chapter 5. Taxing Times
1   Mark Twain, Notebook, 30 December 1902
2   Interview, David Morgan, London, 30 April 2017
3   ibid
4   *Labor in Power*, ep. 1, ABC, 10 June 1993
5   Interview, Paul Keating, Sydney, 1 September 2016
6   Kerry O'Brien, *Keating*, Allen & Unwin, 2015, p. 134
7   Kelly, *Ros Kelly*, p. 66
8   Interview, David Morgan, London, 4 July 2016
9   Interview, Ken Henry, London, 27 June 2016
10 ibid
11 Interview, David Morgan, London, 16 May 2017
12 Interview, David Morgan, London, 3 March 2016
13 Paul Kelly, *The End of Certainty*, p. 157
14 Telephone interview, Martin Parkinson, 29 August 2016
15 ibid
16 Interview, Bernie Fraser, Canberra, 31 August 2016
17 Telephone interview, Martin Parkinson, 29 August 2016
18 ibid
19 Edwards, *Keating: The Inside Story*, p. 268
20 Telephone interview, Martin Parkinson, 29 August 2016
21 Interview, Ted Evans, Queanbeyan, 31 August 2016
22 Interview, Paul Keating, Sydney, 1 September 2016
23 Interview, Ken Henry, London, 27 June 2016
24 ibid
25 David Morgan, *Changing the Tax Mix*, paper given at Australian Tax Research Foundation conference, Melbourne, 27 February–1 March 1985
26 Andrew McCathie, 'Tax Avoidance: Sleeper Issue in Pre-Summit Debate', *The Australian Financial Review*, 4 March 1985

27   Memorandum by David Morgan, 7 March 1985
28   Editorial, *The Age*, 22 February 1985
29   *Keating*, ep. 2, Australian Broadcasting Corporation, originally broadcast 19 November 2013
30   Blanche d'Alpuget, 'Bob Hawke: A Stunning Change', *The Sydney Morning Herald*, 13 April 1985
31   Interview, David Morgan, London, 13 April 2016
32   Address by Paul Keating to Cabinet, 12 May 1985
33   Interview, David Morgan, London, 3 March 2016
34   Interview, Paul Keating, Sydney, 1 September 2016
35   ibid
36   O'Brien, *Keating*, p. 213
37   Interview, David Morgan, London, 3 March 2016
38   ibid
39   Edwards, *Keating: The Inside Story*, p. 275
40   Interview, David Morgan, London, 3 March 2016
41   'A Negative Consensus: From Doubt to Outright Rejection', *The Sydney Morning Herald*, 2 July 1985
42   Andrew McCathie, 'Keating Issues Ultimatum: Put the Nation First', *The Australian Financial Review*, 2 July 1985
43   Report by National Institute of Economic and Industry Research, 4 July 1985
44   *Labor in Power*, ep. 2, ABC, 17 June 1993
45   Interview, David Morgan, 12 June 2016
46   *Keating*, ep. 2, ABC, 29 November 2013
47   Press conference, Paul Keating, 5 July 1985
48   Troy Bramston, *Paul Keating: The Big-Picture Leader*, Scribe, 2016, p. 252
49   Interview, David Morgan, London, 3 March 2016
50   *Labor in Power*, ep. 2, ABC, 17 Jun, 1993
51   Gay Davidson, 'Ros Kelly's Challenge', *The Canberra Times*, 4 August 1985
52   O'Brien, *Keating*, p. 219
53   Interview, Paul Keating, Sydney, 1 September 2016
54   Interview, Bill Kelty, Melbourne, 29 January 2016
55   O'Brien, *Keating*, p. 224

Chapter 6. Hawks Versus Doves

1   *Labor in Power*, ep. 2, ABC, 17 June 1993
2   Paul Kelly, *The End of Certainty*, p. 212
3   Angela Mackay and Stephen Hughes, 'Keating's Home Truths Hit $A', *The Australian Financial Review*, 15 May 1986
4   Editorial, 'Now for the Anti-Banana Cart', *The Australian Financial Review*, 15 May 1986
5   *Labor in Power*, ep. 2, ABC, 17 June 1993
6   ibid
7   Interview, David Morgan, London, 16 May 2017
8   Editorial, 'Mr Keating's Remarkable Budget', *The Australian Financial Review*, 20 August 1986
9   Speech by Jim Carlton, Parliament House, Canberra, 11 September 1986
10   *Keating*, ep. 2, ABC, 29 November 2013
11   *Labor in Power*, ep. 2, ABC, 17 June 1993
12   Interview, Paul Keating, Sydney, 1 September 2016
13   Alan Peacock and Jack Wiseman, *The Growth of Public Expenditure in the United Kingdom*, National Bureau of Economic Research, 1961

14   Troy Bramston, 'Paul Keating's Secret Advice to Britain', *The Australian*, 11 November 2016
15   O'Brien, *Keating*, p. 259
16   Interview, David Morgan, London, 4 July 2016
17   Interview, Paul Keating, Sydney, 1 September 2016
18   O'Brien, *Keating*, p. 296
19   *Labor in Power*, ep. 3, ABC, 24 June 1993
20   Cartoon by Geoff (Jeff) Hook, *The Sun News-Pictorial*, 17 September 1987
21   Interview with David Morgan, London, 16 June 2017
22   Minute by David Morgan to Paul Keating, 30 March 1988
23   Paul Kelly, 'The Fraser Philosophy', *The Australian*, 29 April 1989
24   Minute by David Morgan to Paul Keating, 30 March 1988
25   Minute by David Morgan to Paul Keating, 9 June 1988
26   Report by Joint Economic Forecasting Group, July 1988
27   Interview, David Morgan, London, 16 May 2017
28   Press conference by Paul Keating, Canberra, 23 August 1988
29   'The Beer's on Paul', *The Sydney Morning Herald*, 24 August 1988
30   Minute by David Morgan to Paul Keating, 8 September 1988
31   Paul Kelly, 'The War Between the Hawks and the Doves', *The Australian*, 3 May 1989
32   John Edwards, *Keating: The Inside Story*, Penguin, 1996, pp. 341–4
33   Paul Kelly, 'The War Between the Hawks and the Doves', *The Australian*, 3 May 1989
34   Interview, Bernie Fraser, Canberra, 31 August 2016
35   *Labor in Power*, ep. 4, ABC, 1 July 1993
36   Speech by Paul Keating, Menzies Hotel, Sydney, 21 June 1989
37   Boyer Lecture, no. 4, by Ian Macfarlane, ABC, 3 December 2006
38   F. Scott Fitzgerald, *The Great Gatsby*, Charles Scribner's Sons, 1925
39   Laura Tingle, 'Political Amnesia: How We Forgot How to Govern', *Quarterly Essay*, Issue 60, 2015
40   Paul Kelly, *The End of Certainty*, p. 59
41   Chris Bowen, *The Money Men: Australia's 12 Most Notable Treasurers*, Melbourne University Publishing, 2015, p. 320
42   Interview, David Morgan, Melbourne, 27 January 2017
43   ibid
44   Survey by Australian Public Service Commission, 2014
45   Tingle, 'Political Amnesia', p. 71
46   Interview, David Morgan, London, 25 February 2016
47   Interview, Ken Henry, London, 27 June 2016
48   Speech by Peter Varghese, Department of Foreign Affairs and Trade, 9 June 2016
49   Ross Gittins, 'Budget Office Fills Gap Left by Politicised Treasury', *The Sydney Morning Herald*, 22 July 2018
50   Submission by David Morgan to Independent Review of the Australian Public Service, 2 November 2018
51   Speech by David Morgan, Sydney, 18 January 2014
52   Interview, Paul Keating, Sydney, 1 September 2016
53   ibid
54   Interview, Ian Macfarlane, Sydney, 29 August 2016
55   Interview, David Morgan, London, 3 March 2016

Chapter 7. The Cancer of Hubris

1   Interview, David Morgan, London, 13 April 2016
2   Interview, Ros Kelly, London, 4 October 2017

3   Interview, David Morgan, London, 17 November 2016
4   Interview, Ros Kelly, London, 4 October 2017
5   SIRCA, Share Price and Price Relatives Database, 29 September 1989
6   Interview, Paul Keating, Sydney, 1 September 2016
7   Frank Bongiorno, *The Eighties: The Decade That Transformed Australia*, Black Inc., 2017, p. 97
8   Interview, David Morgan, London, 4 May 2016
9   ibid
10   Sebastian Mallaby, *The World's Banker: A Story of Failed States, Financial Crises, and the Wealth and Poverty of Nations*, Penguin, 2004, p. 129
11   Interview, David Morgan, London, 25 February 2016
12   Edna Carew, *Westpac: The Bank That Broke the Bank*, Doubleday, 1997, p. 294
13   Telephone interview, Helen Lynch, 28 July 2016
14   Westpac annual report, 1989
15   Max Walsh, 'A Counter-Culture Rules at the Bank', *The Sydney Morning Herald*, 28 January 1993
16   Facsimile from Ted Evans, Washington, 12 December 1989
17   Speech by David Morgan at Treasury farewell dinner, Canberra, 15 December 1989
18   Interview, Andrew Cornell, Melbourne, 30 August 2016
19   Carew, *Westpac*, p. 295
20   Note by David Morgan, 'Westpac: Some Learnings, 1990–2007', 5 July 2007
21   Interview, David Morgan, London, 4 May 2016
22   Interview, Ros Kelly, London, 4 October 2017
23   Interview, David Morgan, London, 24 May 2016
24   Speech by Paul Keating to the National Press Club, 7 December 1990
25   Interview, Paul Keating, Sydney, 1 September 2016
26   Interview, David Morgan, London, 4 May 2016
27   Telephone interview, John Uhrig, 30 November 2016
28   Interview, David Morgan, London, 4 May 2016
29   Interview, Brian Johnson, Sydney, 2 September 2016
30   Telephone interview, John Uhrig, 30 November 2016
31   Carew, *Westpac*, p. 393
32   Interview, David Morgan, London, 24 May 2016
33   Interview, Rob McLean, London, 26 July 2016
34   Carew, *Westpac*, p. 403
35   Morgan, 'Some Learnings', 5 July 2007
36   Interview, David Morgan, London, 24 May 2016
37   Sheryle Bagwell, 'The Meteoric Rise of David Morgan', *The Australian Financial Review*, 13 November 1992
38   Interview, David Morgan, London, 1 May 2018
39   Carew, *Westpac*, p. 408
40   Interview, Paul Keating, Sydney, 1 September 2016
41   Telephone interview, John Uhrig, 30 November 2016
42   Interview, David Morgan, London, 4 May 2016
43   Interview, Rob McLean, London, 26 July 2016
44   Stephen Bartholomeusz, 'ANZ and Westpac Turn Things Around to Match Weakened NAB', *The Sydney Morning Herald*, 3 November 2001
45   Interview, Rob McLean, London, 26 July 2016
46   Interview, David Morgan, London, 25 February 2016
47   Interview, Trudy Vonhoff, Sydney, 2 September 2016
48   Interview, David Morgan, London, 24 May 2016

49   Email by Tom Saar, 27 July 2016
50   Interview, David Morgan, London, 19 May 2016
51   Telephone interview, Helen Lynch, 28 July 2016
52   Interview, Bob Joss, Palo Alto, 12 December 2016
53   Kelly, *Ros Kelly*, p. 143
54   Interview, David Morgan, London, 26 April 2016

Chapter 8. Culture Shock
1   *The Australian Financial Review* and Westpac 100 Women of Influence
        Awards, 15 October 2015
2   Interview, Ann Sherry, Sydney, 1 September 2016
3   'Changing of the Guard Brings Fresh Outlook at AMP', *The Sydney Morning
        Herald*, 17 August 2013
4   Interview, Edna Carew, Sydney, 2 September 2016
5   *200: The Westpac Story*, Westpac Banking Corporation, 2017, p. 250
6   Interview, Bob Joss, Palo Alto, 12 December 2016
7   Quotation from George Parker, Palo Alto, 12 December 2016
8   Interview, Bob Joss, Palo Alto, 12 December 2016
9   Interview, Ann Sherry, Sydney, 1 September 2016
10   ibid
11   Interview, Noel Purcell, Sydney, 2 September 2016
12   Interview, David Morgan, London, 26 February 2016
13   Telephone interview, Helen Lynch, 27 July 2016
14   Interview, Phil Chronican, Melbourne, 30 August 2016
15   David Morgan, Westpac development exercise, 1995, p. 1
16   Interview, David Morgan, London, 24 May 2016
17   Interview, David Morgan, London, 4 May 2016
18   ibid
19   Interview, Ros Kelly, London, 4 October 2017
20   Interview, David Morgan, London, 4 May 2016
21   ibid
22   Telephone interview, Karen Miller, 31 October 2016
23   Interview, Ann Sherry, Sydney, 1 September 2016
24   Interview, Bob Joss, Palo Alto, 12 December 2016
25   Robert Hadler, 'Risks for Westpac Man in Reply to NML Plan',
        The Australian, 15 May 1990
26   Interview, David Morgan, London, 4 July 2016
27   Telephone interview, Helen Lynch, 27 July 2016
28   Telephone interview, John Uhrig, 30 November 2016
29   Interview, Ian Macfarlane, Sydney, 29 August 2016
30   Interview, Bob Joss, Palo Alto, 12 December 2016
31   ibid
32   David Morgan, Westpac development exercise, 1995, p. 9
33   Interview, David Morgan, London, 4 November 2016
34   'Joss to Extend Stay at Westpac', *The Age*, 25 August 1997
35   Interview, Paul Keating, Sydney, 1 September 2016
36   Interview, David Morgan, London, 4 November 2016
37   Interview, Bob Joss, Palo Alto, 12 December 2016
38   ibid
39   Interview, David Morgan, London, 19 May 2016
40   Interview, Bob Joss, Palo Alto, 12 December 2016
41   Westpac and Commonwealth Bank of Australia annual reports, 1998
42   Interview, Bob Joss, Palo Alto, 12 December 2016

43 Telephone interview, John Uhrig, 30 November 2016
44 Stephen Bartholomeusz, 'Leaving a Bank That Knows Where It's Going', *The Sydney Morning Herald*, 12 February 1999
45 John Hurst, 'Morgan Will Relish Star Role Centre Stage', *The Australian Financial Review*, 12 February 1999
46 Interview, David Morgan, London, 19 May 2016
47 Interview, Andrew Cornell, Melbourne, 30 August 2016
48 Chris Higgins Memorial Lecture by David Morgan, Economic Society of Australia, Canberra, 11 February 1999
49 Interview, Paul Keating, Sydney, 1 September 2016
50 Interview, David Morgan, London, 25 February 2016

Chapter 9. Risk and Resilience

1 Interview, David Morgan, London, 19 May 2016
2 Westpac annual report, 1999, p. 5
3 Interview, Noel Purcell, Sydney, 2 September 2016
4 Note by David Morgan, 'Executive Office: Purpose, Behaviour, Commitments', 16 March 1999
5 David Morgan, 'Westpac: Some Learnings, 1999–2007', p. 14
6 Ian Rogers, 'Gamble Finally Paying Off for Main-Chance Morgan', *The Australian Financial Review*, 13 February 1999
7 Rogers, 'Morgan Says Westpac Still Follows Joss Blueprint', *The Australian Financial Review*, 19 May 1999
8 Daniel Goleman, *The Power of Emotional Intelligence*, More Than Sound, 2013, p. 64
9 Telephone interview, Helen Lynch, 28 July 2016
10 Interview, Trudy Vonhoff, Sydney, 2 September 2016
11 Lucinda Schmidt, 'Profile: Rob Ferguson', *The Age*, 14 November 2007
12 Mark Westfield, 'Short Walk That Shook BT's World', *The Australian*, 5 June 1999
13 Interview, David Morgan, London, 17 November 2016
14 Interview, Phil Chronican, Melbourne, 30 August 2016
15 International Olympic Committee, 'Marketing Report on the Sydney 2000 Olympics Games', 2001, p. 2
16 Interview, David Morgan, London, 4 May 2016
17 Westpac annual report, 1999, p. 32
18 Interview, David Morgan, London, 4 May 2016
19 Interview, David Morgan, London, 19 May 2016
20 Bill Bryson, 'Down Under Games Are Tops', *The Sydney Morning Herald*, 2 October 2000
21 Siow Lee Sen, 'A Westpac-DBS Merger Will Be a Win-Win Deal', *Business Times Singapore*, 31 October 2000
22 Interview, Ann Sherry, Sydney, 1 September 2016
23 Interview, Leon Davis, Melbourne, 30 August 2016
24 Interview, David Morgan, London, 6 October 2016
25 Colin Powell, *It Worked for Me: In Life and Leadership*, Harper Perennial, 2014, p. 39
26 Interview, Leon Davis, Melbourne, 30 August 2016
27 ibid
28 Interview, Noel Purcell, Sydney, 2 September 2016
29 Interview, Leon Davis, Melbourne, 30 August 2016
30 Interview, David Morgan, London, 19 May 2016
31 Interview, Leon Davis, Melbourne, 30 August 2016

32   Interview, David Morgan, London, 24 May 2016
33   ibid
34   Interview, Trudy Vonhoff, Sydney, 2 September 2016
35   Interview, David Morgan, London, 24 May 2016
36   Interview, Trudy Vonhoff, Sydney, 2 September 2016
37   Kelly, *Ros Kelly*, p. 143
38   Interview, David Morgan, London, 4 November 2016
39   Kelly, *Ros Kelly*, p. 143
40   Westpac First Half Results, 5 May 2001
41   Harvard Law School, 'Examining the Largest Golden Parachutes',
      26 February 2012
42   Bethany McLean, 'Jamie Dimon on the Line', *Vanity Fair*, 4 October 2012
43   Interview, David Morgan, London, 13 April 2016
44   'America's Biggest Banks', *Forbes*, 10 January 2018
45   Interview, Jamie Dimon, New York, 24 January 2017
46   Interview, Paul Keating, Sydney, 1 September 2016
47   Interview, Jamie Dimon, New York, 24 January 2017
48   Interview, David Morgan, Melbourne, 27 January 2017
49   HBO, 'Becoming Warren Buffett', originally broadcast, 30 January 2017
50   Interview, David Morgan, Melbourne, 27 January 2017
51   Speech by James Gorman, University of Melbourne, 2 March 2015
52   Interview, Jamie Dimon, New York, 24 January 2017
53   Interview, David Morgan, London, 17 November 2016
54   ibid
55   Stephen Bartholomeusz, 'Morgan's Instinct Proves a Winner', *The Sydney
      Morning Herald*, 27 August 2002
56   Telephone interview, Ilana Atlas, 22 November 2016
57   Interview, Phil Chronican, Melbourne, 30 August 2016
58   Robert Guy, 'A Good Deal, Now Make It Work', *The Australian Financial
      Review*, 28 August 2002
59   Interview, John McFarlane, London, 21 September 2016
60   Andrew Cornell, 'The Party's Over', *The Australian Financial Review*,
      2 August 2008

Chapter 10. Leaders Throw Long Shadows
1   O'Brien, *Keating*, p. 312
2   Interview, David Morgan, London, 24 May 2016
3   ibid
4   Interview, Noel Purcell, Sydney, 2 September 2016
5   Westpac annual report, 2001, p. 3
6   ibid, p. 11
7   Interview, Noel Purcell, Sydney, 2 September 2016
8   Tony Boyd, 'Westpac's 200th Reveals the Bust That Made the Bank Today',
      The Australian Financial Review, 31 March 2017
9   Milton Friedman, 'The Social Responsibility of Business Is to Increase Its
      Profit', *The New York Times Magazine*, 13 September 1970
10   Interview, David Morgan, London, 25 February 2016
11   Leeora Black, 'Westpac and the Cape York Indigenous Partnership',
      Embedding Human Rights into Business Practice, vol. 2, United Nations
      Global Compact, 2007, p. 19
12   Interview, Noel Purcell, Sydney, 2 September 2016
13   Interview, James Gorman, New York, 10 January 2017
14   Interview, Ann Sherry, Sydney, 1 September 2016

15   Black, 'Westpac and Cape York', *Embedding Human Rights*, p. 18
16   Interview, Ann Sherry, Sydney, 1 September 2016
17   Interview, David Morgan, London, 25 February 2016
18   Interview, Leon Davis, Melbourne, 30 August 2016
19   Interview, Noel Purcell, Sydney, 2 September 2016
20   Interview, David Morgan, London, 13 April 2016
21   Gro Harlem Brundtland, 'Report of the World Commission on Environment and Development: Our Common Future', United Nations, 1987, p. 5
22   Black, 'Westpac and Cape York', *Embedding Human Rights*, p. 20
23   Noel Pearson, 'Our Right to Take Responsibility', 2003, Institute of Public Administration Australia, p. 5
24   Interview, David Morgan, London, 19 May 2016
25   Dow Jones Sustainability Indices, annual reviews, 2002–2007
26   Interview, Leon Davis, Melbourne, 30 August 2016
27   Richard Gluyas, 'Morgan Wants World's Most Sustainable Bank', *The Australian*, 20 March 2006
28   Interview, David Morgan, London, 3 March 2016
29   David Morgan, 'Setting the Scene', address to Westpac executive board, 2003
30   Westpac annual report, 2004, p. 9
31   Speech by David Morgan to Microsoft CEO Summit, May 2004
32   Interview, Brian Hartzer, Sydney, 29 August 2016
33   Interview, Brigitte Costa, Sydney, 2 September 2016
34   Interview, Phil Chronican, Melbourne, 30 August 2016
35   ibid
36   Interview, David Morgan, London, 24 May 2016
37   Interview, Phil Chronican, Melbourne, 30 August 2016
38   Interview, Trudy Vonhoff, Sydney, 2 September 2016
39   Interview, Noel Purcell, Sydney, 2 September 2016
40   Rebecca Thurlow, 'Australia's Westpac Keeps Focus on Home Market', *Dow Jones International News*, 4 November 2005
41   Westpac annual report, 2005, p.8
42   Telephone interview, Jon Nicholson, 19 April 2018
43   ibid
44   Interview, Brian Hartzer, Sydney, 29 August 2016
45   Telephone interview, Jon Nicholson, 19 April 2018
46   Interview, John McFarlane, London, 21 September 2016
47   Interview, David Morgan, London, 1 May 2018
48   Telephone interview, Jon Nicholson, 19 April 2018
49   Interview, Ian Macfarlane, Sydney, 29 August 2016
50   Interview, Brian Johnson, Sydney, 2 September 2016
51   Interview, Brian Hartzer, Sydney, 29 August 2016
52   *200: The Westpac Story*, Westpac Banking Corporation, 2017, pp. 250–1
53   Interview, Jamie Dimon, New York, 24 January 2017
54   Interview, Emma Beames, Sydney, 2 September 2016
55   Interview, Brigitte Costa, Sydney, 2 September 2016
56   Interview, Gail Kelly, Sydney, 30 January 2017
57   Interview, Ted Evans, Canberra, 31 August 2016
58   Interview, David Morgan, London, 28 October 2016
59   Interview, Gail Kelly, Sydney, 30 January 2017
60   Lyndal McFarland and Rebecca Thurlow, 'Westpac Names Gail Kelly as Next Chief Executive', *Dow Jones International News*, 17 August 2007
61   Interview, Gail Kelly, Sydney, 30 January 2017

62 Danny John, 'We're the Bonsai of Bank World', *The Sydney Morning Herald*, 27 July 2007

63 Interview, David Morgan, London, 17 November 2016

64 'Meet the CEO', question-and-answer session with David Morgan, University of New South Wales Business School, 11 July 2006

65 Telephone interview, Ilana Atlas, 22 November 2016

66 Andrew Cornell, 'Exit Morgan the Reformer', *The Australian Financial Review*, 30 January 2008

67 Bill Clinton, *My Life*, Arrow Books, 2005, p. 957; speech by David Morgan at the Sydney Institute, 22 January 2008

68 Telephone interview, Jon Nicholson, 19 April 2018

69 ibid

70 Interview, James Gorman, New York, 10 January 2017

Chapter 11. Life's Third Act

1 Speech by Jane Fonda, 'Life's Third Act', TEDxWomen, December 2011

2 Interview, David Morgan, London, 6 October 2016

3 Interview, David Morgan, London, 1 May 2018

4 Daniel Taylor, 'Sir Alex Ferguson: The Eulogy, the Apology and the Thank You', *The Guardian*, 8 May 2013

5 Cornell, 'Exit Morgan the Reformer', *The Australian Financial Review*, 30 January 2008

6 Interview, David Morgan, London, 28 October 2016

7 Interview, David Morgan, London, 1 May 2018

8 Interview, John McFarlane, London, 21 September 2016

9 Speech by Kevin Rudd, Canberra, 4 February 2008

10 Interview, David Morgan, London, 1 May 2018

11 Interview, Ken Henry, London, 27 June 2016

12 Final report, 'The Future of the Australian Economy', Australia 2020 Summit, May 2008, p. 45

13 Nicholas Stuart, *Rudd's Way*, Scribe, 2010, p. 9

14 Interview, David Morgan, London, 1 May 2018

15 Tingle, 'Political Amnesia', p. 142

16 Interview, Ken Henry, London, 27 June 2016

17 Interview, David Morgan, London, 17 November 2016

18 Interview, Jamie Dimon, New York, 24 January 2017

19 William D. Cohan, 'Checkmate for a Wall Street Wizard?', *Fortune*, 2 September 2009

20 Interview, David Morgan, London, 30 November 2016

21 Interview, Jamie Dimon, New York, 24 January 2017

22 Martin Arnold, 'J Christopher Flowers: After the Storm, the Deals', *Financial Times*, 20 July 2014

23 Remarks by J. Christopher Flowers, 'The Big Fix' conference, New York, February 2008

24 Cohan, 'Checkmate', *Fortune*, 2 September 2009

25 Thomas Heath and David Cho, 'A Dealmaker's Rare Misdeal', *The Washington Post*, 12 October 2007

26 Interview, David Morgan, London, 28 October 2016

27 Interview, Chris Flowers, Melbourne, 27 January 2017

28 Iain Dey, 'City Star in "Phantom Fees" Probe', *The Sunday Times*, 11 April 2010

29 Interview, David Morgan, London, 17 November 2016

30 Jeff Prestridge, 'The Brash Australian Moving in on Banks', *The Mail on Sunday*, 11 October 2010

31   Interview, Chris Flowers, Melbourne, 27 January 2017
32   Interview, David Morgan, London, 30 November 2016
33   Interview, Jamie Dimon, New York, 24 January 2017
34   Interview, David Morgan, London, 17 November 2016
35   Olga Mecking, 'Where Dutch Directness Comes From', BBC, 1 February 2018
36   Kai Hemmerich & Richard D Lewis, *Fish Can't See Water*, Wiley, 2013, p. 18
37   Joris Luyendijk, 'Japanese Banking, A Culture Shock', *The Guardian*,
     7 February 2012
38   Interview, Chris Flowers, Melbourne, 27 January 2017
39   John Gapper, 'Olympus's Deceit Was Dishonourable', *The Financial Times*,
     10 November 2011
40   Note by David Morgan on Japanese corporate governance, 14 September 2018
41   Annual letter to shareholders by Jamie Dimon, J.P. Morgan Chase,
     5 April 2018
42   Paper by Cambridge Associates, 'Private Investments', King's College,
     London, 2018
43   Interview, David Morgan, London, 17 November 2016
44   Interview, Jamie Dimon, New York, 24 January 2017
45   Louis Gerstner, *Who Says Elephants Can't Dance?*, HarperCollins, 2002, p. vii
46   Interview, David Morgan, London, 30 November 2016
47   James Ashton, 'The City's Top Feminist?', *Evening Standard*, 5 March 2014
48   Interview, James Gorman, New York, 10 January 2017
49   David Morgan, 'A Survivor's Guide to Coping in the Corner Office',
     The Times, 16 November 2011
50   Interview, Emma Beames, Sydney, 2 September 2016
51   Interview, Brigitte Costa, Sydney, 2 September 2016
52   Interview, Jamie Dimon, New York, 24 January 2017
53   Interview, James Gorman, New York, 10 January 2017
54   Interview, David Morgan, London, 28 October 2016
55   Interview, James Gorman, New York, 10 January 2017
56   ibid
57   David Rogers & Ben Butler, 'Morgan: Banking Inquiry Can Be
     "Circuit-Breaker"', *The Australian*, 10 April 2018
58   James Thomson & Tom McIlroy, 'Costello Says Banks Have Cruelled
     Company Tax Cut Hopes', *The Australian Financial Review*, 2 May 2018
59   Interview, David Morgan, London, 14 November 2018
60   Note by David Morgan on 'Bank Regulation: Avoiding Unintended
     Consequences', 26 August 2018
61   Richard Gluyas, 'Westpac Cases Question Hayne's Faith in Legal Route
     to Remedies,' *The Australian*, 13 November 2018
62   Interview, David Morgan, London, 14 November 2018
63   Interview, David Morgan, London, 19 May 2016
64   Mathew Dunckley, '"Long and Painful": Costello's Rate Warning
     for Households', *The Sydney Morning Herald*, 20 March 2018
65   Interview, Don Watson, Melbourne, 29 January 2016
66   Interview, David Morgan, London, 25 February 2016
67   Interview, Don Watson, Melbourne, 29 January 2016

INDEX